The
Political Economy
of Mexico

TWO STUDIES BY
William P. Glade, Jr.
AND
Charles W. Anderson

THE UNIVERSITY OF WISCONSIN PRESS
Madison, Milwaukee, and London, 1968

Published by
THE UNIVERSITY OF WISCONSIN PRESS
Madison, Milwaukee, and London
U.S.A.: Box 1379, Madison, Wisconsin 53701
U.K.: 27–29 Whitfield Street, London, W.1

Second printing, 1968

Printed in the United States of America
Library of Congress Catalog Number 63-10531

No. 289-P
1st edition
2nd printing
1st binding
pub: 9-6-63

The Political Economy of Mexico

Preface

These two studies share as a common theme the saga of Revolutionary Mexico and its economic progress. Yet this is not the only bond that unites them either in nature or in purpose. For both authors, the study of contemporary Mexico is not an end in itself but rather a focus which is justified by the pertinence of this setting to the examination of certain problems of interest to the social scientist.

Both of these studies are experiments in the use of interdisciplinary approaches as a way of getting at some of the basic problems of economic development. For Glade, the Mexican Revolution appears as a tapestry, intricately woven of many strands: philosophical, political, artistic, economic. His study, marshaling evidence from the anthropologist, social psychologist, political scientist, and novelist, is an attempt to reproduce something of the design of that revolutionary tapestry and to trace its bearing on the economic process. For Anderson, Mexico's unusual system of public credit institutions provides an opportunity for a sortie into the vast no man's land that separates the traditional concerns of economists and political scientists. His study is an effort to view these economic institutions as part of the political system of the Mexican nation.

For both of the authors, the study of Mexico's economic progress would seem to offer lessons for the student of economic development. Out of a setting and sharing of problems much like those shared by many underdeveloped nations, Mexico has grown and modernized to the point where many now doubt the propriety of its inclusion among the underdeveloped nations. The way in which Mexico exchanged the mantle of the past for the garb of the modern age may be of more than passing relevance to those nations now embarking on the path to development. Glade reflects on the problem of revolution as a possible precondition for economic growth and examines the significance of the Mexican Revolution in the explosive growth of that nation. Anderson, noting the emergence of new types of public institutions throughout the underdeveloped world, which are designed specifically to come to grips with the problems of economic change, suggests that a study of the Mexican development banks may be instructive as we attempt to understand the significance of the "development authorities" and "development corporations" that have come to play such an important role in the political and economic life of the state in the twentieth century.

Credit for assistance received is always in order. Both authors are quite cognizant of the importance of their participation in the Ibero-American Studies Program at the University of Wisconsin in setting the tone and supplying the inspiration for the interdisciplinary approach adopted. The coincidence that these two studies, prepared independently and without knowledge of the other until near the final stages, should have dealt so similarly with the themes developed cannot be dismissed as mere happenstance. Hence, gratitude is due to other members of the faculty of this program for the association and insight that could lead to this outcome. Both authors are also indebted to Professor B. F. Hoselitz of the University of Chicago and to Professor Robert Scott of the University of Illinois who volunteered a number of useful suggestions in their critical reading of the manuscript.

Glade would like to acknowledge his debt to the many people who have, over the years, contributed much to his understanding of Mexico and its cultural history. With a nod to all the rest, suffice it to single out in particular Professor Eastin

Nelson of the University of Texas and Octavio Paz and Edmundo Flores of Mexico. Professors E. E. Hagen of the Massachusetts Institute of Technology and William E. Henry of the University of Chicago generously gave permission to study and cite some especially useful and, at the date of writing this Preface, unpublished research of theirs on Mexican innovators. Professor Henry also gave invaluable aid in the course of several conversations examining various psycho-cultural features of modern Mexico. The conventional disclaimer of the responsibility of all these men for the use made of their advice and assistance is recorded herewith. For typing and proofing the manuscript, the secretarial staff of the University of Wisconsin School of Commerce merits special praise—cryptic notations and the Spanish language were handled with dispatch and cheerful spirit. To Marlene is owed a double vote of thanks for her commendable patience judiciously combined with an optimum amount of nudging.

Anderson would like to thank many friends in Mexican politics, the development banking system, and the National University of Mexico, too numerous to mention, yet each to be remembered for more than the mere contribution of insights for this study. To the staffs of the Rockefeller Foundation, the Food and Agricultural Organization in Mexico City, and the library of the Bank of Mexico go special recognition for services rendered. Yet he alone, of course, is responsible for errors that appear herein. It is also fitting to acknowledge financial support granted by the Research Committee of the Graduate School of the University of Wisconsin, from special funds voted by the State Legislature, and to Karen Stein and Alice Stapp for typing services. Finally, to Jeanie, for exulting with the writer when it went well and commiserating with him when it went badly.

February, 1963   WILLIAM P. GLADE, JR.
Madison, Wisconsin   CHARLES W. ANDERSON

Contents

A Chronology of Modern Mexico

Independence from Spain	1821
The Liberal Reforms	1855–1862
Benito Juárez	1855–1862
The Liberal Constitution	1857
The Empire	1862–1867
Maximilian	1862–1867
Post-imperial Period	1867–1877
Benito Juárez	1867–1872
Lerdo de Tejada	1872–1876
The Porfiriato	1877–1910
Porfirio Díaz	1877–1910
The Revolution	1910–
Period of Violence	1910–1917
Francisco I. Madero	1911–1913
Victoriano Huerta	1913–1914
Venustiano Carranza	1915–1920
Querétaro Constitution	1917
Period of Consolidation	1917–1940
Adolfo de la Huerta	1920
Alvaro Obregón	1920–1924
Plutarco Calles	1924–1928
Emilio Portes Gil	1928–1930
Ortíz Rubio	1930–1932
Abelardo Rodríguez	1932–1934
Lázaro Cárdenas	1934–1940
Period of Industrialization—the Institutionalized Revolution	1940–
Manuel Ávila Camacho	1940–1946
Miguel Alemán	1946–1952
Adolfo Ruiz Cortines	1952–1958
Adolfo López Mateos	1958–

Revolution
and Economic Development

A MEXICAN REPRISE

by William P. Glade, Jr.

Revolution and Economic Development

THE YEAR 1960 was one of special significance for the country lying just to the south of the Rio Grande. As an occasion for spectacular national celebrations and extensive intellectual reappraisal, it marked the fiftieth anniversary of the beginning of the Mexican Revolution. And while the preceding two decades had presented a remarkable record of dynamic economic performance, the profile of which was reflected in innumerable statistical time series, it was in the 1950–1960 interval that one detects a growing awareness among virtually all observers that Mexico had become one of the handful of so-called underdeveloped nations to effect the transition to sustained, more or less self-generating economic expansion.

Before 1950, there was greater room for doubt on this matter. The consecutive impact of exogenous forces—the world depression, World War II, and the postwar period of readjustment—made it difficult to discern the underlying elements of strength that had been built into the national economic structure over the years. At the same time, the incompleteness of the statistical data then available tended to obscure the fact that Mexico, to a large extent, had succeeded in "internalizing" the dynamics of its economy and no longer depended primarily upon external stimuli. That economic growth had taken place was evident enough, and that economic change had occurred was similarly apparent. What was still uncertain was whether or not Mexico had achieved that difficult combination of economic growth

3

and economic change which properly goes by the name economic development.

In this connection it is perhaps of some interest to recapitulate briefly a few of the major judgments and evaluations of Mexico's state of development over the past two decades—all made, it might be added, by competent scholars, most of them long and justly noted as particularly astute and perceptive students of the Mexican scene. In the immediate aftermath of the war, Frank Tannenbaum's *Mexico, The Struggle for Peace and Bread* conveyed a decidedly pessimistic view of the future and suggested that Mexico would have to retrench and retreat to a "philosophy of little things," such as fostering cottage industries, if it were to find some measure of economic salvation in the face of serious impending difficulties brought on by imbalances of industrialization.[1] Tannenbaum was not merely a lone, foreign Cassandra, it should be noted, for a few years before Mexico's "grand old man" of economics, Jesús Silva Herzog, had seen deep social and economic crisis approaching, owing mainly to what he felt were unmistakable signs of moral decay and political corruption.[2] Writing slightly after Tannenbaum, the late Sanford Mosk was less grim in his assessment but nonetheless argued that a sharp deceleration of the pace of industrialization was both inevitable and desirable.[3] Both Tannenbaum and Mosk, probably for the reasons suggested above, seemed to interpret the expansion of the 1940's as principally a result of World War II and to postulate a rather sharp break in government policy between the Cárdenas and the Ávila Camacho administrations, i.e., a distinct shift from agrarian to industrial goals.[4]

Less general in scope than the studies of Tannenbaum and Mosk, but written only slightly later and reflecting a similar tenor in its conclusions, was J. R. Powell's *The Mexican Petroleum Industry, 1938–1950*.[5] By undervaluing significant factors lying outside the framework of firm analysis, Powell pronounced the oil expropriation a failure—even though much of the data presented would quite easily have supported an alternative and more positive interpretation and one, incidentally, more consistent with the course of subsequent developments.[6]

Shortly after 1950, however, one detects a decided shift in the balance of informed judgment, even though at each temporary drop in growth rates thereafter some have tended to read the score as *molto ritardando* where later records suggested rather more a rubato effect.[7] With a few more years of performance to review and having accomplished a magnificent task of assembling hitherto unavailable statistical information, a World Bank group around 1952 expressed skepticism that the boom of the past could be maintained but judged the Mexican economy fundamentally sound.[8] A year or so later, Henry Aubrey could offer Mexico as an example of successful economic development,[9] and in 1958 W. W. Rostow placed the time of Mexico's take-off into sustained economic growth somewhere after the mid-1930's— with the self-evident and significant implication that the crucial preconditions for that take-off were established during the years prior to that time.[10]

The accompanying table, which of course provides insufficient information to prove anything of importance about secular trends, is offered only as a general backdrop to the several foregoing opinions. The table does, however, tend to suggest the gradual attainment of a somewhat more stable pattern of growth. The upturn since 1957 looks especially favorable when viewed in the light of the Minister of Industry and Commerce's recent announcement that the available evidence suggests that Mexico is on the threshold of a new investment boom.[11]

The slowing down in expansion during the late 1950's was attributed by the Banco de México staff to such factors as drought conditions in 1957, a capital flight in 1958 expressive of fears of devaluation, a decline in *bracero* remittances,* and unfavorable price movements in the world markets for a number of Mexico's agricultural and mineral exports.[12] It is also relevant

---

* *Braceros* are the migrant workers from Mexico who find temporary employment in the United States, mostly in agriculture.

to recall in connection with the growth rates of the 1950's that the economy of Mexico's major trading partner, the United States, was rather sluggish for over half the decade, reducing to a relatively low level any spill-over effects of prosperity transmitted to Mexico through international trade channels. In consequence, the reduced incomes of the agricultural and export sectors led to relatively slow rates of expansion of consumer

Rates of Increase in Real National Income

Year	Annual growth rate	Three-year average, ending in year indicated	Year	Annual growth rate	Three-year average, ending in year indicated
1937	3.4		1949	4.7	3.7
1938	1.8		1950	10.7	8.8
1939	5.3	3.5	1951	7.2	7.5
1940	1.4	2.8	1952	−0.25	5.9
1941	12.8	6.5	1953	−1.25	1.9
1942	13.7	9.3	1954	7.6	2.0
1943	4.1	10.2	1955	9.6	5.3
1944	8.9	8.9	1956	7.1	8.1
1945	8.0	7.0	1957	4.0	6.9
1946	7.0	8.0	1958	4.4	5.2
1947	1.6	5.5	1959	4.6	4.3
1948	4.9	4.5	1960	5.7	4.9

Sources:
1940–1959, Annual reports of Banco de México, S.A.
1960, *El mercado de valores*, vol. XXI, no. 9 (27 February 1961), p. 97.
1937–1939, growth rates of real gross national product, from Enrique Pérez López, "El producto nacional," *México: Cincuenta años de revolución, I: La economía*, p. 588.

goods production (though producer goods industries continued, on the whole, to expand at a fairly high rate); this pattern of reaction indicated the continued dependence of the national economy on agriculture and foreign trade, but also afforded indirect evidence of the extent to which Mexico has built up rural markets for the output of its industrial sector. To the extent that foreign investment has become based upon domestic market growth, the foregoing circumstances may contain a large part of the explanation for the steep decline in new foreign investment between 1957 and 1960. While the disturbing decrease in the annual rate of increment in private investment since 1956 (and the rising portion of this investment going into private construction projects rather than into capital formation) may also have been influenced by these exogenous conditions, it may also reflect in addition the increasingly constrictive effect wrought by recent trends in income distribution on market growth and the dampening influence thereof on the attractiveness of private investment in capital formation.

It should be added that the national income data of the table above conceal a serious problem relating to per capita income trends, for the annual rate of population increase has risen from around 2.2 per cent in the first three years given in the table to around 2.8 per cent in the late 1940's and early 1950's, reaching 3.4 per cent by the late 1950's.[13] Still, as P. T. Bauer has remarked, such demographic increases may reflect rising levels of welfare which are not included in per capita income figures alone, and the growth of population not only reflects the increasing capacity of the economy to produce larger outputs, but feeds back into the production process as a stimulus to investment and as an increased supply of labor.

It is also relevant to observe that the encouraging performance of the Mexican economy has been achieved without any really large new discoveries of natural resources of the sort which have customarily triggered a foreign-investment minerals boom (as in the case of Venezuelan oil and the Peruvian Toquepala and Marcona projects)—with the possible though minor exception of the Gulf Coast sulphur deposits, which brought in U.S. capital, and the northern natural gas fields developed by Petróleos Mexicanos. Generally, some 90 per cent or more of total investment has been domestic rather than foreign in origin.[14] During the mid-1930's, in fact, there was foreign disinvestment in petroleum and railways. In any case, the pronounced change in the character of foreign private direct investments leads to the conclusion that the inflow of foreign capital has been largely induced by domestic economic expansion rather than the other way around—a shift in orientation which was described a few years ago by Daniel Seligman. Canvassing the views of U.S. investors, Seligman found that it was the "phenomenal rate" of growth in the Mexican market (an observation contrasting interestingly with the earlier views of Mosk) that induced U.S. manufacturing investment in Mexico to rise from $10 million just before World War II to $240 million in 1956. In that year it represented 40 per cent of total U.S. private direct investment in the Republic, a marked contrast to 1940, when 47 per cent of total U.S. investment was in export-oriented mining with most of the balance in transport, communications, and utilities.[15] By 1959, U.S. manufacturing investment in Mexico had increased to $355 million, representing approximately 47 per cent of the total private direct U.S. investment there.[16] Significantly, U.S. investment also began to flow into local distribution and marketing. Sears, for example, opened its first Mexican branch in 1947 and by 1956 was operating seventeen stores. As a revealing indicator of the breadth of Mexican industrial advance, 90 per cent of sales in the Sears stores in 1955 were of domestically manufactured products.

It is further indicative of both the breadth and depth of this advance that foreign capital is now moving beyond consumer goods manufacturing into the development of domestic heavy or producer goods industries. In this, it is following the main trends in the economy, for while output of consumer goods rose by 60 per cent between 1950 and 1959, the output of producer goods increased in the same period by some 152 per cent. Between 1934 and 1958 there was over a tenfold increase in national crude steel production. The new pattern of foreign investment seems, therefore, to be primarily responsive to conditions within Mexico rather than to market conditions in home countries consuming raw materials or agricultural export products.

In view of this record, it is of considerable interest to the economist to inquire into the process by means of which the Mexican economy has attained that quality of self-propulsion which U.S. foreign economic policy is trying to bring about in other less developed countries and which these countries are ostensibly trying to bring about in themselves. Beyond this, but closely related to it, lies a larger area for exploration, namely, the relations between this economic expansion and the phenomenon of the Mexican Revolution—for twentieth century Mexico has been not only a land in which economic growth has apparently taken root but also one in which a revolution in the fullest sense of that word has been experienced. The question of overriding interest has to do with the extent to which that revolution has been the agent effecting the preconditions for initiation of a process of continuing change and expansion in the economic field.

The question is not without interest for students of any aspect of the social process, and it could hardly be explored definitively without the collaboration of specialists from all the social sciences. Yet, general though the interest in such a question may be, it would seem to be of particular concern to the development economist, for not infrequently among Western economists one finds the view expressed that a revolution—or what for all practical purposes amounts to one—may be a necessary, though not, of course, sufficient, condition for development in many of the economically backward regions of the globe.[17]

W. Arthur Lewis, for example, takes explicit cognizance of this "principle" in his well-known work on economic growth,[18] and S. Frankel made very much the same point when he argued that "technical change as a social consequence" is in some respects a more accurate concept than the conventional phrase, "the social consequences of technical change." [19] Similarly, both Eugene Staley and a prominent international group of economists reporting to the Secretary-General of the United Nations have stressed revolutionary changes in attitudes and behavior, whether accompanied by outright political revolution or not, as prerequisite for economic development.[20] Meier and Baldwin have analyzed the preconditions for development without directly addressing the problem of revolution and its relation to economic development. Nonetheless, a comparison of their "general requirements for development" with conditions actually prevailing in backward regions leaves little room for doubt that they were, in effect, reaching much the same conclusion as the economists mentioned above.[21]

If, then, recent Mexican experience holds a special interest for economists, economists are especially fortunate in the relative abundance of material that has been accumulating over the years relating to this experience. Owing probably to the fact of geographical proximity, this first of the twentieth-century social upheavals has been exceptionally well covered by trained U.S. observers. Equally important has been the fact that, for a retarded region, Mexico has been quite well endowed with a large number of articulate, capable, and self-aware intellectuals who have been actively exploring various aspects of the contemporary Mexican reality since the onset of the Revolution and even before. As a result, the student of Mexico can work with a sizable and growing body of relevant literature, not the least important part of which is the monumental four-volume work of reappraisal currently being published by the Fondo de Cultura Económica.[22] To be sure, not all aspects of the Revolution are equally well covered as yet—economic and political aspects being leaders in this respect, while sociological and psychological aspects are still underreported—but sufficient evidence is in, so to speak, to warrant and sustain a considerable amount of synthetic analysis.

In the end-note documentation, an effort has been made to provide the reader with a fairly comprehensive survey of the literature relating to Mexican economic development. The citation of numerous Mexican studies and the use of extended quotations—in both text and notes—have been employed deliberately to convey something of the way in which Mexicans themselves have read the data of the times, to give, as it were, an idea of how the Revolution looks from the inside.

I

Before examining the hypothesis that the Revolution has been the principal agency of Mexico's rapid economic growth, at least two alternative hypotheses merit some recognition. One of these —herein called, for convenience, the discontinuity hypothesis— holds that the development of an industrial economy in Mexico was achieved more or less in spite of the Revolution or, in a variant of this point of view, after Mexico abandoned the Revolution, presumably at the end of the Cárdenas administration.[23] In some statements of this hypothesis, there is a tendency to identify the Revolution almost exclusively with agrarianism and labor-welfare measures, despite the presence of other goals and groups in the amalgam of Revolutionary interests from the very outset—as indeed some of the proponents of this interpretation recognize.[24] In others, there is a perhaps related tendency to employ such terms as *caudillismo*, socialism (or socialist agrarianism), and capitalism to designate consecutive stages of revolutionary development. In either case, the result is a certain oversimplification which seems to attribute a larger degree of autonomy to industrial worker and peasant interest groups, and even to industrialists, than they may ever in fact have possessed.

It is not at all clear, for example, how, in this explanation, the Ávila Camacho administration could have made such an allegedly sharp break in policy, how political pre-eminence could have passed so swiftly to industrial capitalists, and how the influence of urban workers and *campesinos* * could have receded so rapidly if these latter groups had been truly independent bases of political power presumably occupying a position of dominance in the policy orientation of the Cárdenas administra-

---

* *Campesino* is a useful and broadly inclusive term meaning countryman. As such, it generally refers to rural workers, peasants, and small farmers of modest circumstances.

tion.[25] In retrospect, it seems at least as likely that workers and *campesinos* as organized political forces and even, in a way, Mosk's so-called New Group of industrialists were partly instruments fashioned and sustained by the Revolutionary party-government bureaucracy in the process of pursuing its objectives and seeking a wider area of popular support. Of the several interpreters utilizing the discontinuity hypothesis, it should be said that Tannenbaum, far more than the others, has accorded the party-government bureaucracy a leading role in this period—an interpretation seconded and explored by Eastin Nelson in his "A Revolution in Economic Policy: An Hypothesis of Social Dynamics in Latin America."[26] Johnson has indicated the strategic and catalytic role of Mexican intellectuals and professionals in the early days of the Revolution but perhaps has not emphasized sufficiently the continuing importance of these groups by virtue of their intimate relation to, and their absorption by, the apparatus of government and party in subsequent years. Yet it is perhaps precisely in this matter of recruitment of public leadership that one finds the explanation for the somewhat autonomous or independent direction supplied by the bureaucracy in the face of which other interest groups have tended to play a rather more subordinate role. Nowhere is this signal importance of the "working intellectual" and professional specialist evidenced so clearly as in the operations of federal agencies and other entities in the fields of education and economics. As Octavio Paz has put it, with the Revolution "diplomacy, foreign trade, and public administration opened their doors to an intelligentsia which came from the middle class. Soon there emerged a numerous group of technicians and experts, thanks to the new professional schools," and Mexican intellectuals became deeply involved as counselors and directors in government work: law making, planning, schools, banks, and the like. And in time government officials became involved in and intermixed with industrial and financial leadership as well. Increasingly, especially under Cárdenas, the government assumed

tutelage of the labor movement, and what began as an alliance
under Carranza became a subordination to government by the
1930's. Again in Paz' apt phrasing, both labor and the middle
class until quite recently "lived in the shadow of the State." [27]

Aside from the ambiguities left unresolved in the area of social
and political dynamics, it has been argued that the discontinuity
hypothesis so misreads the data of events both prior to and following 1940 that it is not really in accord with the facts of the
record. Such essentially is the gist of Germán Parra's rebuttal of
Tannenbaum. In any case, because of its focus on political
rhetoric, thought, and events, apparent discontinuities loom
large, while analysis is not carried deeply enough into the economic order to discern the lasting economic significance or
implications of policy and the underlying continuity of economic
development. That is to say, because of its very emphasis on
discontinuities, it is not particularly helpful in elucidating the
gradual establishment of the preconditions for the economic take-
off of more recent years.

If elements of discontinuous change have been, from the economic point of view, overemphasized in the preceding hypothesis,
there is another conceivable explanation which lays stress on
just the opposite, namely, the phenomenon of continuity in a
long-term historic sense. While it is not here contended that any
noteworthy student of Mexican affairs has subscribed to this
hypothesis (herein labeled the historic-continuity hypothesis),
it nevertheless merits some examination on at least two counts.
For one thing, this view, like the one mentioned above, is not
without a certain limited validity. For another, some notion of
what is involved in it is essential to avoid falling into a crude
sort of *post hoc, ergo propter hoc* fallacy in assessing the distinctive contributions of the Revolution to Mexican economic development.

In simplest terms the historic-continuity hypothesis could be
constructed as follows: the principal preconditions for secular
growth were established before the Revolution came to pass so

that the Revolution as such must be construed as of distinctly secondary importance, certainly not as the agency of the take-off. Using the growth line set by the undeniable period of *Porfiriato* * expansion, one could ascribe later periods of production increases to a continuation of developments begun during the earlier era, with the trend occasionally depressed by such factors as revolutionary strife and ensuing social disorganization and occasionally lifted by exogenous forces.

It is perfectly true, of course, that the Mexican Revolution did not begin *de novo* so far as economic progress is concerned, for the forty or so years prior to 1910 had witnessed a marked upsurge on a number of fronts. Especially after 1880, foreign capital had poured into Mexico to develop the country along lines of its comparative advantages: bringing modern mechanization to mining, installing public utilities in the major production and population centers, building railways, and stimulating the expansion of commercial agriculture for export and domestic consumption. Between 1877–78 and 1910, there was approximately a fourfold real increase in foreign trade.[28] Output of refined sugar rose from 25,000 tons in 1877 to 137,000 tons in 1911. Coal mining was begun around 1884 and reached a level in 1910 not attained since. Oil production, which was approximately one million barrels in 1900, was twelve times that amount by 1910.[29] Modern financial institutions were introduced,[30] and railway trackage increased from 578 kilometers in 1874 to 24,559 kilometers by 1910.[31] While the latter was intended primarily, as was general in the pattern of economic colonialism, to move export products to deep-water ports and border points, because of the location of Mexico's principal producing areas and its foreign markets, the railway lines in effect provided the nation with the elements of a trunkline network. Local industries developed quite rapidly as well. The number of textile looms rose from 9,000 in 1880 to 23,000 in 1907, and new enterprises were launched in

* The *Porfiriato* designates the long era, 1877–1910, dominated politically by Porfirio Díaz and his associates.

such varied fields as iron and steel production, glass, paper making, and brewing.[32] Immigrant entrepreneurs played an active role in all this,[33] but the expansion provided some limited opportunities for Mexicans themselves to accumulate industrial experience. In addition, it is possible that the philosophical emphasis accorded material progress by the positivist *científicos* * of the *Porfiriato* was a force in reshaping the neo-Iberian value system in a manner more conducive to economic growth and in increasing the latitude of social tolerance of deviant behavior (i.e., economic-commercial activity as contrasted with traditional aristocratic and landowning pursuits). However, the traditional Hispanic value system was probably never so antithetical to economic ends as the conventional characterization of that system suggests.[34]

Since the inception of the Revolution, the exogenous factors contributing additional impetus to economic expansion have been, primarily, the depression of the 1930's, which admittedly precipitated a similar wave of industrialization in Latin American countries other than Mexico, and World War II, with its attendant influx of refugee capital and human talent, its heightened demand for Mexican exports, and its effective protection of domestic industries from import competition. Other external stimuli of secondary importance have been the rising amounts of foreign investment, the substantial earnings derived from tourism, and the supplementary boost in foreign exchange earnings and domestic demand arising from *bracero* remittances.[35] Without doubt, too, the geographical proximity of the United States, combined with tourism and the *bracero* movement, has facilitated the cross-cultural transmission of new values, tastes, and attitudes and has accentuated the force of the "demonstration effect" in Mexican development in more areas than consumption patterns alone.[36]

---

* *Científicos* is the conventional appellation given the small coterie of top political advisers who, espousing positivism, purported to guide Mexico toward "scientific" development.

Moreover, geographical proximity to the large and growing United States markets has had a beneficial effect on the international transport charges applicable to Mexican exports. Along with the natural resource endowment and the amplifying effect of an evolving supply of productive factors on the range of alternative production functions, location has therefore provided Mexico with a relatively wide range of international goods and enhanced its capacity to expand exports in a diversified pattern. Of all the Latin American countries, only Peru has moved even nearly so far away from monocultural export dependency. Yet, while one must concede considerable importance to the export sector as a provider of foreign exchange to cover growing national investment requirements, foreign trade appears chiefly significant as a permissive, growth-conducive condition which has allowed maximum latitude to the unfolding of the internal growth dynamic. In a different economic context, the rising volume of imports, which has shifted increasingly to producer goods imports (representing, in 1956, 47 per cent of gross domestic investment expenditures), might well have taken the form of a greater inflow of consumption goods.

On balance, however, the historic-continuity hypothesis would seem to underestimate the significance of the primary discontinuity in twentieth century Mexican experience by its failure to take into account the radical shift in the pattern and orientation of development since the Revolution. While certain details of this shift constitute the main focus of the latter part of this study, some of its chief features include:

1. a change from an economic environment in which internally accumulated capital accounted for only about 34 per cent of total national investment to one in which it represents 90 per cent or more (while foreign capital shifted drastically from an export-market to a domestic-market orientation);

2. a recasting of fiscal policy from one in which public expenditures for basic development accounted for 26 per cent or less of total public expenditures to one in which this pro-

portion rose to 82 per cent, with, at least in some periods (e.g., 1940–1951), public receipts covering all current expenditures and a large portion of public investment expenditures as well; [37]

3. a transformation of the institutional framework making for a rapidly widening range of production possibilities and calling forth the participation of more human resources in the economic process in forms other than mere provision of draught power;

4. a pronounced change in the character, distribution, and intensity of national motivation;

5. an elevation of innovation—both in technology and social organization—to a position of centrality in national activity.

Taken together, these and other changes can perhaps most effectively be summarized in terms of one of the Mexicans' most often used expressions for the Revolutionary objectives: Mexicanization of the economy and its enveloping cultural milieu, a concept which is defined in the second section of this essay,[38] and which centers around the function of control.[39]

While insufficient statistical records are available to construct a detailed profile of investment activity since the Revolution began, there seems to be little room for doubt that changes of basic importance have occurred. Especially with the decline of petroleum production after 1921, investment from abroad lost in long-term importance relative to capital generated locally. And export-oriented investment declined in importance relative to that oriented to the economy's internal growth. Domestic expansion, in other words, became less dependent in both respects on the international market mechanism.

That heavy costs have been incurred, at least over the short run, is undeniable, but the result of Revolutionary policy has been substantial achievement of its proclaimed objective of Mexicanization as well as of its attainment of a more diversified economic structure imbued with a greater measure of resiliency

and a wider horizon for further advance. In view of the crystaliz-
ing tendencies observable in the social and political structure
of the late Porfirian era, there seems to be scant evidence that
this radical transformation would have been effected more or
less automatically in the absence of revolution. In this sense,
the Porfirian framework of economic advance seems open to indictment on two main counts. First, if one considers the concept
of infrastructure as comprising two parts, economic overhead
capital and social overhead capital, the expansion obtained in
the former component was combined with substantial neglect
of the latter. The result of this serious investment imbalance was
manifest in the Revolution itself—evidence that the *Porfiriato*
had failed to construct a productive social organization viable
over the long run. In other words, the continuing failure to
make the total investments necessary to support rising levels of
output over the longer term in effect meant an overstatement of
net national returns prior to 1910 at the expense of an under-
statement of the current social costs involved. The failure to
cover all costs led eventually to a detrimental impact on levels
of national output in the form of revolutionary upheaval and disorganization. From the long-run social point of view, therefore,
the Porfirian system was fundamentally uneconomic in its allocation of resources because of its attempt to postpone the meeting
of certain (social) costs of production and to defer necessary
supporting (social) investment outlays.

Secondly, the growing institutional rigidities of the *Porfiriato*
combined with the increasing supplies of productive factors to
produce a system in which the capacity for growth in aggregate
output was disproportionate to the capacity for change, so that
genuine economic development, which involves both growth
and structural change (with the latter providing a feedback to
the former), was possible only to a limited degree.

Furthermore, even the capacity of Mexico to receive and benefit from several of the secondary external stimuli of the past three
decades is not unrelated to the shape of Revolutionary economic

policy. The *bracero* movement, for example, with the high degree of labor mobility it implies, is hardly conceivable without the abolition of the system of latifundia and debt peonage. And certainly the work of Revolutionary governments, bent on integrating the nation by extending the network of transport and communications (using the latter term in its social process sense as well as in its technological sense), has been a further essential ingredient in generating *bracero* dollar incomes. Government programs of this sort together with efforts to improve public sanitation and government promotional activity have also contributed mightily to the more or less continual expansion in tourist-industry earnings, a development that was dependent, in addition, upon the success of post-1920 administrations in creating an environment of social and political stability. Moreover, the Revolutionary preoccupation with and cultivation of *indiginismo* * have functioned to preserve what, from the viewpoint of cultural heritage and tourism at least, is an important national asset.

While World War II ushered in a period of accelerated industrial growth and provided foreign exchange reserves to fuel the investment boom of the postwar period, it added little that was essentially new to the Mexican scene and served rather to push pre-existing economic trends along at a more rapid rate. Furthermore, it can be demonstrated fairly readily that developments during the 1930's had, albeit unintentionally, prepared Mexico to turn to account wartime conditions by increasing the elasticity of supply of both international and domestic goods through construction of industrial capital, accumulation of entrepreneurial experience, and development of an industrial labor force. One might well wonder if industrial growth could have proceeded at such an accelerated pace after 1940 without these prior developments in building a fairly substantial indus-

* *Indiginismo* refers to the concatenation of efforts centering on the Indian communities: the study of their cultures to ascertain their distinctive values, cultivation of Indian folk arts and crafts, the formulation of policies designed to rehabilitate the Indian population, and the like.

trial nucleus. Thus, while large new investment outlays were often precluded because of wartime dislocations in the import supply of capital goods, productive capacity had been built up sufficiently during the 1930's that output—and, along with it, exports and dollar exchange reserves—could be expanded considerably with relatively low levels of additional investment, though part of the explanation probably lies in capital consumption as well (especially in the transport sector). Gross national product in constant pesos, for example, rose from 20,721 million pesos in 1940 to 34,084 million pesos in 1946 while the marginal capital-output coefficient for the 1941–1946 period averaged only about 1.5.[40]

In short, examination of the evidence highlighted and organized by the two alternative hypotheses would appear to lead back to the central hypothesis under consideration: namely, that the Revolution was an historic social fact uniquely and intimately related to the phenomena of economic development. Before attempting to define the significant relations in this area, however, it is appropriate to sharpen the focus by explicitly excluding from consideration a number of tangential issues.

For one thing, there is no intention of looking into the general question of whether or not a revolution, in whatever form it may take, is a precondition for economic development either in Latin America or in the backward areas as a whole. There are, of course, examples of revolutions which have led to long-term economic retrogression, as in Haiti after the 1790's. And in some countries, e.g., Sweden and Denmark, development has come without revolution.

Neither is there any concern in this study with the extent to which the Mexican Revolution and the economic policy directives flowing from it may have resulted in malallocation of resources. The spectacular growth rates in particular industries and sectors are not in themselves valid indicators of the general process of expansion. In some instances, they may have been achieved at the expense of growth in other industries and sectors which would have contributed more to long-run growth in total national output. In a period of experimentation conducted under intense social pressure rendering action imperative, and in an environment characterized by deficient economic information and a rudimentary development of technical economic competence during the earlier revolutionary decades, defects in this area—even substantial ones—are to be expected as a matter of course. A sophisticated theoretical understanding of development processes is, after all, itself a comparatively recent development. The real question is how, despite the more or less inevitably large quota of errors of judgment, inconsistent policies, and administrative deficiencies, the growth process has been initiated with success.

It is also irrelevant to the purpose of this study to examine the evidence of residual backwardness. One can without difficulty discover regions of continuing deep poverty, as in communities of the central and southern portions of the country. One may point out correctly that 40 per cent or so of the population is illiterate. And it has been claimed that real income for the bottom 20 per cent of the population has declined both relatively and absolutely in recent years.[41] But poverty has historically been an unexceptional condition in Mexico, and it is the exceptional phenomenon of the march out of poverty which merits analysis. The interest, in other words, is rather in investigating how, despite all odds and a high and rising rate of population increase, real income per capita doubled between 1939 and 1956,[42] and how, with almost no educational resources to speak of in 1910, Mexico has managed to teach over one half of its population to read and write. In a way, the whole matter of perspective has been most effectively stated by Carlos Fuentes in his remarkable *La región más transparente,* a novel which provides much useful insight into the workings of the Mexican Revolution. Looking out the window of his modern office above the vast expanse of Mexico City, one of the central characters of the book, a newly rich banker of humble origins, reflects,

Out there still remain millions of illiterates; barefoot Indians; people in rags dead from hunger; *ejidatarios* ° with a miserable parcel of land arable only in the rainy season, without machinery, without loans; unemployed people who leave for the United States. But also there are millions who have been able to go to the schools which we, the Revolution, built for them; millions for whom the *tienda de raya* [the company store of the *hacienda*] was abolished and for whom urban industries were opened up; millions who in 1910 would have been peons and who now are skilled workers, who would have been domestic servants and who now are typists with good salaries; millions who in thirty years have moved up from the common people to the middle class, who have automobiles and use tooth paste and who can spend five days each year in Tecolutla or Acapulco. Our industries have given work to these millions, our commerce has given them roots. We have created, for the first time in the history of Mexico, a stable middle class, with small personal economic interests, which is the best surety against revolts and rioting. People who do not want to lose their job, their car, their nest egg, for anything in the world. These people are the sole concrete work of the Revolution. . . . We established the foundations of Mexican capitalism. . . .[43]

Admitting the many defects of the times, the banker asks, "Would you have preferred that in order to avoid these evils nothing had been done?" and goes on to make the telling point that things were done and by Mexicans themselves working under difficult conditions.

II

The matter in question—the role of revolution in changing the Mexican institutional order "from one in which capital formation and the introduction of modern economic organization is difficult or impossible to one in which capital accumulation and the introduction of new production processes appear as 'natural' concomitants of general social progress"[44]—is one which leads directly to the heart of the relations between economic processes and other social processes as they interact within an evolving

° *Ejidatarios* are members of the *ejidos* or collective farms. In some *ejidos*, lands are owned and worked in common. In others, lands are owned collectively but worked individually on allotted parcels. Some *ejidos* combine elements of both practices.

total complex. Accordingly, the following discussion is an attempt to trace and appraise the impact of the several components of the Revolution on two sets of variables, sociological and economic, which bear on the capacity of the Mexican economy to produce ever larger outputs over time. The discussion employs a "field" concept of interacting forces rather than the more mechanistic concept of cause-and-effect relationships; this is done because of the complexity of the relations between the great structural changes in social, political, and economic institutions which took place in the first thirty years of the Revolution and the rapid economic growth of the past two decades.

The initial impact of revolution was negative, or, perhaps more accurately, permissive: it shattered the pre-existing institutional framework. This may well have been its major value, for it is difficult to escape the conclusion that the primary growth-constricting factor in the pre-1910 period was the social structure of that era. The repression of initiative, the underutilization of labor power, the limited possibilities of capital accumulation, the direction of public investment, and the narrow range of investment alternatives seem each to have had their origin in the prevailing set of social relations. By reason of its explicit repudiation of the whole organizational pattern of Porfirian society, the Revolution opened up the possibilities of change along a wide front in the cultural complex of Mexico, changes which, cumulatively, were to amount to a fundamental restructuring of the system of social relationships. And while the actual details of Revolutionary policies were evolved pragmatically over the years, this broader significance of the upheaval was perceived even before the older period came to a close, especially among an articulate group of professionals and intellectuals, which class was to provide much of the leadership and ideology in ensuing decades. Their growing discontent with the existing order found expression in a number of areas of life.

The Flores Magón brothers and others working with them in

the labor movement adumbrated a large portion of the Revolutionary goals of economic development and social justice in the pages of *Regeneración,* a periodical founded in 1900, and in the Liberal Party platform issued in exile from St. Louis. The important *Los grandes problemas nacionales,*[45] written by Andrés Molina Enríquez and first published in 1908, gave voice to essentially similar views. While agricultural and labor reform was seen as the most pressing issue by these and other writers of the times, both Molina Enríquez and the Liberal Party group indicated their awareness that industrial expansion was constricted by the Porfirian structure and that all sectors would benefit from changes in the national market brought about through agrarian reform. Though originally Francisco Madero had viewed the most necessary changes as those relating to political freedom, by the third edition (1909) of his book, *The Presidential Succession of 1910,* he began to concede the pressing need for social reorganization. Even the realm of philosophy and ideology was undergoing reconstruction during this period through the work of Wistano Luís Orozco, Antonio Caso, and others associated with the Ateneo de la Juventud (a society of intellectuals). The ideas and concepts of these and similar groups began to be pulled together in various plans and decrees prior to 1917 and in effect were synthesized in the 1917 Constitution.[46]

In the first instance, then, by combining fluidity of social organization with the existing potential for growth inherited from the nineteenth century, and by increasing the capacity of Mexico to receive and turn to account later technological and economic developments, the Revolution can be taken, at the least, as a necessary though not a sufficient condition for development. In this broad sense, it was perhaps somewhat analogous to the longer-term significance of feudalism in Western Europe: while the resource base and the inherited technological and organizational knowledge of classical civilization (enriched by culture contact and by borrowing over the course of ensuing centuries) provided a basic growth potential for Western Europe, the dis-

integration of the archaic institutional fabric of the Mediterranean world, which found its logical culmination in the late
Roman Empire and Byzantium, opened the door to further
changes and new forms of social organization amid the in-
terstices of a decentralized, fragmented feudal order.

As the following pages will suggest, however, the Revolution
appears to have achieved something more than merely a "liberation" of the growth potential of the economy. In several respects
it has indeed constituted or supplied the motivating force to
realize and to increase that potential for expansion. The prominent sociologist, Lucio Mendieta y Núñez, while conceding that
much of the advance in modern Mexico has been attributable to
its sharing of the global development of science and industry,
views the Revolution's meaning in essentially these terms, assessing it as

a stimulus, a type of reaction which awakened the energies of the
Mexican people, saving them from the morass in which they lived and
which, whatever the failings of that great movement, . . . established
in the national life a climate of improvement and an orientation, which
seems definitive, toward social justice.[47]

Of central importance in this catalytic role was the Revolution's impact on the national power structure and decision-
making process. The overthrow of Díaz brought into control
a group which had occupied a position of marginality in the
narrow social structure of the *Porfiriato;* the group had in large
measure grown up in the heightened tempo of economic activity
of that era, although its roots were in the earlier reform period
following the Mexican-American war. Lucio Mendieta y Núñez
has noted the emergence of this group, aptly described as a
white-collar proletariat, which in the context of prerevolutionary
Mexico was not able, on the basis of achievement, to advance
to the rather limited number of higher posts in national economic and political life, these being reserved in the main to
foreigners and Mexicans well connected in family relations.[48]
The memorable phrase—poor Mexico, mother to foreigners and

stepmother to Mexicans—depicts with considerable accuracy
both the objective situation and the widespread subjective reaction to it. The Revolution was the vehicle by means of which
this subordinated group—consisting of intellectuals and native
business and professional persons—was to move into the top administrative posts of an aggressively interventionist government,
which by its actions was to increase the number of significant
decision-making positions and increasingly to fill these positions,
despite the continuing importance of political influence, with
technically qualified nationals.

Not only does this new group appear to have been the most
creative, innovation-minded, and, relatively speaking, the most
technically competent native group on the Mexican scene, but
also its dominant motivations implied a shift in the ends to
which power would be exercised and resources utilized. It was,
in other words, a group precommitted to change and experimentation. With its accession to power, the Revolutionary leadership, fueled by the pressure of popular aspirations, could and
did bring the full resources of the state to bear upon the promotion of change and innovation in social organization, economic
relations, political processes, and general cultural values.

In the three decades following the beginning of the Revolution, by means of far-reaching reforms carried out by the central government and through organization of the major interest
groups into an overwhelmingly dominant political party, the
new middle groups at the helm of the government and party
bureaucracies were able ultimately both to eliminate the effective
power of the landowning and foreign elite of the *ancien régime*
and to reduce materially the independent power basis of that
other bane of Latin American political history, the regional
caudillo. The land redistribution program effectively disposed of
the older native aristocracy, so far as its traditional basis of
political power was concerned. The expropriation of major foreign investment holdings in land, petroleum, and railroads, together with the new importance of labor legislation and central

government intervention in labor-management disputes as opposed to collective bargaining procedures (with the obvious potential for differential enforcement of the new labor legislation, especially with respect to foreign concerns), eliminated the prerevolutionary power position of the foreign capitalists. The role of government in the field of labor and its control of tariff and import policies as well as its provision of industrial credits gave somewhat similar leverage over domestic industrial interests. Central government control of the land redistribution program, of the irrigation and road-building programs, and its pre-eminent position in the supply of agricultural credit undermined the role of the regional *caudillos,* whose position was further eroded by the gradual "domestication" of the military into a nonpolitical, professional arm of the government.[49]

In this manner, the federal government established its control over competing power structures and created a relationship of direct dependence on the machinery of government among the major interest groups in national life—the *ejidatarios,* the small farmers, urban labor, and the industrialists—for in so linking the central government with the people, it reduced the independent role of other potential focal points of popular loyalties: local landowners, state governors, military leaders, labor and peasant leaders, and the like. It is from these developments and from the enlistment of a rather large portion of the available national leadership talent in public administration that it appears warrantable by way of hypothesis to assign a certain measure of independence to the Revolutionary bureaucracy which, in its control of the administrative mechanisms and political processes of an interventionist state, has provided Mexico with a creative intellectual leadership of a "leftist" but essentially pragmatic and nondoctrinaire character. And within this hypohesized framework of relations, elements of continuity appear as relatively more significant and those of discontinuity as relatively less significant in the historic record of the past half-century. Accordingly, such phenomena as "the emergence of the middle sectors" and the New Group of industrial entrepreneurs appear as part and parcel of a larger social process of cumulative change along a new continuum initiated by the Revolution, for their locus of origin is clearly in the revolutionary process itself: directly in the Revolutionary bureaucracy, indirectly in the policies pursued by that important segment over the years.

The key to comprehending the action program of this new type of national leadership lies in the scheme of values to which it has been fundamentally committed and of which the 1917 Constitution was a summation. Far from merely delineating the framework of a new politico-legal structure, the articles and clauses of this document linked the concept of democracy directly to economic, social, and cultural improvement and in essence represented a statement of aspirations and a blueprint for achievement. In the nature of the case, the several goal-components of the Revolution have been closely interrelated, the more so as they are all suffused with or even, in a sense, subsumed under a more comprehensive value: the quest for national identity or *Mexicanidad* in cultural values and forms. In political and economic goals, this central Revolutionary value, Mexicanization (the realization of *Mexicanidad*), has implied:

1. erection of a socio-politico-economic structure in which decisive control over resource use is vested in purely domestic or national institutions—the attainment of national autonomy or independence in economic as well as in political affairs;

2. restructuring of the national economic system to "internalize its dynamic," that is, a regrouping of the dominant factors and forces of economic life to the end that these become responsive primarily to conditions prevailing within the national borders rather than without;

3. progressive elaboration of a more democratic arrangement of the structure of opportunity with broader participation in decision-making processes; and

4. construction of a pattern of economic organization in which the benefits of economic growth accrue primarily to

Mexicans and are translated into rising material standards of living for the population at large.

On the conviction that "history teaches us that the struggle for national redemption cannot be begun without a radical revision of the confused system of values," [50] as early as 1910 a group of young intellectuals organized the Ateneo de la Juventud to begin to work out a distinctively Mexican *Weltanschauung* in reaction to the prevailing positivism of the Porfirian period "which could never satisfy our ambitions." [51] Drawing on the wellsprings of Hispanic culture, the group studied the personality and work of outstanding Spanish American thinkers, not to focus on the nature of man so much as to comprehend the ways and implications of culture, for what was involved essentially was a perspectivist concept of philosophy in which

philosophy is not the quest for certainty, but rather the search for a *point of view* on human life. And as every point of view reflects a determinate climate of culture, philosophy is necessarily a contextual affair. In short, there is no philosophy in general for perspectivism; there is only philosophy in particular, e.g., Mexican, etc. The obvious moral . . . is that henceforth Mexicans should look at the world from a *Mexican* point of view and thus put into practice on a national scale the Socratic dictum: Know Thyself [italics added].[52]

In more recent years, the Grupo Hiperion (another society of intellectuals), working under the general leadership of Leopoldo Zea, has attempted to utilize existentialist concepts for a description of *lo Mexicano* and to derive a humanistic sort of philosophy from Mexican experience in accordance with Zea's "circumstantialist" belief that "any particular philosophy whatsoever is born out of the problems of human experience." The initial results of this exciting effort were published in 1952 in a series of books under the general heading of *México y lo Mexicano*.[53] In a remarkably parallel contemporary development, intellectual understanding of the socioeconomic reality of Mexico has been enhanced by a long series of studies ranging from the early Molina Enríquez book through the "Estructura Económica y Social" studies sponsored by Nacional Financiera to the *México: Cincuenta años de revolución* volumes referred to earlier.[54]

Intensive efforts to socialize the Revolutionary perception of *Mexicanidad* have proceeded along several lines: notably in the government patronage of the fresco muralists of the 1920's and the mosaic muralists of the 1950's, in aggressive promotion of a "socialist" system of public education, and in the continuing *indiginismo* efforts of Revolutionary administrations.

In the first of these, lavish subsidization of the production of a public art explicitly placed art in the service of social change, for the great murals—pictorial testimony to national problems, solutions, and goals—were seen as vehicles for keeping the spirit and ideals of the Revolution in motion for illiterate as well as literate segments of the population.

In the second area of action, quite early in the Revolutionary period and in response to the 1917 Constitution's commitment to popular education, the central government undertook what was, relative to the available resources, a massive educational effort in establishing and supporting a system of rural and urban elementary and secondary schools, technical and industrial schools, and institutions of higher education. Prior to the Revolution, there were only a few thousand schools in the whole Republic, and few of these were in the rural areas where some 80 per cent of the population lived. In less than five years after the establishment of the Ministry of Education in 1921 (which superseded an earlier agency), federal action had established over a thousand rural schools, serving some 65,000 students, in addition to which an even larger number of other rural schools had been opened under the auspices of the states and private sponsors operating in accordance with Article 123 of the Constitution. By 1934, the number of rural schools had risen to over 8,000, and in 1947 the number reached 13,700.[55] By 1935, three central agricultural schools and nine regional agricultural schools were operating. The National University was reorganized in 1929, a National Economics School was established in 1935, and in 1936 the National Polytechnical Institute was created. Supplementing the formal educational system was an active *alfabetización* campaign against illiteracy, in which hundreds of volunteers were enlisted to conduct basic instruction in improvised classrooms in patios, public squares, the homes of workers, and even on mountainsides.

On the one hand, the investment in education had an important effect in fostering upward social mobility and growth of a middle class and in increasing sharply the supply of Mexican nationals available for filling positions in the economy requiring higher technical competence. Theodore Schultz has ventured the opinion that the rate of return on capital invested in improving the quality of the human factor of production is probably much higher than that used to increase the stock of reproducible goods and cites Mexico as a specific example of a country which has achieved significant increases in productivity by a wise allocation of resources in this direction.[56]

On the other hand, an equally meaningful economic value of the effort has been the program's explicit objective of using the schools to effect attitudinal changes compatible with social modernization. The sociologist Wilbert Moore reports that "Education seems to be part of the contemporary aspiration even of the impoverished sectors of the Mexican population . . . [and] the schools may be credited with success in overcoming the apathy and fatalism long charged to the Mexican peon."[57] Other students of the Mexican scene have attributed a major role to the new schools in fostering a sense of community solidarity and a heightened national consciousness in rural communities[58] and feel that the schools together with the new political relationships established after 1910 have, along with other developments, drawn even the more isolated rural villages "increasingly into the main stream of national life."[59] "New games learned in the school emphasize teamwork, competition, scoring, definite goals, loyalty, sportsmanship, and physical exercise. In contrast, the traditional games were characterized by quiet play, little or no physical skill or exertion, and little competition."[60]

While it has been charged that education in more recent years has changed from an agency for inculcating Revolutionary aims and cultural change to a more prosaic teaching of the 3 R's, it would appear that by then the general forces making for cultural change had already acquired a probably irreversible momentum and that the evolving complexity of Mexican society called for increased attention to technical preparation. Even so, this development in itself is a part of the process of cultural change and one, moreover, comprehended by the larger goals of the Revolution. To interpret this shift in emphasis as evidence of a weakening of the Revolution does not, therefore, seem justifiable. In short, apart from its direct effect upon increasing productivity through raising the level of technical competence, education in Mexico has also operated to upgrade the national capacity for successful economic performance by heightening the geographical, social, and intersectoral mobility of labor (and management) and by affecting in an economically advantageous way the interplay of initiative and incentives through emphasis on achievement motivation.

A related development of considerable importance has been the concerted effort made throughout the Revolutionary period to incorporate the indigenous population into the national community, working thereby to a resolution of the difficulties posed for economic, social, and political development by a dual society. Though the Spanish crown had employed the church's mission movement to achieve a limited sort of assimilation, the serious problems of social dualism had been largely neglected throughout the nineteenth century, and planned acculturation may be said really to have begun with the Revolution's repudiation of nineteenth-century *Malinchismo.** From the early cultural missions through the Department of Indian Affairs to the more re-

* *Malinchismo* means the uncritical acceptance of European and North American norms with an unrealistic disregard for the cultural conditions actually prevailing in Mexico. The *científicos*, especially, were addicted to *Malinchismo*. The term is derived from the name Malinche, the Indian woman who betrayed her people to become the mistress of Cortés.

cently established Instituto Nacional Indigenista, one discerns a progressive sophistication and growing effectiveness in national-action programs in this critical area. The literature on the subject is extensive, but the guiding precepts of the movement have been set forth lucidly by Alfonso Caso in his *Indigenismo*.[61] In essence they are the systematic integration of indigenous communities into the economic, social, and political life of the nation by furnishing them with "cultural elements of positive value, in the government's view, as replacements for cultural elements which are valued negatively in the indigenous communities themselves." While the early experimental efforts of the cultural missions to promote general cultural development in Indian communities inevitably fell short of their objectives, it is noteworthy that even one aspect of their failures—the rather high percentage of rural dwellers exposed to their influence who migrated to the cities instead of returning, as anticipated, to their villages to spread the teachings of the missions—may have had a positive economic effect by increasing the elasticity of labor supply to urban-centered modern economic activities.

At the same time, the rejection of *Malinchismo* in favor of indigenous and national values has enhanced the status of the mestizo. In consequence, *mestizaje*, or racial mixture of European and Indian ancestry, has become more effective as a solvent for the older ethnic differences and hence an aid to upward social movement. Indeed, *mestizaje* has come to be so closely associated with *Mexicanidad* as to be virtually identified with it. For example, George Foster records that in the village of Tzintzuntzan the older distinctions between Indians, mestizos, and *criollos* (persons of pure Spanish ancestry), have tended to fall into disuse as all have come to think of themselves as, first, mestizos and, later, more simply as *Mexicanos*.[62]

Associated with this general Revolutionary drive towards Mexicanization have been three interrelated factors of cardinal importance for the economic order: one relating to motivation (achievement), one relating to social structure (an expanding open structure with increasing room at the top and middle levels), and one relating to social process (general upward mobility on the basis of intellectual and economic competence). The phrase, *forjando patria*, the title of an early Revolutionary period book by Manuel Gamio, furnishes a striking indication of the relation of the first of these to the larger movement of the times, a relation which is clarified further by developments in the field of public art which, in Mexico, has been to a pronounced degree reflective of the surrounding social realities. Appearing as a not infrequent element in the great protest and propaganda murals of the 1920's, the value of achievement was an even more recurrent motif in the sophisticated thematic complexity of the murals of the 1950's. These latter works, in stressing the cultural inheritance of the Mexican people by recreating in pictorial references the life history of the nation, have the rather clear intent of using this tradition to engender pride and self-confidence. Those of the new University City, in particular, seem to point the way to a future rich with the promise of renewed greatness through national effort.

Though I have been unable to discover any published studies which focus directly and primarily on this matter, the indirect evidence adduced from a variety of fields would appear unmistakably to point to the pre-eminent position accorded achievement motivation in contemporary Mexico, if one uses the concept of "achieving" in its common-sense meaning of accomplishment, ambition, or assertiveness rather than in the more narrowly circumscribed sense in which D. C. McClelland talks of *n* Achievement in a recent book, *The Achieving Society*. In a study of international management, for example, J. Fayerweather, who earlier had made a special study of executive behavior in Mexico, observes that in Mexico "an aggressive drive for progress is common," in marked contrast, he adds, to the situation in many other less developed countries.[63] According to some still unpublished but extraordinarily interesting research conducted by E. E. Hagen, James Abbegglen, William E. Henry, and Louis Schaw in Mexico,

in which leading business innovators and executives were inter-
viewed and given thematic apperception tests, this drive for
progress appears to relate more to an almost narcissistic or ego-
centric drive for power and personal domination rather than to
n Achievement in the McClelland sense. As the psychologist
William Henry observes, however, in the present and recently
past Mexican cultural context, the *n* Power motivation may be
more germane to activity which is, in the social sense, describable
as "achieving" or "getting things done" than the *n* Achievement
motive proper. Similarly, the somewhat vestigial particularistic
and diffuse norms which distinguish the Mexican entrepreneurs
from their contemporary *gringo* counterparts may also be at least
partially functional in the setting in which business enterprise has
been conducted in Mexico. That such traits and the Mexican executive's limited perception of the role of collaborative authority
would constitute a condition inimical to effective operation of
large corporate undertakings in a more modern economic system
is therefore not altogether relevant to explaining the take-off
period of Mexican growth. The same research does provide some
evidence, though, that the personality of the Mexican business
leader and his perception of his role are currently undergoing
a distinct transformation. In any case, for these reasons the concept of achievement motivation employed in this essay includes
both *n* Achievement and *n* Power. Both, in other words, seem
operationally relevant to economic accomplishment in the period
of growth in question.

Turning to another field, one finds that a fairly heavy emphasis
on achievement motivation (with some emphasis on affiliation
motivation) has been built into the Revolutionary educational
effort as described in the previously cited studies by Sanchez and
Booth, and a similar priority of value is implicit in the constructive existentialism of Zea and other philosophers. Not at all atypi-
cal is the rather soaring expression of this, along with other Revolutionary values, in *Pensamiento y dinámica de la revolución
Mexicana,* a collection of essays by the Mexican economist, Ra-

món Beteta. Pages 74–76 of this work are especially noteworthy for a brief but revealing statement of the meaning of the Revolution to the vanguard of Mexican intellectuals.

Significantly, too, the rather extensive body of Revolutionary period literature has both rejected the nineteenth-century tendency toward self-denigrating *Malinchismo* and has affirmed new social and psychological values which are "the two most powerful constants contained in all the novels of the Revolution." [64] Even among the many writers acutely troubled by the distance between Revolutionary ideals and reality, F. Rand Morton detects a continuing hope or elemental optimism which rests on a basic belief in democracy, in open-ended possibilities for improvement, and in man in his Mexican incarnation. Thus, even though no content analysis has been made of Revolutionary literary works to code them for such psychological variables as *n* Achievement, *n* Affiliation, and *n* Power, it would not appear that the value postulates incorporated therein are incompatible with the hypothesized motivational changes here under discussion.

It is not, of course, altogether true that achievement (or achievement-power) motivation was absent from the prerevolutionary cultural climate. That it was a significant value among the *científicos* of the *Porfiriato* is clear, as Leopoldo Zea notes in his *El positivismo en México*.[65] Furthermore, the several accounts of the antecedents of revolution in Mexico indicate that the frustration or repression of this motivation among the subordinated middle groups by the narrow Porfirian structure was a key factor in precipitating the overthrow of Díaz. It also seems reasonable to infer from the work of John Gillin that achievement motivation has been at least latently present, and often overtly so, in Ladino society, for in his study of the basic components of the ethos of Latin American culture, Gillin finds (a) a concept of the individual which sees each person as having the right and even the obligation to fulfill himself by pursuing his own "inner-directed" goals and (b) a prevailing awareness of the (limited) opportunities for upward mobility within the accepted hierarchically organized system of social stratification.[66] To note the presence of achievement motivation in the pattern of Ladino culture in no way implies, it must be added, a contradiction of the frequently remarked traditional disrepute attached to manual labor or utilitarian productive pursuits. The point is rather than within the older social organization the limitation of opportunity blocked its expression for low status segments of the population, the secure position of the dominant elite reduced the pressure on its members for action, and for the rest the expenditure (often prodigious) of energy directed toward achievement not unnaturally was channeled toward culturally approved forms of achievement, which is to say toward those activities for which the pattern of society provided rewards: military adventure, literary creation, and legal and political maneuver. The Brazilian maxim cited by Vianna Moog in his *Pioneiros e Bandeirantes*—"he who works has no time to make money"—says a great deal about the relation of achievement to the structure of opportunity in traditional Latin American society in general.

There is considerable evidence that a type of achievement motivation which relates importantly to utilitarian work concepts has been latently present in at least some of the major Indian subcultures of Mexico and Latin America—a matter worth recalling in view of the often-implied laziness and indolence of the indigenous populations. The developments recounted in Robert Redfield's *A Village That Chose Progress* [67] bear upon this point, as does Oscar Lewis' finding, in his well-known study of Tepoztlan, that the rural Indian finds security in his devotion to work and that in the village culture no social stigma attaches to manual labor. It is interesting to recall that the matter finds some corroboration in studies of other indigenous cultures in Latin America. Sol Tax, in his *Penny Capitalism: A Guatemalan Indian Economy*,[68] has described the presence of a very strong commercial orientation and acquisitive bent among the Indian cultures of a neighboring country, and Allan R. Holmberg, writing about an area farther south (in Peru), has commented that "to accumulate wealth in an agrarian society like Vicos . . . the peasant must work hard and be frugal. It is through physical labor that he gains dignity and it is through frugality that he accumulates wealth." [69]

Though it is true that in some cases—the Lewis study of Tepoztlan, for example—a relatively "favorable" indigenous concept of work seems to go hand in hand with a near absence of any strong achievement motivation,[70] there is also the suggestion that this situation may be construed as a low level of motivation based on a probably realistic assessment of available opportunities—perhaps conditioned as well by the notably poor quality of interpersonal relations.[71] Where economic opportunity presented itself, the results appear to have been different. Charles M. Leslie observed in this connection that the Indian population of Mitla had, in common with many other Indian communities, a pronounced pecuniary orientation and that, with the expansion of local coffee cultivation in the late nineteenth and early twentieth centuries, commerce became increasingly a major focus of community interest.[72]

To the extent that one can draw valid inferences from these and similar studies for the value systems and motivational structure of indigenous peoples, it would appear that the alleged Indian "passivity" has been only partially an inherent cultural value springing from his perception of the relation of man to the universe. It has been also an adaptive mechanism or response to a singularly oppressive and unrewarding social structure which both narrowly constricted the range of economic opportunities available to the Indian population and held to a minimum the resources, including those of education and technological know-how, necessary for getting ahead. The pattern of income distribution prevailing under the Porfirian and earlier dispensations wrought an additional negative effect. Altogether, therefore, the available evidence leads to the conclusion that historically "backward" Indian masses were behaving more rationally in terms of their environment than has sometimes been supposed. Thus, a paralysis of productive motivation and a weak interest in exertion would derive from simple ignorance of available opportunities, malnutrition, limited economic capabilities, and the lack of any clear-cut correspondence between expended effort and accruing results (owing to appropriation of increased output by the entrenched elite) as well as from such factors as habit, tradition, and "prerational" or "precommercial" values. The former might well have been, in fact, the objective basis for confirmation and validation of the latter.

Among the landed aristocracy—*los grandes terratenientes*—the economic expression of achievement motivation was similarly repressed, for in the main these non-innovating absentee owners received their income on the basis of ascription rather than achievement. For some, access to the top political and economic posts (and the formal and informal emoluments thereof) came by virtue of having the right family connections, so that the assignment of leading economic roles was a matter of status prerogatives rather than technical competence. Many appear to have been vested with sufficient free income from their extensive property holdings (often hypothecated and rehypothecated for additional ready cash) that the marginal disutility of efforts to increase the low prevailing level of productivity was often in excess of the marginal utility of the additional income to which such efforts would have given rise—in a sense, the same relationship which held true for the actual workers of the land. The long-run effect of land redistribution was, among other things, to change these marginal relations in a manner conducive to increasing the outlay of productive effort—particularly after education, market participation, and increasing involvement in national life were able to affect the consumption patterns of the rural population and hence the marginal value of additional income.

While it cannot be said, in the light of the foregoing analysis, that the Mexican Revolution introduced achievement motivation into the cultural complex of the nation, it did, by initiating apparently irreversible and contagious changes in attitudes and organizations and by injecting a dynamic character into popular aspirations and expectations, "liberate" the expression of this motivation in several respects. Such was the magnitude of this liberation, however, that it seems appropriate to speak of it as a qualitative rather than a merely quantitative change.

As might be expected, achievement motivation has appeared most strongly in the new middle class which, Lucio Mendieta y Núñez finds, has come to place a high value on education, science, technical competence, and rising material standards of living and which has provided leadership in all areas of social activity: politics, intellectual life, the arts, and, of course, industry and trade.[73] It was this group, of course, which the Revolution brought to the top of the power structure, displacing a small elite of achievement-oriented *científicos* and comfortably affluent, nonstriving absentee landowners, for amidst the chaos of the first decade or so of the struggle, there emerged from the officers and the rank and file of contending factions a group of people bent, quite simply, on getting ahead. Over the long run, this shift in the incentives and desires of the people at the helm was to provide Mexico with a technologically-minded leadership in both public and private activity and in both managerial and labor groups. Again Carlos Fuentes' *La región más transparente* furnishes much insight into the appearance of this group in the context of the Revolution and the relation of its motivation to the Revolutionary goals. In the words of a new Mexican millionaire who had earlier fought in the battles of the day,

And it was our lot simultaneously to defend the postulates of the Revolution and to make them work to the benefit of the progress and the order of the country. It is not an easy task to reconcile the two things. What is very easy is just to proclaim revolutionary ideals: land redistribution, protection of the workers, whatever you please. Then, it was our turn to go into the difficult question and to realize that the only political verity is compromise. That was the Revolution's moment of crisis. The moment in which we had to decide to begin to build and construct, even if it meant tarnishing our consciences. To sacrifice some ideals in order that something tangible would be accomplished. And we proceeded to do it in a good and proper fashion. . . . The

Porfirian period had offered no roads ahead to any of us; it had closed the doors to our ambition. Now the time had come to get up in arms. . . . Our hour had come, but always working for the country, not gratuitously as those had during the old regime.

. . . [I]t was necessary to work hard, to serve the country. Otherwise, why should we have made the revolution? Not to sit down and contemplate the triumph of our ideals but to work, each one in his own field. . . . [W]e all felt that the moment had come to make great resolutions, to arm ourselves with an ambition beyond all tests.

. . . In those days there were no enterprises with Northamerican participation which might protect you against all eventualities. Then we gambled with our lives every day . . . not with easy politicking but with guts, guts, and more guts.[74]

Striking though this new orientation has been among the members of the Mexican bourgeoisie, the incidence of achievement motivation has by no means been confined to this group alone. The investigation of lowerclass families made by Oscar Lewis in his *Five Families* [75] would seem to indicate that it has played a role in the social dynamics of the "culture of poverty" as well— in this instance, in the urban variant of that subculture. Still more important, however, has been the change in rural attitudes, for one finds in the widespread and intense adulation of Madero at the commencement of the Revolution a generalized popular attachment to Revolutionary ideals and the first significant expression at the popular level of the new concepts of democracy and brotherhood.[76] Following a rather long period during which public attention was distracted by events and personalities, the Cárdenas program of land redistribution and nationalism (e.g., the petroleum expropriation) appears to have reawakened with new intensity the rural public's aspirations and its interest in political and economic issues. With enthusiastic approval of Cárdenas and his policies, the rural population identified more closely than ever before with the goals of the Revolution and gave expression to a sense of vigorous forward movement.[77]

Not surprisingly, one finds distinct evidence of these changes in the available anthropological and sociological literature. The

Redfield study of the Yucatan Mayan village of Chan Kom is
directly relevant, for though a number of influences contributed
to the striking development of Chan Kom, Redfield's account
leaves little doubt that it was the Revolution and associated conditions which were of decisive importance in releasing human
psychic and physical resources (which in turn mobilized additional nonhuman resources) for modernization and expansion.[78]
Corroborating evidence for this change in motivational structure
is supplied by Clarence Senior's Land Reform and Democracy [79]
as well as by Leslie's study of the Zapotec Indians of Mitla. In
the latter, the Revolution is seen as accelerating the trend in
which power, prestige, and wealth derived from commerce and
the provision of specialized services of all kinds: "Money com-
peted with sacred rituals and kinship in defining social relationships," and "an individual's status was determined more and more
by individual achievement, less and less by the possession of land
or even by the system of town service." [80]

Undoubtedly the social significance of achievement motivation
has been enhanced and reinforced by the Revolution's emphasis
on democratic organization and procedure with all that they
imply for widespread participation and accumulation of experience in the decision-making process. Moreover, the new value
assigned to a higher level of aspiration has been accompanied
by the fostering, through extensive organizational innovation and
assistance in mobilizing necessary material means, of group and
individual action to realize those aspirations. In Land Reform
and Democracy, Senior describes important developments along
this line in the organizationally and motivationally retarded rural
sector (pages 89–165), and similar efforts can be found in a
variety of other fields: e.g., the work of the Banco del Pequeño
Comercio del Distrito Federal.[81] In this sense, achievement motivation has been reinforced by establishing a closer relation between action and reward and by encouraging a heightened capacity (and awareness of capacity) for goal-directed behavior.
Even in places in which directed or guided social change has

been minimal, there is evidence that the Revolution, by reducing the level of affluence and power of cacique families and by redistributing hacienda lands, has had a considerable psychological impact on the population in the direction of strengthening attitudes of independence and initiative and, conversely, reducing those of submissiveness.[82] In the Tepoztlan case, Lewis attributes to the Revolution's impact on village life "a general rise in the standard of living, the expansion of educational facilities, as well as a weakening of the older concepts of authoritarianism and a corresponding strengthening of democratic values"[83]—in short, the creation of an environment in which achievement motivation has practical meaning.

During this transition, substantial operational difficulties have been encountered in a variety of forms—in village factionalism, in bureaucratic power-seeking, in irresponsible and corrupt behavior—but these in themselves may be taken as indicative of the radical nature of the attempted change in question, a change of inestimable long-term economic import demarking a sharp break with the traditional pattern of paternalism and its associated lower status values of passivity, endurance, and quiescent acceptance. The costs of these difficulties—reflected, for example, in such forms as the heavy operating losses incurred by pioneering institutions like the Banco Nacional de Crédito Ejidal[84]— may perhaps be validly viewed as part of the investment in social change and reorganization. Together with expenditures on education and indigenous assimilation, they represent an allocation of resources to improvement of the social framework within which economic processes are conducted—perhaps a necessary condition for long-term national economic growth.

Of no little consequence for the change in values and motivation has been the use of a mystique of revolutionary nationalism, buttressed by government tutelage of organized groups, to provide a consensus mechanism for concerted, collective action. In this respect, modern Mexico has been quite distinct in reducing the debilitating, bitterly partisan factionalism so much in evidence in other Latin American countries. A dramatic case in point is the Cárdenas program, which did more than merely engender a feeling of national pride and independence. By rallying the support of practically all sectors of Mexican society (in the petroleum expropriation), it contributed outstandingly toward the building of a spirit of national group solidarity. And in providing such a mystique, the Revolution has been able to work part of the way toward the transmutation of the motivation for individual achievement into cooperation for group and national achievement. In the process, it has probably mitigated the contraproductive aspects of Hispanic individualism and personalism,[85] which elsewhere in Latin America have been charged with being "inimical to the emergence of social relationships which would enable individuals to act concertedly in the pursuit of common goals and interests."[86]

Apart from providing appropriate social conditions for the more effective interplay of achievement aspirations and goal-centered action and in addition to developing a mystique for a more socially beneficial coordination of individual action of this sort, the Revolutionary emphasis on an open and expanding social structure has served in at least two other ways to link the expression of achievement motivation more closely with national development objectives. A recent and impressive study of contemporary conditions in Latin America observed that there tends, in the region in general, to be an overproduction of intellectuals "whose frustrations at not being able to find what they regard as employment suitable to their talents contributes in no small measure to political instability in Latin America."[87] Though a similar condition is not entirely absent from contemporary Mexico, it seems nevertheless true that in this respect the situation is probably far more favorable in that country than elsewhere in Latin America. While the cited statement could be applied with accuracy to prerevolutionary Mexico, owing to the more or less steady and rapid expansion of both private and public sector activity since the mid-1920's, there has been a continuing call for competent and trained persons to staff the higher and middle echelons of management and administration. Energy which has constituted a potential source of discontent and disruptive agitation has, therefore, tended in large measure to find outlets in channels of constructive employment, as, for example, in some of the agricultural training institutions and the national railway enterprises.

Secondly, as later sections of this paper will illustrate, with the over-all expansion of the social, economic, and political structure there came a widening range of socially approved channels for the realization of achievement. The nation which had historically been so productive of generals and politicians began forthwith, in response to the new range of opportunities appearing in the environment "when administration replaced revolts," to generate men of enterprise in commercial and technical fields as well. For by providing strong incentives for sizable numbers of the population to break with traditional patterns of behavior, Revolutionary developments called into being the latter-day counterparts of Pirenne's medieval *deracinés*—culturally uprooted people freer to make those innovations in behavioral adjustment required by the new situations into which they had been thrust.

The expansion of petroleum activity and the educational system during the Obregón administration enlarged the nucleus of white-collar employees, skilled laborers, and teachers, while the irrigation and highway programs launched under Calles required (and trained on the job) still greater numbers of engineers, skilled construction workers, technicians, and white collar employees. Both mestizos and Indians participated in this socio-economic ascent. The enormous stimulus given by the Cárdenas administration to banking activity, the transport system, irrigation programs, land redistribution, and the establishment of other new government enterprises during the 1930's and thereafter all led to a notable rise in activity in the contruction industry and an enlargement of the governmental apparatus. In the process, there was a further substantial increase in the number of banking functionaries, civil servants, engineers, technicians, and agronomists.[88]

Such occupational trends were accelerated by World War II, the policies of post-Cárdenas administrations, and the derivative expansion of new industrial and commercial enterprises. Withal, technological and economic skills were increased and diffused to the benefit of the quality of labor and management, and the national enterprises and other government operations in effect generated and trained their own continuing supply of leadership —not only for the exercise of bureaucratic or public initiative but, with the movement of government technicians into top industrial and financial posts in mixed and private enterprises, for private initiative as well. The case of Miguel Alemán—son of a general, who was president and who also is a leading industrial entrepreneur—is especially relevant.

In addition, during this time energetic friends and relatives of political leaders—a "buccaneering new group from the middle class," Maddox aptly calls them—not infrequently used their informal connections with government to reduce risk levels and launch new ventures or expand old ones on the basis of profitable government contracts and "gifts" of capital from the public treasury. Often with backgrounds as workers, foremen, or soldiers, these individuals were, Maddox observes, "motivated to act boldly to attain positions of prestige and status," sometimes intermarrying with older families when the solvents of time and money had, in demonstration of the Talmudic insight, brought respectability.[89] From the dispossessed elite whose younger members sought to recoup lost fortunes in land by turning to commercial, financial, and industrial activities, and from the growing ranks of Mexican nationals employed as managers by foreign-owned concerns conscious of the implications of the new nationalism, came others of those key figures in the Schumpeterian scheme of changes, the latter group in particular supplying the economy with experience in modern production engineering, in the careful computation of costs and returns, in market analysis, in the scientific appraisal of alternative opportunities. And in a circu-lating process of cross-fertilization, the induced expansion of private sector activity has fed back as another recruitment source for public sector leadership. The present relevance of these changes is, of course, the close linking of achievement-motivated endeavor with the requisites of economic development.

Though many are available, two examples will suffice to illus-trate the various sources of economic leadership tapped in con-text of Revolutionary social reorganization. With the upheavals of the early period, among the landed families moving northward for security were the Bermúdez. Relocating in Ciudad Juárez, the family was able to establish a new basis of livelihood in industry (distilling) in partnership with Kentucky interests—owing to the fortuitous circumstance of the passage of prohibition in the United States. With the repeal of prohibition, the Kentucky investors withdrew, and the Bermúdez family continued to operate the enterprise. Later on, A. J. Bermúdez was to become the outstand-ing director of the nationalized oil industry, Petróleos Mexicanos, and, still more recently, the director of the government program to develop the northern border cities.

The rediscovery in 1935 of the important Tehuantepec sulphur deposits, at least second in size to any known deposits in the world, occurred when a former general of the Revolutionary army, Alfredo Breceda, and his engineer partner, Manuel Urquidi, began to explore Baja California for antimony but encountered sulphur deposits instead. As their interests gradually turned to sulphur, the two men began to search the Mexican geological archives for some clues to deposits of the mineral. In the process, they uncovered old manuscripts of the Mexican Eagle–Royal Dutch Shell Company which reported the discovery of sulphur incidental to drilling for petroleum in the Tehuantepec Isthmus in 1904. Because of his status as a war hero, Breceda was able to obtain concessions to a sizable amount of land in the area. After initial unsuccessful attempts to raise capital, in 1942 Bre-ceda formed a venture to develop the resources with the three

Brady brothers (a lawyer, a geologist, and a financier), who had operated in the Central American area as oil deposit finders. Thus was set in motion a development which was to lead to the production of over a million tons of sulphur in 1957, placing Mexico in second place among world producers.

To be sure, the manifest vulgarity of some of the *nouveaux arrivés*, with their eyes always on the main chance, has not escaped scathing criticism. The jeremiads against their unaristocratic or allegedly unproletarian values and behavior (their ambition, their social climbing, their undisguised "materialism") have echoed in Mexico the laments which have almost always accompanied their rise in other societies. But whatever their deficiencies from other perspectives, the point remains that their characteristic motivation and behavior correspond more nearly to the exigencies of material progress than the earlier cultural *Gestalt*. And questions of taste aside, the notable figures who have appeared on the economic scene to build new industrial empires have tended generally to win social approbation from a community which views their individual successes as active ingredients in the task of building a modern Mexico.

Associated with these trends in motivation and behavior is mounting evidence that increased social mobility, linked not infrequently with occupational and geographical mobility, is a reality as well as an ideal. One of the case studies in Lewis' *Five Families*, for example, traces the emergence of a wealthy industrialist from a background of poverty and deprivation, and examples of somewhat more limited mobility can be noted in several of the other case studies. In *Life in a Mexican Village*, Lewis discovered that the Revolution "brought about a general lessening of social and economic class differences," which were fairly rigidly drawn before 1910, and that the upward social and economic mobility had been not inconsiderable. Not only was there a much larger group of small landholders and *ejidatarios* than previously, but also the number of upper-group families had increased with at least half of the families in this group having worked their way up to this category since the Revolution.[90] Elsewhere two Mexican sociologists have indicated the effects of the Revolution on increased social mobility into the growing rural and urban middle class,[91] and José Iturriaga's *La estructura social y cultural de México* presents some striking evidence of the heightened fluidity in class structure arising from Revolutionary social and economic conditions.

The Revolution, during its stage of conflict, on destroying the directing role of the upper classes tied to the Dictatorship, replaced these classes by means of the phenomenon of the vertical circulation of "elites" or social capillarity, which emerges from the whole process of bringing about a violent change in an established order. But along with it, the Revolution created, equally importantly, the economic and juridical conditions which were to give to the middle classes—enlarged with the downward movement of some of the sectors of the upper classes—greater possibilities for development, in those matters which bear on the numerical size of this class as well as in those matters which relate to its traditional structure.[92]

Even by 1940, the class structure of the nation had undergone considerable change.[93] Between 1895 and 1940, an interval in which national population rose from 12.7 million to 19.6 million, the number of persons in the rural upper class (1.05 per cent of total population in 1895, 0.48 per cent in 1940) had actually declined by 41 per cent while the large rural lower class (76.6 per cent of total in 1895, 60.7 per cent in 1940) had grown by almost 23 per cent. During the same period, however, reflecting the modernization of the economic structure and industrialization, the urban upper class (0.39 per cent of total population in 1895, 0.57 per cent in 1940) had grown by 124 per cent and the urban lower class (14.2 per cent of total population in 1895, 22.4 per cent in 1940) had risen by 145 per cent.

Of still greater economic significance, both in terms of supply of skills and market demand, was the changing position of the middle class. Directly linked to the programs of agrarian reform and modernization, the rural middle class (only 1.7 per cent of total in 1895, 3.8 per cent in 1940) increased by 245 per cent in the period in question while the urban middle class (6.1 per cent of total in 1895, 12.1 per cent in 1940) rose by 207 per cent. Even with allowances for statistical inaccuracies and class differentials in survival rates, which are only partially offset by differential birth rates, the general inferences to be drawn from Iturriaga's figures seem valid. Since 1940, according to calculations made by Howard Cline, the trends observed by Iturriaga have been subjected to acceleration. Though the methods of estimation employed by Cline are not strictly comparable with those of Iturriaga, his analysis is nonetheless indicative of the general order of magnitude of change.[94] In Cline's reckoning, the upper classes, by 1960, had come to constitute somewhat over 6 per cent of the total population with the middle class ranging from around 25 to 33 per cent of the total. Interestingly, Cline detects a transitional group of upwardly mobile individuals, some 20 per cent of the population, between the lower class and the marginal middle class.

The economic implications of the foregoing summary account of Mexican sociological changes are clear and of fundamental importance. Both incentives and initiative have been positively affected, with production-increasing consequences on the supply and quality of entrepreneurial and labor factors. New values and policies have been, therefore, significant instruments for effecting a transition from the growth-inhibiting social-structural pattern of the late nineteenth century to one more compatible with modern forms of economic organization, a transition aided and abetted by the growing bureaucratization (and, presumably, Weberian rationalization) of major areas of Mexican life: in the formation of political leadership in the ruling party, in an expanding and expansionist governmental administration, and in economic activity in many ways dominated by new public enterprises and public policies.[95]

To summarize these developments in Parsonian terminology, the Revolution fostered a shift from ascription to achievement as the basis for distributing income, and from particularistic to universalistic standards as the basis for distributing political and economically-relevant tasks among performers. In addition to the quantitative and qualitative impact of these shifts on the supply of human factors, they bear rather directly on the facility with which these factors are shifted from one region to another, from one occupation to another, and from one economic sector to another in response to changing economic circumstances. The drop in the agricultural labor force from 70 per cent of the total in 1930 to 65 per cent in 1940 and 52 per cent in 1960 is indicative of the degree of mobility which has been required. The increase in factor supply elasticities and in the intersectoral and geographical mobility of labor has functioned to improve considerably the operation of the market mechanism and thereby influence the efficiency with which the parts of the economic system operate and interact.

Needless to say, the foregoing developments must be viewed as trends or tendencies, not as a completed transformation of social relationships. Nepotism and other forms of ascriptive association are still to be found in both governmental and private activity, and, in contrast to the prevailing modalities of United States business organization, even Mexican business enterprises, and the interpersonal relations obtaining therein, contain a strong residue of diffuse, affective, particularistic, and expressive elements (as contrasted with specific, neutral, universalistic, and instrumental relations), as mentioned earlier. Nevertheless, it is not uncommon for ascriptive relations—for example, the appointment of a kinsman to a business post—to be backstopped with achievement-based appointments to insure technical efficiency. Despite a certain degree of cultural lag in some of their values, and given the relatively conservative base upon which the financial and business community originally rested, economic leadership has moved far toward modern motivations and values.

Finally, it is evident that the nationalistic character of the Revolutionary movement together with the broad area of congruence between politically significant new class interests and

social goals has assisted the shift from self-orientation to collec-
tivity-orientation in the performance by the new elite of its social
role. This, along with the technical competence of the new elite.
has affected positively the character of economic guidance imparted by the government, increasing the level of systemic operating efficiency.[96] The efficacy of this relatively higher caliber of
governmental economic leadership has been reinforced by four
parallel, interrelated developments which, like the trends described above, have their origins in the Revolutionary program:
(1) the deliberate and progressive Mexicanization of the economic system, (2) the adoption and elaboration of a policy of
aggressive state interventionism, (3) the evolution of political
instruments for building a viable consensus on national policy,
and (4) the formulation and implementation of economic and
social policies productive of "industrial goodwill."

III

The economic counterpart of the political and cultural nationalism described above is found in a long series of measures,
dating from the basic legal framework established in the 1917
Constitution and continuing to the present day. Designed to effect
a corresponding Mexicanization of the national economic structure, they represent a reaction to the *Porfiriato,* at the close of
which over one half of the total national wealth was owned by
U.S. and European interests. Foremost of the measures instituted
in this basic transformation of institutional control was the land-
reform program, which for many interpreters, both Mexican and
foreign, *was* the Revolution. While one may reasonably object to
equating the Revolution totally with only one of its manifold
expressions, it is difficult to overestimate the long-term significance of this profound change in the dynamics of economic,
political, and social life in Mexico. Indeed, it seems likely that a
full understanding of all the implications of this radical step is
only just beginning to be realized, for the difficulty in evaluating
the land-reform program lies in the fact that its effects have not

been confined to the agricultural sector. Perhaps, even, its most important consequences have been manifest outside that sector. Certainly the depth and breadth of the perception of its meaning has undergone considerable elaboration between, say, the early writings of Tannenbaum and the monumental work of Eyler Simpson, not to mention scores of earlier Mexican analyses of the subject, and the more recent appraisals of such writers as Nathan Whetten, Clarence Senior, Edmundo Flores, Marco Antonio Durán, and Joaquín Loredo Goytortúa.[97] There seems to be no reason to believe that this progressive sophistication of interpretation and comprehension will not continue.

For present purposes, the significance of the land-reform program may be sketched in rather quickly. Despite incipient industrialization and the spectacular production achievements of various mineral enclaves, prerevolutionary Mexico was basically an agrarian nation, not only in terms of the overwhelming preponderance of population involved in agriculture and the share of total national product originating in the agricultural sector, but also in terms of the dominant tone of national life. The most important relations of production were those controlled by the prevailing system of land tenure, and with land ownership went ownership of the government at both the national and local level, including the right to make and enforce (or not to enforce) laws, the right to tax or not to tax, the right to control and limit the amount and direction of social investment.

In this system, the large traditional haciendas and, to a lesser extent, the newer commercial plantation dominated the rural scene, controlling almost all of the privately held arable lands, pastures, and woodlands. Something in excess of one fifth of all privately held land was owned by foreign interests, though the exact extent of foreign holdings is not known. Some authorities have even claimed that a majority of hacienda owners were not Mexicans, in which case the Mexicanization aspect of land reform is accentuated.[98] In any event, absentee ownership by a small domestic upper class and foreigners, both with seemingly little

capacity to identify with the interests of the underlying population, was the general rule, and the huge majority of Mexicans
were alienated from access to the available national means of
production except on the terms laid down by the owners.
Monopolistic ownership of land provided the basis for a monopsonistic purchase of labor, and various techniques of debt
peonage were employed to obtain a captive labor force and to
reduce the mobility of labor. Both sets of conditions tended to
perpetuate the use of backward agricultural techniques, for an
extensive exploitation of land and labor factors could in some
measure substitute for productivity-lifting organizational and
technical innovations. While this tended directly to depress the
rate of domestic capital formation, the weakness of the pressure
on landowners to utilize their income for reinvestment rather
than for consumption purposes had an additional, indirect
dampening effect on the capital formation variable. At the same
time, pre-emption of vast tracts of land in the haciendas posed
substantial obstacles to the mobility of capital in agriculture.

By isolating a considerable portion of the population from
any significant direct participation in the money economy and
concentrating money income in a few hands, the hacienda system
had a constricting effect on consumer goods markets and worked
to fragment the economy into a multitude of atomistic, self-
sufficient, quasi-feudal units. Development of an integrated national economy was thereby impeded in several respects, and
for the bulk of the population there was little or no room for
the effective interplay of incentives and initiative, for the ac-
quisition of experience in economic decision making, or for
training to elevate the level of production skills and abilities.
Neither did the majority of Mexicans participate in the process
of public policy formation and administration.

Against this backdrop, starting in 1916 the government moved,
at a generally increasing rate up to the peak year of land redistribution in 1937, to reorganize the pattern of land tenure and
to place more Mexicans in control of the means of agricultural

production, and, by eliminating the power basis of the traditional oligarchy, to free the political process so that public policy formation could thereafter respond to a radically different configuration of domestic interests. In this program, which has given the Mexican Revolution its strong agrarian coloration, the logic of land reform appears to derive both from the logic of revolution and from the requirements of general development. Since the very concept of revolution involves radical change in the relations of production (as well as, perhaps, in the mode of production), and since in an agricultural economy the primary relations of production which are to be changed are necessarily those in agriculture rather than those in the less central sectors of activity, almost by definition anything other than the land policy employed would not have been revolutionary, in the sense of opening the system to changes of far-reaching significance. Moreover, in a context in which agriculture is the dominant activity, it seems economically sound to accord some initial emphasis in a development program to those organizational changes which may prepare the way for upgrading its performance. Because of the relative capital-output ratios in industry and agriculture as well as the nature of intersectoral relations, by this means real income of the majority is apt to rise somewhat more rapidly and consistently than in instances in which a premature industrialization is launched on the basis of an archaic agricultural system.

Midway through the Cárdenas administration, with the most pressing demands for land met and with the former grip of the domestic and foreign *hacendados* (hacienda owners) materially reduced, the logic of the program led to a sharp reduction in the annual amounts of land redistributed, though the 1938–1946 average was well over one million hectares annually and each administration since Cárdenas has redistributed a greater quantity of land than any of the pre-Cárdenas administrations. For example, in the first three years of its term of office, the López Mateos administration distributed some 6,774,000 hectares of land, an amount equal to 15 per cent of the total distributed since 1915.

If one is concerned to find evidence of a policy break in the evolving goals of the Revolution, the drop in annual land redistribution would suggest that it began well within Cárdenas' term of office rather than with Ávila Camacho; but rather than attribute any major reorientation of the Revolution or, indeed, its abandonment to this period, it seems more logical to construe the course of Mexican land reform as a simple matter of doing first things first. In the very nature of the case, a relatively high rate of land redistribution, such as that of 1935–1938, could not, of course, have been maintained indefinitely, and by the end of 1939, when almost twenty-five million hectares had been distributed, the historic function of the land program—the destruction of the latifundia as the dominating factor in Mexican society and the traditional barrier to agricultural and general economic progress—had been largely achieved.[99] Thus the inescapable decline in annual land redistribution rates and the consequent relative increase in prominence of other policies and actions is in no way inconsistent with a long-run basic continuity of goals.[100] As will be seen later on, long before 1939 governmental programs were supplementing land redistribution with efforts to foster agricultural modernization and the settlement and development of new lands, thereby anticipating the Ruiz Cortines "March to the Sea" program of the 1950's.

In the older regions especially, the haciendas were replaced by a variety of types of ejidos, some of which were later parceled out or distributed in fee simple to the members. Figuring prominently in the newer regions of agricultural settlement have been small-to-medium sized individual property holdings ranging from only a few hectares to upwards of a hundred or two hundred hectares in size. The division is not absolute, however, as small and medium individual holdings are also found in the older areas just as new ejidos have been established in regions more recently opened to settlement. Both types of properties have also been established in the earlier as well as in the later periods of reform. For example, during the 1930–1940 period, in which large numbers of *ejidos* were created, the number of small, non-*ejidal* properties increased by 368,711, a gain of 44 per cent,[101] and while many of these small properties are too limited in size to permit effective exploitation, some, not infrequently owned by the merchants and professional people of the towns and cities, appear to be sound commercial undertakings drawing capital (through their owners' urban connections) from the nonagricultural sector.

Over the past three decades or so, these twin products of the Revolution have played fundamentally different roles, in effect reflecting a strategy of technological dualism by means of which the government has pushed for a more rapid national growth through concentrating capital investment in modern sectors of activity.[102] The *ejidos*, which were the major instrument for breaking up the haciendas, have functioned to absorb rural unemployment, thereby providing some work and a means of subsistence for millions of the agricultural population. Devoted to crops the production coefficients of which are relatively variable, they have been able to produce some output on a low-capital, high-labor-input basis. Thus, though there are some exceptions, particularly among the more heavily capitalized *ejidos* of the newer regions, the *ejidos* have "economized" on scarce capital resources and allowed capital to be applied with greater effect in the modern agricultural enterprises where capital-output ratios are more favorable but where production coefficients are more capital-intensive and relatively more fixed. As it is also likely that the reinvestment quotient is higher in the modern agricultural enterprises, initial allocations of capital to them have probably promoted with greater certainty a continuing and self-sustaining process of growth in agriculture. Hence, while the *ejido*, because of its factor combinations, is not the most productive agricultural unit in the nation, it is nonetheless productive in the sense of generating some output and, given the scarcity of cooperant factors of production, may constitute under the circumstances a not unreasonable use of abundant labor resources.

The non-*ejidal* properties of over five hectares in size have, for their part, constituted the major source of increased agricultural output. In 1950, when the distribution of cultivated land between *ejidos* and other properties was about 50-50, the value of total output was divided, in percentage terms, 37-63. Part of the difference in average productivity of the *ejidos* as compared with the non-*ejidal* properties may lie in the level of capitalization, for in 1950 the non-*ejidal* properties had an average per hectare capital investment of 337 pesos in contrast to the 138 pesos average for *ejidal* properties.[103] Another intervening variable of importance undoubtedly is location, for the large majority of *ejidos* are in the less favorable regions of the country and themselves differ markedly in efficiency from those *ejidos* situated in the newer irrigated areas. In contrast, the individual properties include both the nuclei of the reduced haciendas in the older areas (which holdings not uncommonly retained the best of the land of the older hacienda) and the new commercial farms and ranches established individually and in colonies in promising new regions.

From the standpoint of agricultural output alone, therefore, the Mexican agrarian reform suggests at least two lessons. First, freedom of institutional organization in the new agricultural regions was probably more helpful than the *ejido* in the old, though the over-all reform, of which the *ejidos* were a basic instrument, relates directly to the new-land colonization programs in a number of ways—as later paragraphs will indicate. For one thing, the reform laws broke up latifundia control of these new lands, and for another the population pressure (itself partly a consequence of higher food consumption by the *ejidatarios* of the older areas) made the new-land drive increasingly urgent. At the same time, release of the population of the Mesa Central from the bondage of debt peonage on the old haciendas furnished the basis for the increased geographical mobility reflected in migration to the new areas while the political dynamics of agrarian interests in the Revolutionary government insured government attention to the problems of agriculture.

Secondly, the changing role of the hacienda remnants illustrates that the evaluation of agrarian reform must include a look at what happens on lands not redistributed as well as an examination of trends on redistributed properties, for there is some evidence that reduction of the extent of *latifundismo* and the freeing of labor (by opening up access to alternatives of self-employment and nonagricultural employment) have not infrequently tended to exert an economic pressure on the hacienda remnants to attain a more efficient management of productive factors. Incidentally, the reduction of the possibilities for appropriating income from mere extensive land ownership and monopsonistic exploitation of labor has meant that, since the reform, income for consumption and savings has derived rather less from absentee ownership and rather more from direct participation in the processes of production—further evidence of the shift from ascription to achievement in the assignment of economic rewards.

It should also be remarked that the capital investment and output trends in these individually-owned agricultural properties would seem to refute the notion that the agrarian reform drove capital out of agriculture on anything other than a short-term basis. It was, after all, the breakup of the large extensively exploited land holdings which, along with the government's credit, road building, settlement, and irrigation programs, made land available and economically attractive for these newer, more capital-intensive private units. Furthermore, their security—and thus the feasibility of investing in them—rests fundamentally on the general political and social stability brought about in the rural sector by the use of the *ejido* program to appease the pressing land hunger of the rural population. This latter aspect, indeed, might well be considered a vital political precondition which not only has permitted the concentration of increased public and private capital investment in certain parts of the agricultural sector for maximum productivity but also has lain behind much of the capital formation which has taken place with greater investment security throughout the rest of the economy.

As one would surmise from the foregoing, simple redistribution of land did not alone suffice to solve Mexico's agrarian problem even though it did, in the longer run, contribute to agricultural modernization. The compelling demand for land which had become the source of endemic agrarian unrest had to be met, in the main, by giving the *campesinos* the land which they were on. In effect this meant initially leaving much of the population on the poor and semiarid lands of the Mesa Central which, prior to the Revolution, had been able to supply a few large owners with adequate income only when exploited on the basis previously indicated. The precarious economic position of the new properties which replaced the haciendas is depicted by the statistics for 1940, which reveal that 60 per cent of the acreage sown was not harvested—74 per cent of the loss being attributable to drought, 15 per cent to freezes, and the balance to other causes.[104]

Furthermore, though some of the stronger rural population centers received sufficient lands for their needs—allocations which allowed for a modest degree of development and some redistribution of income and wealth—and though these fortunate centers accordingly began to manifest a discernible economic and social improvement, most of the population initially received insufficient amounts of land. In these cases, subsequent population increases were to lead in a relatively few years to excessive land division and the "pulverization" of many *ejidos*. In addition, because of the shortage of land in the more densely populated portions of the central region, many people remained without land altogether.

On the other hand, while land redistribution was not per se a complete solution to the problems of the times, neither was it, in and of itself, the root of the major ills which afflicted the agricultural sector during much of the Revolutionary period. To utilize the post-1910 declines in agricultural output as an indictment of the institutional reorganization involved in the agrarian program seems for a number of reasons to be a somewhat simplistic and partially inaccurate view of the totality of complex forces operating in the environment during this period. Because of its truncated perception of this totality, the rather too hasty condemnation of land-tenure changes also overlooks, it may be argued, long-run factors which have more than compensated for the short-term difficulties encountered.

The major output declines in the 1910's and 1920's occurred, of course, before the redistribution program had gained very much momentum, though to be sure, the anticipation of reform uncertainties probably discouraged investment on the part of existing land owners. In the main, however, the declines seem chiefly attributable to the difficulties of carrying on production in the midst of violent civil warfare. Labor supplies were dislocated by the recruitment of manpower for the various armed factions, and the areas traversed by the armies were subject to recurrent if temporary evacuations. The general organizational disorder led to the breakdown of the rudimentary financing and marketing apparatus as well as to the marked deterioration of the transport network. The latter was seriously impaired not only by disinvestment in capital equipment but also by the actual destruction of rolling stock and roadbeds. The flight to the cities of hacienda managers was probably an additional contributing factor as was the destruction and using up of various forms of agricultural capital, such as sugar mills, under conditions which precluded their replacement. After the cessation of armed conflict and a partial recovery in production levels in 1922–1928, there followed new declines which seem not unrelated to a continuation of the capital deterioration induced by the conditions described above, to the impact of the *cristero* * rebellions, and to the decline in agricultural prices and temporary depression of urban-sector activity which were part of the general world crisis.

After another period of partial recovery in 1931–1934, the balance of the decade—encompassing the period of most intensive land redistribution—was marked by sporadic fluctuations in agricultural output which appear to relate mainly to climatic conditions and to some continuation, in the 1931–1936 period, of the pre-existing declining trend in maize production.[105] By the late 1930's and the early 1940's, agricultural production was clearly beginning to benefit from the general return of peaceful conditions, a strengthening of agricultural prices, the provision of credit from new governmental credit institutions, the highway and irrigation programs, and related developments.[106]

That this last-mentioned recuperation, which has carried up to the present day, could have commenced so soon after the intense reform activity of the mid-1930's itself furnishes a clue that, veiled by the more conspicuously dramatic events of the period and unreflected in the erratic behavior of statistical time series, new forces were set in motion which were working in the general direction of agricultural modernization. One of the perhaps unexpected consequences of agrarian institutional reorganization had begun to appear in the national demographic trends. In all likelihood, an undeterminable but significant part of the crop declines was apparent rather than real and represented a decline in marketed output rather than in production, for the increase in rural population after the early 1920's suggests a marked increase in survival capacity owing to higher rural food consumption as well as to the modest improvements introduced

* The *cristeros* were religious zealots who, in the 1920's, rose in armed protest against the harshness of the government's anticlerical policies. They were also in opposition to various reform policies, or at least to the form these policies took.

in medical and sanitation facilities. Granted that certain problems arose from this increase in rural consumption so far as supplying the urban sector was concerned, in at least two ways this development might be counted as a net gain. By partial alleviation of the age-long underfed condition of the *campesinos*, it may well have increased the work efficiency of the rural labor force so that both the quality and the quantity of labor resources benefited. This, plus the heightened mobility of rural labor once debt peonage was abolished, has probably also been a relevant factor in increasing the supply of labor to the urban sectors of the economy, while the *ejido's* provision of a stake in the country has possibly been a factor in restraining the rural-urban migration to relatively more manageable proportions.

Above all, however, the effective change in the distribution of real agricultural income provided the population pressure which A. O. Hirschman and Colin Clark, among others, have recognized as a galvanizing force in stimulating an accelerated pace of change and growth.[107] This it could effect because the government, by the very nature of its origins and goals, was deeply committed to doing something to improve the conditions of agriculture and the burgeoning Mexican population working therein. In promoting the organization and growth of the Confederación Nacional Campesina as one of the corporate sectors of the Revolutionary party, the government had both established a principle of solidarity among the formerly disunited rural population and provided the *ejidatarios* with an instrument for more effective political action. Thereby the rural population was brought into an unprecedented participation in national political processes where it could exert a continuing, if varying, pressure for steps to improve the agricultural sector. In distinct contrast to, say, the urban-centered reform movements of Chile and Uruguay, the Mexican government began at a fairly early period to make a relatively heavy commitment of resources along the several complementary lines necessary to "complete" the agrarian revolution. It did not, in other words, contemplate that mere

land redistribution would substitute for a broad-front attack on
the conditions of agricultural backwardness and limited land
resources, though in view of the available resources, the other
ingredients of agricultural reform and rehabilitation—rural education and agricultural extension, new credit and marketing
channels, application of capital-using production techniques, and
absorption of redundant rural population in industry—were
necessarily long-range developments. Thus, while the land-tenure
reform, in releasing land from latifundia idleness or low-intensity
utilization, had increased the effective supply of land by increasing its institutional availability, these supplementary developments (especially the investments in highway construction, land
clearing and drainage, fertilizers, irrigation, and in housing and
civic amenities in the new colonization centers) were to add
further to the land supply by increasing its technological availability.

In 1925, to integrate the nation and stimulate agriculture and
industry, a national highway construction program was launched
which was, over the years, to improve considerably the existing
roads and to bring about a more than twofold increase in the
total number of kilometers of highways. In the next year, the
National Irrigation Commission (later raised to ministry rank)
was organized to add, in about three decades, over two million
hectares of irrigated land to the few hundred thousand then in
use. Aside from the creation of private investment opportunities
in the external economies springing from this infrastructure construction, the prevailing high marginal propensity to consume
occasioned a high spending multiplier for the public works outlays, thereby providing a feedback stimulation to investment
in the form of rising market demand. Assuming, as seems reasonable at such low income levels, a high income elasticity of demand
for agricultural products, much of this secondary stimulation returned to agriculture, as well as to domestic industry and commerce and to imports.

In consequence of these changes, Mexico is one of the few
developing countries in which agricultural output has more or

less kept pace with industrialization. In spite of rapid urbanization (the four largest cities have grown about 5 per cent annually
since 1940) and an extraordinarily high rate of population increase, and in spite of substantial increases in per capita food consumption,[108] the Banco Nacional de México research department
could report in early 1961 that the 1960 national agricultural output was sufficient to meet internal needs.[109] In 1959 goods originating in the agricultural sector had accounted for 415 million
dollars of Mexico's 723 million dollars total goods exports.[110]

With such a record of performance, it seems questionable to
imply, as has been done on occasion, that agriculture has some-
how been neglected since Cárdenas in the rush of industrialization. The provision of agricultural credit, and auxiliary services,
both of a technical and marketing nature, expansion of the highway and railway network to outlying parts of the country, the
increase in irrigation and electrification, the elaboration of agricultural extension services and expansion of rural education
facilities—all these efforts and others were continued and often
intensified in the years since 1940. The Banco Nacional de
Comercio Exterior and the Compañía Exportadora e Importadora Mexicana,* which had been established by the government
in 1937 to work toward several goals, among them the fostering
of agricultural production, increased the volume of their operations significantly, and the area irrigated from projects of the
National Irrigation Commission and the Ministry of Hydraulic
Resources rose from 20,000 hectares in 1930 to 267,000 hectares
in 1940 to 2,610,000 hectares in 1958.[111] The establishment of
the new regional development commissions supplies still further
evidence of the government's continuing concern with agricultural progress, even though in some cases the commissions have
not lived up to the original expectations. The Papaloapan and
Tepalcatepec commissions were established in 1947, with the

---

* Later on the name of CEIMSA was changed to Compañía Nacional de
Subsistencias Populares (CONASUPO). Over the years its chief function
became that of marketing low-priced food staples and, in time, other goods
consumed by low-income families.

Río Fuerte and Grijalva commissions being added in 1951 and 1953 respectively. In roughly the same period, the government had also created the National Colonization Commission (1946), the National Maize Commission (1947–1949), and the National Coffee Commission (1949), all devoted to the task of expanding agricultural output.

After 1940 the government began a campaign to improve agricultural technology, giving special attention to replacement of the traditional Egyptian plough with more modern ploughs and to increasing the number of tractors. By the end of the 1950's, Mexico had more tractors than any other Latin American country, surpassing even Argentina whose agricultural acreage was about double that of Mexico.[112] It should be noted, too, that one of the earliest enterprises established by the Nacional Financiera was Guanos y Fertilizantes (1944) which, along with the later addition of other public fertilizer manufacturing companies, lifted national production of fertilizers from 13,000 metric tons in 1945 to 265,075 metric tons in 1958. The packing plants, sugar mills, and other food-processing industries established with Nacional Financiera support also bear directly upon agricultural development.

Agricultural investment as a percentage of total investment rose from 13.3 per cent in 1939, after a brief relative decline in the early 1940's, to 19.5 per cent in 1950,[113] but, more important as an indication of government interest in the field, public investment in agriculture rose from 46 per cent in 1939 to 60 per cent of total investment in agriculture in 1946, dropping back relatively thereafter as private investment forged ahead to take up the investment opportunities provided by government investment and export market conditions.[114]

Thus, the Revolution precipitated a relatively heavy and long-term program of public capital formation in agriculture which in turn, through its repercussions on the national pattern of investment opportunities, has induced a fairly substantial amount of private capital formation in the same sector. As an index of these achievements in agriculture, between 1945 and 1959 the area planted in the twenty-one principal crops increased 78.3 per cent. The average yields in these crops rose 42.5 per cent. The total physical volume of agricultural production rose by approximately 154.2 per cent, and the value of output by 123 per cent.[115]

As the figures suggest, the pattern of land use has undergone considerable modification—mostly in the direction of a more intensive utilization of land resources. Increasingly, the extensive cultivation of the haciendas of the Mesa Central has been replaced by such activities as dairying and the intensive cultivation of cereals, fruits, vegetables, sugar, and alfalfa, with a tendency to shift maize production to the marginal lands. The previously unutilized lands of the north have become with irrigation an important provider of foreign exchange earnings as well as of maize and wheat for the domestic market.[116] There were, of course, special factors contributing to this general expansion— the vicinity of the large U.S. market for products like tomatoes, the opportunity to increase cotton output under the umbrella provided by U.S. agricultural policies, and the opportunities for coffee production during the boom of the 1950's. But the capacity to act on these opportunities derived unquestionably from the basic national agricultural program of reform and modernization. The upshot has been, therefore, a more dynamic and diversified agricultural structure, whose quantum of resources and productive potential have been augmented considerably. And through taxes on agricultural exports, relatively low prices on agricultural goods, including price ceilings on foodstuffs, and relatively low wages, the agricultural sector has been a major source of capital formation for the economy at large as well as for that plowed back into its own expansion.[117]

The contribution of the land-reform program to building a democratic pattern of interpersonal relations and to bringing about a greater measure of social equality and occupational and social mobility has been noted earlier in this discussion.[118] More broadly viewed, it has—assisted by education, transport, and communications expansion—drawn the rural population out of

its former isolation and increased its exposure and vulnerability
to the forces making for cultural change in such crucial areas
as values, organization, knowledge, and patterns of taste and consumption (affecting, e.g., the substitution ratio of material goods
for leisure and the preference for commercial goods over home-
made goods).[119]

Of paramount importance in this connection, especially over
the longer run, is the reform's removal of the repressive and
deadening effects of the latifundia system—with its paternalistic
authoritarian structure and caste-type social relations—on incentives, innovation, and the exercise of individual and group
initiative. In marked contrast to the traditional organization under which the chances for self-improvement by the rural population were virtually nil, the evolution of post-1910 agricultural
organization has provided a context in which the opportunities
to make economically relevant decisions have been far more
widespread and in which the incentives to exercise initiative and
to innovate have been materially stronger (i.e., pecuniarily meaningful) for larger numbers of persons acting as individuals and
as groups. Increasingly, the *campesino* has become an active
rather than a passive agent in the production process. The positive repercussions of this on the quality of labor effort expended
in the rural economy are important enough. The long-term
productivity-increasing effects of a more rapid rate of agricultural innovation and accelerated rural entrepreneurial formation
in the more propitious new system can hardly be overvalued.[120]
Somewhat paradoxically, it would appear that the land reform
also increased the supply of entrepreneurial initiative to, and
capital formation in, nonagricultural sectors of the economy [121]—
and this over and above its market effects in inducing or eliciting
an increase of investment, initiative, and output in these sectors.
For one thing, the reform eliminated the hacienda as an outlet
for savings with strong leakage into consumption, and, by removing more or less effortless rural land ownership as a secure

source of income for consumption spending, it established the practical necessity for an active management of savings (i.e., investment) to obtain income to support desired levels of consumption. Edmundo Flores has pointed out that the older land-owning families, whose urban properties were not affected by the agrarian expropriations, began to receive higher rents with the growing migration to the cities. As the large public works program and urban expansion raised the returns on investment in construction industries, fortunes deriving from urban land ownership began to be invested in cement, glass, iron and steel, and other construction industries.[122] To a significant extent, then, the older landowning group abandoned its passive *rentier* role to become actively involved in new financial and industrial under-takings, including those induced by domestic market growth.

Over the years, too, the institutional and technical changes associated with the land reform have served to give rising numbers of the rural population access to the market and, reciprocally, the market access to them. In other words, a major economic aspect of the cultural changes ensuing in the wake of agrarian reform has been that of bringing a progressively larger portion of the rural community into potential and actual contact with and participation in the national market mechanism on both the supply side, as providers of labor and agricultural products, and the demand side, as users of capital and consumers of other manufactured goods.[123] Commercialization of rural life has, in consequence, been intimately related to the Revolutionary objective of "national integration" in a way conducive to stimulating a broader and more diversified pattern of development. By virtue of the increased tempo of general cultural change, for example, the change in rural tastes and consumption patterns alone has been remarkable:

More and more rural people sleep on beds instead of on the ground, wear shoes instead of huarachos or going barefoot, use store-made pants, instead of home-made white cotton *calzones*, eat bread in addition to *tortillas*, grind their corn in mills instead of by hand, drink beer (or the ubiquitous "colas") instead of *pulque*, use doctors instead of *curanderos*, and travel by bus or train (or bicycles) instead of on foot or by burros.[124]

To an extent, these shifts merely involved the displacement of home manufactures by modern factory goods of, in many cases, demonstrably improved quality. In the process, however, this gradual transformation of rural consumption habits, reinforced by the growth of rural population and relatively more widely distributed rising real incomes (especially among the more acculturated groups located away from the stronger indigenous culture areas) has contributed to the rapid growth of a market demand, highly elastic with respect to income, for the goods of industries serving the domestic market.[125] This, in turn, has encouraged capital formation and the introduction and utilization of modern technology in the industrial sector, thereby enabling the economy to shift to production functions of higher and rising levels of productivity. In this sense, therefore, the agrarian reform, in opening the rural sector to far-reaching innovation and helping to propel the economy into the stage of increasing returns, has been a strategic measure for development—

a catalyst which in chain reaction changes the pattern of income distribution and of the availability and utilization of resources, alters the structure and composition of supply and demand, exercises a profound impact on the rates of population growth and capital formation, and, in general, liberates forces which positively affect the most important variables of an economy.[126]

This, too, is the full meaning behind Flores' statement that

This spatial structure (of the new agricultural regime) is the concrete and measurable foundation of a fluid social organization responsive to economic incentives and to individual and collective initiative. The positive interaction between spatial patterns and social and occupational patterns permits one to predict a more intensive utilization of resources, an increase in external economies, and an increase in the rate of capital formation.[127]

By strengthening reciprocal market relations between the agricultural and nonagricultural sectors, it would appear that Mexico has attained a more or less workable balance which has redounded to the benefit of both sectors.

IV

While the Mexicanization of nonagricultural sectors of the economy has been undertaken in a more piecemeal and, with one exception, a less dramatic fashion, the cumulative impact of these measures has been substantial over the long run.

With the establishment in 1925 of the Banco de México to act as the sole bank of issue and to perform both central and commercial banking functions, the government made its first move to Mexicanize the money market by subjecting the major banking institutions of the country, and the supply of money, to the control of federal monetary policy. In so doing, the locus of the economic power residing in money and banking institutions (some of which were foreign owned) was shifted from the private discretionary authority of bank owners and savers and the vagaries of international trading relations to Mexican public control, to be harnessed to the accomplishment of national economic objectives.[128] Through the commercial operations of the Banco de México and those of the Banco Nacional de Crédito Agrícola y Ganadero, established by the government in 1926 to initiate a national system of agricultural credit, the government moved directly to modify the operations of the money market to a degree greater than that permitted by reliance on central banking controls alone.

With the banking reform of 1932, the Banco de México retired from commercial operations but strengthened its central banking powers. Subsequent years saw the initiation and development of a broad array of government banking institutions operating directly in and extending the coverage of the national money market: the Banco Nacional de Crédito Ejidal (1935), the Almacenes Nacionales de Depósito (1936), the Banco Nacional de Comercio Exterior (1937), the Banco Nacional de Fomento Cooperativo (1941), the Banco Nacional Cinemategráfico (1941), the Banco del Pequeño Comercio del Distrito Federal (1942), the Banco Nacional del Ejército y la Armada (1946), the Financiera Nacional Azucarera (1953), the Banco Nacional de Transportes (1953), the Fondo de Garantía y Fomento a la Industria Mediana y Pequeña (1954), the Fondo de Garantía y Fomento para la Agricultura, la Ganadería y la Avicultura (1955), and the Fondo de Garantía y Fomento del Turismo (1957). In 1960, the government announced the organization of a system of regional agricultural banks.[129] The goals of this progressive intervention have been twofold: to give access to the money market to groups and sectors of the economy not served, not servable, or served only partially by existing private credit institutions; and to channel an increasing volume of short-term and medium-term credits into areas accorded a high priority in the national development effort. In the process, the general increase in credit availability has tended to lower the over-all level of short-term loan rates, while selective intervention has tended to change the structure of these rates, so that domestic enterprises not able to tap foreign financing sources and local private institutions are less disadvantaged than formerly.[130]

Beginning in the early 1930's, the government also moved to effect an equivalent domestication of the capital market or, perhaps more accurately, to build a national capital market to overcome the pre-1910 heavy dependence upon foreign capital. The operations of the Banco de México in financing governmental deficits had in effect "domesticated" the public capital market, while a number of the institutions listed above have also operated in the field of longer-term financing. Indirectly, the assistance given new firms through short-term and medium-term credits has helped to bring these firms to the point at which they could begin to accumulate capital internally.

In 1932, the government authorized the establishment of private *financieras* * to mobilize longer-term funds for industry. With

---

* *Financieras* are somewhat like investment banks but also buy and hold securities for their own account and engage in lending activity.

the establishment of the Banco Nacional Hipotecario Urbano y de Obras Públicas in 1933, the government sought to intervene more directly in the capital market. Originally this bank was intended to finance popular housing, local public works, and— in line with the 1933 declaration of Revolutionary party goals and the six-year plan—new industrial enterprises. In 1933, the Nacional Financiera was organized and (in 1934) charged with developing an organized capital market for public bonds and private securities, and two years later (1936) President Cárdenas set up a Fondo de Fomento Industrial in the Banco Nacional Hipotecario Urbano y de Obras Públicas to provide industry with those elements necessary for its development. In the following year, 1937, the Banco Obrero de Fomento Industrial was constituted for similar ends. In practice these early efforts at fostering a flow of capital to industry were mainly experimental in nature as was the 1941 Fondo de Fomento a la Industria y de Garantía de Valores Mobilarios. Modification of the private *financiera* law in 1941 enabled these institutions to expand the scope of their operations (with government backing since 1945), and in the same year the Nacional Financiera was converted into a government industrial investment bank. Over the years, additional steps were taken to strengthen the capital market. In 1947, the establishment of private savings and loan institutions was authorized, to be followed two years later by a reform permitting deposit banks to grant longer-term credits. In 1950, the Patronato del Ahorro Nacional was instituted to conduct an aggressive program of selling national savings bonds to raise funds for industrialization.

A good picture of the government's role in these matters is presented in the statistics on bank financing, the total volume of which, in 1953, was 13,323 million pesos. Of this total, government banks provided 7,695 million pesos. Private credit institutions—including deposit and savings banks, mortgage banks, investment banks, and capitalization companies—led in the field of short-term credits, providing 3,208 million pesos, compared with 2,599 million pesos from government institutions. In medium-term and long-term financing, however, government banks contributed 5,096 million pesos with only 2,420 million pesos coming from the private institutions.[131]

By means of the foregoing measures, the Revolutionary governments have endeavored to erect the domestic financial infrastructure necessary to support a modern complex economy—to provide, as it were, a financial seed bed in which new domestic enterprises could take root and flourish. Through their relation to the central bank, the government credit institutions have been important agents of public capital accumulation; and through the guarantee programs initiated by government as a backstop for private lending activity, and through such measures as Nacional Financiera's flotation of "participation certificates" on the stock exchange, the government programs have also assisted in eliciting a greater mobilization of private savings for investment. By imparting a greater measure of certainty and security to the financing of new undertakings, through government lending agencies and government-supported private lending institutions, it seems reasonable to assume that additional capital formation has been induced on the part of private firms and individuals. In sum, in creating the basic financial instruments of capital mobilization, the Revolutionary program has increased the aggregate rate of domestic capital formation, in both the public and private sectors of the economy, and, moreover, built the institutional means of directing that capital formation to those areas in which its long-run contribution to lifting the level of productivity in the national economy is relatively great.[132] Very likely, too, the increased facility of obtaining financial support, combined, in some institutions, with the provision of auxiliary services such as economic studies and technical and marketing assistance, has contributed to increasing the supply of entrepreneurs willing to act upon the available economic opportunities. In some cases, where the provision of a favorable environment has for one reason or another failed to call forth private entrepreneurs, the banks (especially Nacional Financiera) have assumed all or part of the entrepreneurial role as well.

Complementing the Mexicanization of agriculture and finance, a variety of tactics have been evolved to effect a similar extension of national control, and sharing in benefits, to the industrial sector proper. In a few cases this has involved nationalization, but in others it has meant the formulation and implementation of policies designed to foster domestic replacement of foreign supply sources and/or a greater participation by Mexican nationals in the operations and fruits of foreign-owned enterprises. The profit-sharing law passed in early 1962 adds yet another instrument for progress towards these goals. In all cases, however, it seems clear beyond any reasonable doubt that Mexicanization has been the paramount objective, even where nationalization has been employed as a means to this end.[133] The point is worth emphasizing, for during the 1930's, particularly, there was a tendency to interpret government action as directed toward the narrower goal of nationalization and "socialization." [134] Even today it appears to have been necessary on several occasions for the present incumbent of the presidential office to make specific pronouncements with a view to clarifying the meaning of government policies and correcting this misinterpretation.[135] It is noteworthy that official policy has never, not even during the "radical" 1930's, really raised serious objection to those types of foreign investment thought to be "beneficial" to the Mexican nation and operating in conformity with the laws of the land: i.e., manufacturing, distribution, and urban real estate.[136] There was, in fact, some increase in foreign investment in these fields between 1930 and 1940 and still more, of course, thereafter. By maintaining free exchange convertibility and unrestricted repatriation of profits and by granting new enterprises customs protection and tax exemptions, the government has, indeed, favored their growth. The opposition that foreign investments in these fields have encountered has more often stemmed from nationalistic propagandists and competing domestic capitalists than from a "socializing" state.[137]

Of the several branches of the industrial sector, the railways were the first to be inducted into the process of Mexicanization. The first decade after 1900 had, in fact, brought an increase in the native personnel employed in operating the system, and during the same period the government made its initial entry into ownership and control of a part of the network. Owing to a variety of circumstances, however, the largely foreign-owned railway lines were encountering increasing financial difficulties by the turn of the century, and during the years of civil strife following 1910 conditions in this key activity became progressively worse in almost all respects.[138] National and international economic conditions added further to the weakness of the railways. By the mid-1930's the system was on the verge of total collapse, and indeed there were those who felt, not without reason, that chaos and ruin were already complete.[139]

As a more or less unavoidable salvage operation, the president decreed in 1937 the complete nationalization of several lines which had been partially government owned heretofore, a step which was extended to other lines in the following year. In this case, the immediate reason for Mexicanization is clear. It was simply an effort to ensure the continued operation of a basic technological component of the national economic structure.

In subsequent years, national railway policy has come to encompass certain broader goals, albeit often in a faltering manner. A program of constructional and organizational renovation, comprehending consolidation, modernization, and extension of the network, has been carried on in an effort to repair the cumulative defects which began to emerge almost from the time the first lines were built. The hoped-for result, which has in part been already realized, was a more efficient transport structure serving a larger portion of the Mexican Republic. In working toward a pricing policy in which the state would cover capital costs, with railway revenues set to attempt to cover operating costs, the government seems to have hoped to bring about a more complete and efficient utilization of capacity (i.e., to move to a lower point on the average total cost curve) and to use cheap transport services as a means of stimulating agricultural and industrial development. In other words, railway policy has, in effect, aimed at lowering firm production costs through subsidizing a relatively low delivered-cost of raw and semiprocessed materials and other producers goods, and at creating an economic and geographical expansion of the national market through increasing the physical accessibility of remoter market areas and helping to lower the delivered price of finished goods in all markets. Insofar as the consequent market expansion has facilitated an increase in scale of production in modern industrial and agricultural activities, one may reasonably infer that it has enabled a number of these industries and firms to obtain over the long run further reduction of production and marketing costs—the familiar phenomenon of external and internal economies of scale making for decreasing costs and increasing returns.[140] The geographical expansion aspect has also, in opening new regions to settlement and resource development, had the "frontier effect" of increasing the supply of attractive investment opportunities in these new regions, in addition to its market effect of increasing investment opportunities in older regions.

Moreover, by facilitating a more rapid and certain flow of goods to markets, railway policy—and the highway construction program which has similar economic implications—has in all probability reduced the relative amount of capital tied up in inventories, releasing it for other investment purposes. Thus, just as the land-reform program eliminated status-oriented latifundia expansion (with its associated conspicuous leisure and consumption) as one major traditional outlet for savings, transport developments have probably reduced the relative attraction of another traditional alternative for capital: inventory speculation and inventory investment for nonspeculative purposes.[141] The relative attraction of more socially productive avenues of investment has accordingly been enhanced by negative measures as well as by positive ones. Finally it should be noted that government control of railway purchasing and investing policies has been used to increase the market demand for the output of—and, accordingly, to promote investment in—certain domestic capital goods industries: the iron and steel industries and the locomotive and railway car works.

The nationalization route to Mexicanization was employed in a rather more dramatic fashion in the 1938 expropriation of the petroleum industry. Prior to the events of that year, the level of national production had been generally falling for about a decade and a half. Foreign capital had begun to move to other areas such as Venezuela, export demand and petroleum prices were dropping, and there is some basis for believing that the 1930's, at least, witnessed some actual disinvestment in the Mexican area—a factor which renders dubious the possible effectiveness of conventional fiscal techniques as a means of redirecting the orientation of this enclave activity and capturing a larger share of its earnings for domestic purposes.

From the Mexican point of view, the industry—which had been primarily geared to export markets and had done relatively little to cultivate domestic consumption and which had tended to rely upon continued employment of highly paid foreign technicians and managers—was declining to the general detriment of national development aims.[142] Against a background of conflicting national and company goals and incompatible property concepts, a protracted and involved labor dispute led eventually to a refusal by the companies to comply with a ruling of the supreme court. In the sensitive political climate of that time, the decisive issue of national sovereignty had thereby been raised. Nationalization was decreed, therefore, under a set of circumstances which indicate distinctly its instrumental relation to the goals of Mexicanization.[143] Labor difficulties, a retaliatory international boycott, the withdrawal of trained technicians and movable capital, and the accumulated costs of previous years of disinvestment and rapacious exploitation of reserves all took their toll, and the initial years of operation of Petróleos Mexicanos were difficult ones indeed.

Gradually, in the 1940's and 1950's, a new pattern of development began to take shape.[144] Investments in exploratory and development drilling restored an upward trend to reserves and production, which, unlike the high levels of output in the earlier oil boom, were obtained in a manner consistent with sounder conservation practices. As a consequence, the national resource base was broadened in a strategic area, for with a concerted effort to renovate and expand refining capacity and to build a domestic distribution system the industry became the major source for meeting, as well as a technique for stimulating, growing national energy requirements. In the process, foreign exchange was released for other uses, and such social costs as deforestation and erosion were reduced through fuel substitution.

Throughout the period of nationalized operation, the petroleum industry has been employed as a multifaceted instrument of development. In its training and recruiting policies, it has both contributed to a wider diffusion of technical and managerial skills among the domestic labor force and provided opportunity-incentives for advancement to more productive types of labor. By increasing the geographical availability of petroleum products and by maintaining a low price policy—which has not, however, prevented financing a substantial portion of new investment out of internally accumulated funds—the industry has been used to stimulate general industrialization and mechanized agriculture. Additional impetus to industrialization has come from the deliberate policy of utilizing a sort of technological multiplier to develop the backward and forward linkages of Pemex's operations. On the one hand the company's investment program has become, for example, an important demand component for the output of the national siderurgical industry. Altogether, in 1957, around 50 per cent of the requirements of the petroleum industry were procured from local supplying industries whereas most requirements had been imported only a decade or so earlier. In the other direction, the output of Pemex has been used in recent years as the springboard for launching a substantial effort in the petrochemicals field.[145] Thus, investment opportunities in broad new areas of the economy, sectorally and geographically speaking, have been created or enhanced by the external-economy impact of petroleum policy on energy availability, cost structures, and supply and demand certainties. The increased amount of public-sector capital formation has been thereby co-joined with positive effects on private-sector industrial capital formation, both of them, moreover, in areas of relatively high productivity with potentialities for future growth. Over and beyond these effects upon the amount and direction of investment have been the productivity-increasing repercussions on the supply and quality of entrepreneurial managerial and labor factors. All things considered, it is evident that Mexicanization of the petroleum industry has been a factor of no mean importance in leading the economy to a new factor endowment conducive to the employment of more modern production functions.

A somewhat similar economic rationale lies behind the gradual nationalization of the electric power industry in which government investment programs have been employed to anticipate and push general industrialization through increasing the aggregate energy resource base, spreading its geographical availability, and encouraging, through low price policies, the growth of industrial users of electric power. In part, government intervention was required because of the deferred profitability aspect of this development-oriented policy, and in part government became a major provider of hydroelectric power as a consequence of its multipurpose river basin development programs.

Public action in this field began in 1937–1938 with the establishment of the Federal Electricity Commission, to be extended further in 1940 with the purchase by the government of the

Chapala Electric Company. Soon after its inception, the FEC initiated a heavy investment program which in roughly two decades was to add over a million kilowatts of installed capacity to the 922,824 kw. capacity the two major foreign privately-owned public service companies had installed between 1900 and 1959.[146] By 1959 the government was in charge of plants having 48 per cent of the total national generating capacity of 2.8 million kw.[147]

During 1960, both of the major privately-owned public service companies were purchased by the government in a move that grew out of long-standing disagreements concerning rate levels and investments for capacity expansion. Two features of their nationalization serve to distinguish it from the earlier precipitous petroleum expropriation and denote a marked refinement in the economic application of intervention. For one thing, the two decades of operating experience and personnel-development accumulated by the FEC facilitated the smooth transition to public ownership and national management. For another, the undesirable capital repatriation effect of the petroleum case was reduced by means of an interesting purchase arrangement in which one of the companies involved agreed to reinvest its capital, jointly with Mexican capital, in national industrial development.[148]

Apart from dealing with the immediate conflicts of interest, the step was viewed as a desirable one which, by leading towards administrative and technical unification of the domestic electric power system and facilitating the modernization of older plants, would provide a closer articulation of electric power programs with national development needs. There seems also to have been implicit in this move the idea that nationalized operation would enable the necessary capital accumulation to be effected at lower long-run cost to the economy than either of the alternatives of domestic private operation or operation by foreign-owned private concerns. In the case of the former, insufficiency of capital resources and managerial capabilities rendered private domestic operation unfeasible. Government had, as noted above, already acquired the essential managerial know-how and could through various forced saving techniques raise larger amounts of internal capital, on more favorable terms, than could domestic private interests. As an alternative to foreign private direct investment, external public borrowing was a cheaper method of obtaining funds from the international capital market—an advantage of some relevance to the nationalized operation of the petroleum and railway industries as well.[149]

In 1960, nationalization was also effected in the distribution of motion pictures under circumstances which tend to support the equation of nationalization with Mexicanization. As the developmental import of this measure is palpably remote, however, it will not be treated further.

V

Contrary to the view which holds the goal and the fact of industrialization to be a comparatively recent development in Revolutionary history, dating essentially from the Ávila Camacho administration of the early 1940's, a case can be made that the initiation of the industrial revolution in Mexico was an implicit component of the economic nationalism with which the Revolutionary program was imbued from the very outset. Just as a close scrutiny of the record fails to support the notion that agrarian reform was in any real sense abandoned after the Cárdenas government left office, so also an examination of the economic ramifications of Revolutionary policy between 1920 and 1940 reveals that, long before the alleged policy shift of the 1940's, the government had been progressing more or less steadily toward the construction of an economic system in which industrial production would play an increasingly important role. Even as early as 1913, an important steel company had been established in Mexico City to utilize scrap, the export of which was prohibited by the government. It is difficult, in other words, to find much in the post-Cárdenas administrations which was not present at least implicitly in Cárdenas' policy. And both Ávila Camacho and

Alemán were essentially followers of the bold *Plan Sexenal* laid down in 1934, rather than innovators. Among other things, the Six-year Plan had called for "a coordinated system of genuine national economy," for domestic elaboration of raw materials being exported in an unprocessed or semiprocessed form, and for creation of a national system for the generation, transmission, and distribution of electric power.

That the industrial revolution could appear as a dramatic expansion originating in the fifth decade of this century is accountable partly in terms of the cumulative nature of that phenomenon, reinforced by the exigencies of wartime conditions and, in the postwar period, by the increased availability of external funds and equipment. That it was indeed dramatically evident so soon after 1940 is testimony to the extent to which the ground work had been laid in preceding years. Moreover, its strong coloration by those enduring policy hallmarks of the Revolutionary period, Mexicanization and interventionism, both of which figured so prominently in the foregoing sections of this essay, constitutes further evidence that the roots of industrialism in Mexico are inextricably bound up with the objectives and the program in practice of the whole Revolutionary movement.

Though in this case, unlike the others, foreign capital has generally been favorably received, it has been welcomed because of the wide contributions such companies as General Motors, Quaker Oats, Goodrich, Woolworth, and Sears could make to the domestic Mexican economy—in adding to the national stock of capital, in transferring new skills and techniques to their Mexican personnel and native emulators, and in innovating modern industrial production and marketing practices. Unlike the rather limited diffusion of benefits which ordinarily accrued to the host country from traditional enclave operations, these new investments have tended to increase productivity more broadly in the recipient economy. And by substituting factor movements for trade flows, they have helped to shift the factor endowment of that economy in the desired direction. Accordingly, foreign investments in these fields have been viewed as assisting in the realization of national objectives. Even so, it is significant that they have come in under the same inducements available for domestic enterprises rather than in response to the lavish concessions so often tendered foreign capital in the past; and they have, in addition, been subjected to policies designed to insure their fuller integration into the national economic scene. Thus, despite the acceptance of foreign capital as an important auxiliary in building the new industrial superstructure, the abiding objective of industrial policy remains the same as that of agrarian and financial policy: the erection of an economic apparatus primarily serving Mexican needs, fully subject to national control, and with widespread participation by Mexicans in its operations at all levels.

Most of the material presented earlier in this study relates to the preparations for and the early initiation of industrialization in the Mexican economy. At several points, the reader may recall, the bearing on this matter of the topic under consideration has been indicated. Yet, at the risk of belaboring the obvious, a brief recapitulation may be in order to sketch out the strategy of industrialization developed pragmatically in the course of Mexican experience up to the early 1940's.

In roughly the second and third decades of the Revolution, the government launched an agrarian reform and a large-scale program of infrastructure construction to increase both social overhead capital (i.e., facilities for health, education, and public administration) and economic overhead capital (including both financial institutions, such as a banking system and a capital market, and technological components such as transport facilities, irrigation systems, and, latterly, basic energy industries). On the one hand these programs worked to increase the quantity, the quality, the supply-elasticity, and the mobility of productive factors as well as to reduce various other imperfections of the market mechanism. On the other hand, the combined impact of the agrarian program, the educational effort, the public works programs, and other factors of general cultural change was to make for a quite rapid expansion of the initially small domestic market, while striking a rough sort of balance in the intersectoral or reciprocal market relations which exist between the agricultural and nonagricultural parts of the economy. The interaction of the spreading "external economies" and the rising market demand in turn brought about a concurrent increase in marginal efficiency of capital in the industrial sector and drastically lowered the investment-inhibiting "specific uncertainties" formerly prevailing in the Mexican economic environment.[150] Additional ingredients for a forced draft industrialization effort were injected by the expansionist monetary and fiscal policies of the 1930's which, together with the proliferating government banking system, enabled the government to accelerate the pace of domestic capital formation in both the public and private sectors (through forced savings and induced increases in voluntary savings) as well as to canalize that capital formation into the desired areas.[151] In other words, government policies functioned both to create industrial investment opportunities and to increase the availability of liquid capital for acting on them.

By 1941, the general direction of economic change had, in short, served to build an economic environment favorable to industrialization—especially in the basic construction industries and in light industries catering to the growing consumer markets.[152] Beyond this, however, a variety of special measures had been introduced to enhance the relative attractiveness of investments in the industrial field and to induce thereby a higher rate of capital and entrepreneurial formation in this area. As early as 1920, the government announced its intentions along this line by passing a law giving tax relief and import duty exemptions to certain new industrial ventures. Supporting presidential decrees were issued in 1926 and 1932. Considerably amplified by another presidential decree in 1939, the promotional measures of this category were formalized in the 1941 Ley de Industrias de Transformación.[153]

The rate of return on capital investments in new industries was elevated still further by the protective tariff policy which was employed with increasing frequency by the Cárdenas and subsequent administrations, the shift to protective duties having been made possible by the growing importance of the income tax and other direct taxes in the fiscal system. At the same time, the investment-inhibiting specific economic uncertainties, already materially reduced by market growth and infrastructure investments, were lowered additionally by the security afforded against competing foreign imports.[154] Lest mistakes of still inexperienced domestic investment judgment result in strong domestic competition in certain new areas, security against this possible entrepreneurial deterrent was embodied in the 1936 Law of Industry Saturation, which authorized the President to close by decree the entrance of new firms to any field. Not only did such protectionist measures tend to raise the marginal efficiency of capital in industry, but they very likely spurred industrial investment in a more indirect manner as well. For one thing, by reducing specific economic uncertainties, they probably lowered the risk premium component of the market interest rate for industrial borrowing, accentuating the contemporaneous downward pressure on costs of industrial loan capital exerted by the impact of monetary expansion and government bank lending policies on credit availability. The fall in the time discount, in turn, had favorable repercussions on the economic feasibility of investing in long-term, lower-yielding industrial projects. In the second place, the consequent higher domestic industrial price and profit levels probably induced some transfer of income from consumption channels into investment and reinvestment. In the third place, the combination of monetary expansion, exchange convertibility, and restrictions of consumer goods imports would appear to have imparted an element of subsidy to capital goods imports and domestic capital formation.

It is also noteworthy, in the light of later developments, that under Cárdenas the state began to assume a greater measure of direct responsibility in leading the economy forward through public entrepreneuring, supplementing the as yet deficient endowment of native private entrepreneurs. Aside from the aforementioned state entrepreneuring in finance, railways, petroleum, and electric energy production, which marked an intensification of the Calles infrastructure program, the administration of the 1930's took the lead in organizing the new *ejidal* agricultural production units and in promoting rural industrialization ventures such as the Zacatepec and El Mante sugar mill cooperatives.

As one would expect from surveying the economic forces set in motion by Revolutionary policies, the progressive expansion of industrial activity is strikingly revealed in the index of the physical volume of manufacturing output for the period in question.[155] After reaching a prerevolutionary high of 43.0 in 1910, the level of output declined to a low of 27.2 in 1918. By 1922, however, the 1910 level had been recovered. In 1931, the index stood at 78.0, which was also approximately the volume of production in 1934 after a rather sharp fall during 1932 and 1933. Following a pause in 1935, in which year the index registered 76.0, a new wave of expansion carried manufacturing output steadily upward to 100 in 1939 and 105.1 in 1940.[156]

Behind this record of growth lay trends of inestimable importance for the accelerated industrial expansion of the 1940's and 1950's. A nucleus of enterprises in iron and steel, cement, paper, and in textiles, shoes, beer, tobacco, soap, sugar refining, and flour milling had been substantially expanded from their Porfirian base, and new enterprises, both domestic and foreign in ownership (e.g., Ford, Simmons), had arisen to produce rubber items, household furnishings, metal goods, window glass, foodstuffs, and other products. An expanded resource base and higher income levels provided the elements for rising amounts of domestic capital formation, while a new pattern of investment opportunities was beginning to pull that capital into fields with a higher potential for long-run productivity increases and reinvestment. A growing industrial labor force was acquiring through in-job training and technical schools a wider variety of skills, and the general expansion of activity and economic opportunities created a vacuum which in turn tended to pull that labor force upwards into positions of higher technical competence. In this upgrading of human resources, a supplementary impetus was provided by the Federal Labor Law of 1931, which required that 90 per cent of the workers in each skilled and unskilled category in all enterprises be Mexicans. Though managerial personnel were not included in this law, immigration permits have generally been issued to foreign administrators, managers, technicians, and specialists only on condition that similarly qualified nationals were not available. In consequence, even the new foreign-owned plants attracted to the Republic have generally pursued a policy of providing increasingly wide employment opportunities to Mexican workers.[157]

The spread of economic opportunities meant also a wider participation in microeconomic decision-making and was almost certainly a condition making for a higher rate of domestic entrepreneurial formation during these crucial years. Perhaps, indeed, it is this facet of the experience of the 1920's and 1930's which provides a large part of the answer to the intriguing question left hanging in Mosk's path-breaking study: namely, how it was that in such a comparatively short period a considerable number of aggressive new entrepreneurs could emerge to capitalize on the favorable investment opportunities of the early 1940's.[158] Moreover, the gradual accumulation of entrepreneurial experience in this field was an important factor in reducing the specific uncertainties of new industrialization to manageable proportions. In these several respects, then, by the early 1940's an industrialization process had been established which could feed upon itself for further expansion.

The post-1940 period of industrial growth is so well known as to make a descriptive summary of it superfluous. Suffice it to say, by way of recalling its general dimensions, that the index level of manufacturing output, which stood at 105 in 1940, had risen to 174.6 by 1946 and to 270.6 in 1951, soaring to around 370.2 in 1959.[159] Within this record, which represents in part the impact of exogenous stimulants and in part the pay-off period of earlier developments, some older industries experienced tremendous expansion and whole new fields of industrial activity made their appearance on the Mexican scene. The present discussion will focus upon those aspects of this process which relate it to the distinctive policy framework of the Revolution. Taken in conjunction with the interpretation offered above of the pre-1940 period of industrial growth, the ensuing discussion will, it is felt, strengthen the view that industrialization, far from being an alien child, adopted by the Revolution in its later years, has been a creation of the Revolution itself. Coming forth as a product of the structural changes wrought by that phenomenon, it bears the unmistakable genetic markings of its parentage.

The Mexicanization of the nation's industrial superstructure, which began with early special incentives to spur the growth of domestic industry, the Labor Law of 1931, and the nationalization of basic industries, acquired another dimension in 1944. A presidential decree of that year gave the government discretionary authority to require 51 per cent Mexican ownership in all Mexican companies. Even though the requirement has been imposed in only a limited number of fields, its potential application seems to have been instrumental in encouraging foreign-owned concerns to share ownership with domestic investors.[160] In the same year, by a decree dated August 8, 1944, operations by which Mexican nationals acquired foreign-owned enterprises were exempted from the income tax—a further inducement for Mexicanization.

Related action of a more compelling character was taken in December 1960 with passage of a new mining law. Under the terms of its provisions, future mining concessions are to be granted only to government enterprises, mixed public-private corporations, or Mexican corporations which have a majority of their capital subscribed by Mexican nationals. To encourage existing mining corporations, which are almost 90 per cent foreign owned, to increase Mexican participation, a 50 per cent reduction in production and export taxes was authorized for companies having at least 51 per cent Mexican ownership, and present mining rights were declared to terminate without compensation in twenty-five years for companies in which nationals do not own a controlling interest.[161]

Two other recent examples of Mexicanization policy may be cited as further evidence of the continuing interest of Revolutionary governments in this goal. As in the case of a number of policies described earlier, their effect is to strengthen the appeal and to increase the availability of industrial investment opportunities in the domestic economy. To encourage increased local assembly of automobiles and the incorporation of a greater number of locally-manufactured parts in assembled vehicles, the Ministry of Industry and Commerce, in a decree of November 1, 1960, issued a blanket prohibition against the importation of completely assembled automobiles and indicated its intention of considering the percentage of locally-produced parts in domestically assembled units when granting import quotas to assembly plants or importers.[162] A few months later, in early 1961, the government established the Programa Nacional Fronterizo under the direction of A. J. Bermúdez, the capable administrator responsible for so much of the success of Petróleos Mexicanos.[163] Designed to link the high per capita income areas of northern Mexico through the national market to the industrial center of the nation, the program proposes a variety of measures to accomplish this integration.[164] For example, the Almacenes Nacionales de Depósito, a government warehousing company, will construct warehouses in the important border towns to facilitate the smooth supply of domestically-produced goods to local markets. Special measures will be taken to promote the establishment of new industries in border towns not already enriched by foreign trading activity in order to raise the purchasing power of the area further. To lower the delivered price of domestically-produced goods in these markets, freight rates will be adjusted downward, and tax exemptions will be considered for those goods competing with U.S. products coming in over the border.

As a continuing contrapuntal accompaniment to the leitmotiv of Mexicanization, interventionism has been fully as pronounced a feature of the post-1940 period as it was of the preceding years. The two have, in fact, been mutually reinforcing. On the one hand, Mexicanization has served to bring the controlling factors of national economic life under the purview of the state, enhancing the effective application of controls and interventionary measures. On the other, intervention by the state has been the propelling force in accomplishing the Mexicanization of the economy.

To a large extent the ready recourse to government economic action and state direction of economic life appears to have been an inevitable outgrowth of the necessity of meeting serious internal pressures in Mexican society and making good the Revolutionary commitment to effect fundamental institutional reorganization within a fairly abbreviated span of time—for accelerating, in other words, the relatively slow "normal" pace of institutional change and evolution while holding internal conflicts to a tolerable level. In this capacity, the state may be thought of as the vehicle for expressing those large collective interests which exist as something over and above the sum total of individual interests, and intervention thought of as the instrumentality for abridging the operation of the market mechanism to achieve social and economic objectives not attainable—at least in the short run—within its automatic functioning.

Apart from this larger rationale, however, many of the features of state intervention in Mexico would seem to have developed from the practical exigencies of advancing the tempo of economic growth in the context of a backward society. Some measures have been directed primarily to improving the market mechanism and extending its coverage in the economy, while others have been taken, as it were, in lieu of market-centered operations, to supplement the defective operation of the market and to modify the structure of economic opportunities both geographically and functionally. In this area, the extra-market activity of the state may be viewed as arising out of the disparity between existing conditions and those postulated as essential for effective market behavior.[165]

In neither case, however, has state intervention been confused with "statism." That vigorous intervention is in no necessary way incompatible with privately directed economic growth and that, indeed, under some circumstances such activity may be prerequisite for private-sector development would appear to be amply borne out and confirmed by the facts of Mexican experience.[166] And while such intervention may take and, in the Mexican context, has taken a wide variety of forms, both direct and indirect, as indicated earlier, the form of direct entrepreneurial intervention, which in some ways has been the most striking feature of Mexican policy, merits special consideration in this brief survey of industrialization.

In the post-1940 period, the state entrepreneuring which began in railways, agriculture, and banking before 1930 and which spread to rural industry, petroleum, and electric power under Cárdenas was pushed further into the industrial structure of the nation. Altogether, nearly four hundred undertakings, exclusive of the publicly guided *ejidos*, are government or mixed (government-private) enterprises.

A significant portion of this bureaucratic entrepreneuring has been conducted under the aegis of Nacional Financiera after the widening range of light industries arising in the 1930's and early 1940's had begun to underscore the logic of developing industrialization in depth. To provide domestic supply support for these new industries, thereby alleviating production bottlenecks and maintaining a workable balance in the national industrial structure, the state began in the early 1940's to forge the way in developing the basic industrial underpinnings of the economy. By means of this vertical extension of industrialization, the foundation was also laid for further derivative horizontal industrial expansion.[167]

Throughout its life, the role of Nacional Financiera has been conceived as essentially that of an indispensable instrument of development rather than as a means of socialization. As its record makes clear, the reliance on state initiative in undertaking new industries stems more from the character of prevailing economic conditions than from ideology, except insofar as it derives from the Revolution's endorsement of industrialization and rapid economic growth and its acceptance of state intervention as a valid means to those ends. Thus, economic leadership by public servants of high competence has been both a means of economizing on scarce entrepreneurial talent and a "demonstration" technique which, by showing the way to new forms of industrial ventures and removing much of the uncertainty necessarily attaching to them, has value in cultivating a spirit of enterprise among private entrepreneurs and potential entrepreneurs. Moreover, in the fields of investment in which Nacional Financiera has been especially prominent, a number of factors—the larger capital outlays required, the more complex operations which rendered new ventures technically more difficult to launch, and the higher risks deriving from uncertainties of costs and production flows as well as from the greater market imponderables (i.e., greater than those encountered in industrialization to substitute for consumer goods imports)—all placed the minimum effort required well beyond the capicity of the private entrepreneurs and investors of a still newly developing economy. It would also appear that state-directed industrialization has been utilized as a means of insuring maximum plowing back of profits into further expansion —a distinct advantage in view of the observed tendency in some underdeveloped areas for private capitalists to hold undistributed earnings in industry to a minimum, to the detriment of long-term growth. In this connection, it should be observed that Nacional Financiera has over the years, largely through accumulated earnings, increased the original capital of three million pesos granted it by the National Treasury to 734,555,078 pesos (capital and reserves) in March 1961.[168]

Finally, the rapid and comparatively smooth pace of institutional change and economic growth in Mexico would have been almost inconceivable in the absence of certain valuable contributions to the process which have their basis in the social and political policies of the Revolution, contributions beyond those already taken into account earlier in this essay.

Through a variety of arrangements by means of which the major interest groups have been institutionalized, the dominant political party presiding over this era of massive change has succeeded in evolving a workable method of collaborative economic guidance.[169] By virtue of its internal structure, the P.R.I. affords representation to organized labor, peasants, and the bureaucracy, and over the years a number of formal, quasi-official organizations of other groups have been conceived and promoted outside the P.R.I. by government initiative to establish regular channels for the representation of their interests before the party and government agencies.[170] Among other functions, they work with the government in drafting legislation and making policy decisions. The Mexican Employers Association, for example, was established under the terms of the Federal Labor Law of 1931, and in 1936 and 1941 the government enacted laws which made membership obligatory in the chambers of commerce and industry, which, in turn, were organized into national associations: the Confederation of National Chambers of Commerce and the Confederation of Industrial Chambers. In these organizations, the Minister of Economy controls the establishment of chambers and determines the chamber to which various industrial plants should belong. Another powerful organization, the Mexican Bankers' Association, works closely with the Banco de México and the Nacional Financiera and appoints some of the members of the National Banking Commission, the National Securities Commission, and the Stock Exchange.

Since within this structure the means have been provided for the chief social and economic groups to express their views with some hope of influencing national policy, group action has been steered into regular, more or less orderly political channels. Reciprocally, the national policies emerging from the give-and-take of party debate have borne at least a tolerable measure of correspondence to the respective aspirations of participating interest groups. In thus institutionalizing the formation of a viable, if shifting, national consensus and in institutionalizing the recruitment of national leaders (largely from within the ranks of the party and government bureaucracies), the P.R.I. and the government have managed to construct the organizational basis for a high degree of longer term continuity in policy. Incorporation of the pragmatic mutual accommodation of myriad interests within an all encompassing framework, in other words, has meant that Mexico has been able to avert the paralyzing accentuation of class divisions and conflicts which has so often developed elsewhere in Latin America when divergent class attitudes and goals become crystalized in polarized political parties. While this built-in rapport with the major sectors of Mexican society has undoubtedly been used on occasion to serve narrow interests, it seems more than merely a facile generalization to say that it has, on the whole, demonstrably served truly national objectives even more.

For the new investing groups in Mexico, the foregoing arrangements represent a socially acceptable vehicle for taking action to reduce those primary uncertainties and risks which inhibit the commitment of liquid assets to industrial plant and equipment.[171] For the rising middle groups, the system is a means of pushing dynamic economic policies to provide an expanding array of more desirable employment alternatives. For the *campesinos* and urban workers, it constitutes an agency for raising minimum security levels and obtaining collective assistance for efforts to realize aspirations of upward mobility.

In the latter area, particularly, the Revolution may well have made one of its major contributions to long-term economic development. The land redistribution policy, the labor security measures, and the health, education, and welfare programs all have been instrumental in building that intangible but vital agent of production in the absence of which the other factors are unable to operate effectively—industrial good will.[172] Without this ingredient, as Commons has observed, the operating efficiency of the economy is substantially lowered by disunity and industrial strife, by "soldiering," strikes, and sabotage. From the historical experience of Mexico, one might add to the contraproductive effects of industrial ill will such costs as a passive but noncreative acquiescence of rural labor to the traditional scheme of things, agrarian revolt and disorder, and domestic uncertainty levels which contribute to a high liquidity preference and encourage capital exports in quest of security.

If only for its effects on conditions of loan capital availability, the creation of industrial good will would have marked a substantial step forward in Mexico's advance to modernization, for through its impact on liquidity preference and risk levels it opened up a whole new range of investment alternatives to exploitation. Its influence on productivity levels, however, has been far more widespread than this alone. For one thing, the increase in savings and capital formation obtained through fiscal policy and the distribution of income has, thus far at least, been obtained without provoking overt negative reaction from lower income groups imbued with a rising level of expectations, despite the restraint of popular consumption. For another, the incalculable benefits flowing to the economy at large from the quieting of rural unrest are so patent as to make elaboration of the point needless. Suffice it to mention that for all the severe stresses which have inevitably accompanied the accelerated pace of social and cultural change over the past three decades, the last revolt of any consequence took place in 1928–1929. The years since have witnessed the more or less steady growth of political democracy and social stability, with free speech, relatively peaceful elections, and a heightened sense of national unity. Unlike the forced draft industrialization programs of many other nations, that of Mexico has been carried out, and its challenges met, with essentially voluntaristic rather than coercive or compulsory methods.

In yet another area, the long-term soundness of early investments in industrial good will would appear to have been demonstrated. The available evidence indicates that the Mexican labor
unions, with strong political support from the government's labor
policies, have materially facilitated the transfer of manpower
from agriculture into industry and have helped to integrate the
new workers into the life of the factory, the community, and the
nation.[173] In this transition, government and organized labor have
fostered labor mobility by providing an urban alternative to the
low level security arrangements of traditional agricultural life,
and the relatively high wage levels enforced in industry have
exercised a drawing power which experience suggests could not
have been provided by lesser wage differentials, given the as-
sorted cultural barriers to labor mobility. In addition to taking
on part of the function of labor recruitment, the unions, operating
within the framework of national labor policy, have also been
successful in bringing about significant reductions in the costly
labor turnover so characteristic of most underdeveloped areas.[174]
The machinery provided by government for the settlement of
labor-management disputes has helped to contain the costs of
work stoppages within reasonable limits.[175]

Thus arises the paradox that the strongly entrenched labor union
may be a positive factor in industrial development . . . the labor organization in Mexico, through the very nature of the occupational
heterogeneity of its membership, is a strategic instrument of social
control and change. The wide extension of sindicatos into the rural
villages, their support of village schools, adult literacy campaigns,
adult education in agricultural education and marketing improvements—all this bespeaks the influence of unions toward social innovation. When to this is added local and national direct political
participation, the sindicato becomes a major source of innovation and
national economic development.[176]

Furthermore, if the new behavioral sciences approach to the
problem of motivation and human organization in the field of
production has any significance at all, it is to point to and underscore the relation of morale and a creative commitment of energy

to the job at hand—both components of the concept of industrial good will—to the efficiency of labor in the processes of production. Thus the observation that labor productivity in Mexico, once essential training has been acquired, is generally fairly high for an underdeveloped area may bear more than a coincidental relation to the social policies of the Revolutionary period.

Because of the multitude of influences emanating from the climate of industrial good will, therefore, the costs of the land-reform, labor, and welfare programs have in effect represented investments in labor resources and productivity-increasing social reorganization, which, like more conventionally conceived investment outlays, have contributed importantly to the capacity of the Mexican economy to produce a growing surplus over the long run.

VI

In the endeavor to evaluate the contribution of the Revolution to Mexican economic development, certain conclusions stand out with compelling clarity. The first among these is negative: namely, that the essence of that contribution did not lie in any one change or even in a limited number of marginal changes affecting the relations between resource inputs and output. Rather, the fundamental significance of the Revolution lies in the nature of revolution itself as a comprehensive social phenomenon which initiates a process of sweeping change and transformation among virtually all the components of the cultural complex. In Mexico this burst of energy has led to nothing less than a thoroughgoing restructuring of the whole economic environment and a corresponding radically new pattern of economic interaction.

To be sure, not all aspects of the economic order were immediately affected to the same degree, but by launching a continuing social process of open-ended, cumulative change and by introducing a more or less total reorientation in the direction of that change, the Revolution gradually extended its influence to all the critical factors in economic life. The pattern of motivation and incentives, the structure of economic opportunities, the distribution of investment preferences, the resource base, the range of production alternatives, the appropriation and utilization of the economic surplus—all of these have been profoundly affected by the half-century of Revolutionary development following 1910. More importantly, it would appear rather definite that on balance they have been not merely modified, but modified in a manner conducive to long-term economic growth. The reconstruction of Mexico has been, in other words, a reconstruction for achievement.

By viewing the Revolution in its totality, moreover, it is possible to discern the underlying continuity of development following the sharp break with the past during the turbulent years of 1910–1917. Retrospectively, the Revolution emerges, on the one hand, as an institutional rupture prerequisite for the fuller and more effective utilization of the material and technical inheritance from the antecedent era. On the other hand, it appears as the basic source of those important changes which have led to a progressive expansion and elaboration of the productive apparatus during the past four decades. The essential unity of the 1910–1960 period, therefore, lies in the intimate genetic relationship existing between the Revolution and the phenomena of cumulative change which have more or less ineluctably carried Mexico across the threshold into modern industrial civilization.

Within this larger frame of reference, shifts of investment, differential sectoral expansion, and the like take on the aspect of "normal" adjustments to external conditions and the evolving exigencies of a dynamic domestic environment. That the domestic environment has been so dynamic and has necessitated a continuing redefinition of tactics, if not of strategy, is itself a reflection of the success of the Revolution in building an economy and a society possessed of a strong forward momentum.

There were, of course, substantial costs involved in the work of the economic reconstruction, costs that loom with particular prominence when one judges short periods of the Revolutionary era in terms of a static framework of analysis. But it is easy to overstate their magnitude, and the compensating advantages have counted for more in the longer term. The aggressive economic nationalism of the period, for example, and the preoccupation with domestic reform may occasionally have deterred the inflow of foreign capital and the technical assistance which came as an adjunct of direct foreign investment activity. Yet, as Ashworth and others have shown, the transfer of capital and skills from the metropolitan economies to the periphery through traditional channels declined appreciably in the interwar period for reasons essentially extraneous to conditions in the less developed regions. In addition, one misconstrues the real situation by thinking in terms of a fixed aggregate supply of capital, partly foreign and partly domestic, so that a sacrifice of foreign-capital contributions is equated with a corresponding reduction in the total capital available to the economy. Were this the case, many of the measures of the Revolution would stand indicted as an uneconomic sacrifice of already scarce resources.

Considering all things, however, the short-term negative effects on traditional external borrowing came as part of a general institutional reordering which induced an intensification of domestic capital formation. Similarly, in the case of entrepreneurial and skilled labor factors, the same set of events which tended to reduce the import of these productive agents from the outside worked to increase the elasticity of supply and the quality of these factors available from within. The post-1910 economy, therefore, after the initial period of readjustment, could begin its new wave of expansion on the more substantial and reliable base of increasing amounts of internally-generated resources. The expansion of twentieth-century Mexico has been a Mexicanized expansion. If in the process there have been deviations from the optimum allocational pattern as constituted by the international distribution of comparative advantages, the measures related to those deviations have also been instrumental in extending the range of opportunities for shifting underutilized resources from less productive to more productive employment. From the con-

comitant increments of the surplus, the restructured Revolutionary economy has forged a more socially rewarding set of comparative advantages.

Like Cortés, the Mexican people in opting for revolution burnt
their ships behind them. Also like the audacious *conquistador,*
they have not regretted the action, for they have marched ahead
to discover anew the promise of Tenochtitlán.

Bankers
as Revolutionaries

POLITICS AND DEVELOPMENT BANKING IN MEXICO

by Charles W. Anderson

Bankers as Revolutionaries

Bankers, almost by definition, are not revolutionaries. Yet throughout the world, wherever economic development and related social reform has become *the* political issue, leaders of credit institutions have been called on to play a key role in the process of social transformation. Since the end of World War II, the "development corporation" or "development bank" has become a characteristic appendage to the political structure throughout the newly developing world.[1] Established outside the conventional framework of the state as an independent agency, such institutions may become a center of power and of decision-making authority whose importance cannot be overlooked.

The justification for the establishment of such public credit agencies runs a by now familiar course. (1) In underdeveloped societies, the state is the only social institution that can accumulate sufficient capital resources to impel economic change. (2) The state can use its ability to control authoritatively the allocation of resources so that the scarce potential available may be most rationally employed in stimulating economic growth. (3) Where desires for economic growth have not permeated the entire society, the state is the logical instrument of tutelage and action for those limited elites who understand and seek economic development. (4) Productive activity on the part of the state, to paraphrase Gunnar Myrdal, may serve to break the cycle of cumulative and circular impoverishment and create self-generating growth.[2]

The notion that bankers may act as revolutionaries, however,

has a special significance in modern Mexico. The recent history
of this nation affords many lessons for the student of economic
development. Not the least of these is the role that development
banks have played in carrying forward that process of economic
transformation which Mexicans summarize as the Revolution. An
organization chart of the executive branch of the Mexican government notes the existence of fifteen public credit institutions,
formally part of the governmental apparatus, capitalized by government funds, and designed to fulfill certain public purposes.

This is, then, a case study of this system of politically controlled credit institutions in a rapidly modernizing society. It is
not an undertaking in economic analysis. Rather, the Mexican
government banking system will be viewed as part of the political
system of modern Mexico. We shall attempt to locate and explain
the role of these institutions within the process by which authoritative public decisions are made in Mexican society.

The focus on a single nation is a matter of convenience and
not of direct intent. For the function of this study is to delve into
some problems of broader concern to both political scientists and
economists as they approach problems inherent in the desire for
rapid political, economic, and social change present in various
parts of the world. These problems may be described as follows:

First, a vast no man's land exists between the historic concerns
of the disciplines of political science and economics. Robert Dahl
has taken his fellow political scientists to task for their neglect
of this problem. "For all the talk and all the public curiosity
about the relations between business and politics, there is a remarkable dearth of studies on the subject. What *is* written is
more apt to come from the pen of a sociologist, an historian, a
lawyer or an economist than from a political scientist.[3] Joseph
Cropsey also points to the dilemma: "That politics and economic
life have much to do with each other is a remark matched in
self-evidence by the parallel observation that political science and
economics are of mutual interest. All the more striking then is

the difficulty one meets in attempting to state with precision how politics and economic life, how political science and economics, are related." [4] Economists too have been concerned, as evidenced by much of the recent writing on the problem of economic development.[5] It is imperative, if the social scientist is to build a framework of understanding about contemporary social processes, that a start be made toward creating a body of theory which will link together the preoccupations of these two disciplines.

Second, this concern for the development of a new political economics, if you will, becomes most striking when applied to the so-called "underdeveloped" or "newly emerging" nations (though its relevance to highly developed, industrialized societies is, of course, beyond dispute). The concepts of "economic development" and "political modernization" are vitally interrelated themes. In regions where the revolution of rising expectations is appearing in full force, virtually all questions of political analysis must at some point hinge on the apparent desire to use political institutions as instruments of rapid economic development. Furthermore, the study of the conditions under which rapid economic growth does or does not take place is directly affected by the nature of the political regime in the system under consideration.

Third, in the newly emerging nations, new types of public institutions have been developing that are involved with planning, regulating, and directly stimulating economic growth. In approaching these institutions, the analyst frequently seems uncertain in the use of his tools. Ostensibly, the institutions pertain to the political order, for they emerge out of the process of authoritatively determining public means and ends. Formally, they belong to the institutional structure of the state. Yet their function seems to be exclusively economic, their effect to pertain only to the economic order of the society. The analyst is stymied. Either he describes their obvious relationship to the political order (usually with considerable attention to administrative and legal structure) or he analyzes their consequences for the economic system. The gap is seldom adequately bridged.

Among such "newly emerging" institutions in the "newly emerging" world are the public development authorities. In some of these nations, public development programs are concentrated in a single agency or development authority. Such has been the case, for example, in Chile, where the pioneer *Corporación de Fomento de la Producción* has been in existence since the 1930's; in Nicaragua, where the *Instituto de Fomento de la Producción* serves as a central clearinghouse for development programs; and in Cuba, where the *Instituto Nacional de la Reforma Agraria* has become virtually a state within a state. In other Latin American nations, public economic programs are spread among a number of development banks or authorities. In Costa Rica, such institutions have been established in the fields of central banking, electric power, social insurance, public housing, tourism, and commodity and production regulation. In this case, the overt justification for the establishment of multiple development agencies was that the power concentrated in a single organism "might come to rival that of the state itself." [6]

The Mexican case pertains to the latter category, for this is a nation in which multiple development banks have been established. Yet it is hoped that analysis of this system will shed light on the case of the single development authority as well. Quite simply, the Mexican case was selected because the relatively "public" nature of politics in that country, and the multiple system of development banking institutions, made the political processes that surround such institutions more accessible to analysis. It should be reiterated that this is a case study, whose relevance extends beyond the particular example under consideration insofar as it serves to explain the political process that surrounds all institutions of this type.

Our purpose is to understand the Mexican development banks as part of the political system of that nation. Throughout, we shall be concerned to show how economic and political processes are related in the activities of these institutions. We begin with the assumption that the development banks perform an economic function and that this function represents an exercise of political power. The specific problems that require analysis follow from this initial assumption.

1. *The acceptance of development banking as a legitimate exercise of political authority.* We should have much less difficulty in describing relationships between economic and political functions did not modern man, perhaps unconsciously a Parsonian, perceive the state and the economy as distinct social systems. At base, the modern understanding of the state seems to be that of a legitimate monopoly of force, capable, within defined limits, of being used as a means of social control and as a repository of authority, and able to make commitments concerning appropriate forms of behavior for its citizens or subjects. The economy would seem to be accepted as a system of contractual exchanges of things of value.

The notion that the state should never act as a participant in the economic system has seldom been seriously entertained, except perhaps by anarchists or utopian Marxists. The state's ability to use its authority to buttress economic relationships, as in the legally binding character of contracts, is generally accepted. Furthermore, the state is usually recognized as a participant in the economic system, gaining resources through taxation and expending them for functions which it performs. Yet no problem has seemed to perplex man more during the past two centuries than that of establishing the boundary conditions of the two systems—the state and the economy—in specifying the legitimate extent of state economic activity. The question is one of determining both the extent to which the state may act as a participant in the economic order (should the state undertake the ownership and operation of productive enterprise?) and the extent to which the state is obliged to act according to the conventions of the economic system (if the state is to build roads, may it do so through forced-labor levees and the commandeering of materials, or must it contract for goods and services in the market?).

Hence, rather than engaging in the old debate of whether development in Mexico has come about predominately by capitalistic or by socialistic means, we shall be seeking out the reasons for the acceptance of development banking as an appropriate exercise of public power in modern Mexico, and evaluating the difference that development banking makes in the relationship of government to economy. In so doing, we shall look to the ideologies and interests of the component forces in the power structure of modern Mexico, and observe how the present development banking system of that nation reflects their approaches to the role of the state in the economic order and their demands on the state for economic activity.

2. *The relation of the development banks to the political system of Mexico.* The use of an economic instrument such as development banking by the state as a form of political power makes a difference in the relationship of the government to the rest of the society within which it operates. However, the incorporation of such a process into the governmental mechanism will also have an impact on the way the political system of a nation is itself structured. As we set about locating the development banks within the Mexican governmental structure, we shall be attempting to understand the impact of economic process on political system. In understanding the relationships between elements in the Mexican political apparatus, we shall of course give attention to the legal and constitutional forms which such institutions have been given as well as to the political processes which set the context for the operation of institutional patterns. Of particular interest, however, in terms of our objectives, will be understanding the use of financial techniques in establishing political relationships.

We shall observe the interaction between legal, political, and economic processes in attempting to determine the relationships of influence which affect the development banks, the manner in which other institutions exert influence over bank policy, and the reciprocal power of the banks within the political system. We will need to know how conflicts over bank policy are resolved, the degree to which the banks act autonomously, and the measure in which they are held responsible to political leadership, in view of the political and economic processes which serve to reinforce both autonomy and control.

3. *The use of credit as a political sanction.* Although the old distinction between politics and administration has gone out of favor among political scientists, it would seem that there would still be some point in making an analytic distinction between those things that happen in the course of making a decision on public policy and the events that follow from this act, when efforts are made to transform an abstract formula into a working social reality. Insofar as we shall examine the development banks as part of the process by which authoritative decisions are made in Mexico, so it would also seem pertinent to examine the instrumental character of these institutions.

It is apparent that the inclusion of the banking device in the political system is a mechanism of great utility in assuring the effective implementation of basic policy decisions on the course which the economy, and hence the society, shall take. The denial or bestowal of credit in a rapidly modernizing society may have a profound influence in directing individual performances toward activities deemed consistent with public purposes. The conditions or assurances which private lenders conventionally attach to their investments to reduce risk of default become, in this new context, important mechanisms of social control. In a sense, then, government credit becomes a sanction, a means of effecting compliance with decisions taken on public purposes.

Credit is like many other powers which are derived from government's role as a participant in the economic system. In a sense, the economic capabilities of government become optional strategies to be used by political leaders in place of those powers characteristic of the state (consent based on legitimate authority or severe deprivation based on monopoly of force) in making political decisions effective. "The power to tax is the power to destroy"—and the sanction implicit in that phrase is but one of many potential powers deriving from government's capacity as an economic actor which can be used to enforce policy if deemed legitimate in terms of the boundaries established between the polity and the economy.

The study of the political art of finding techniques appropriate to given ends is a fascinating aspect of the study of politics. In this study we hope to show how Mexican policy makers found in development banking a carrot and a stick of great utility, one which could provide political direction and regulation of the development process without doing violence to the formal precepts and conventions of liberal society.

Evolution of the Development Banking System

Our first problem is to understand the political factors that account for the emergence of this extensive development banking system in Mexico, to ask why such instruments have been accepted as legitimate mechanisms of public policy in this nation, and to describe the specific political situations that account for the existence of particular banks. (For a précis of functions of these various banks, see the Appendix.)

While the Mexican Revolution of 1910 is usually understood as an experiment in political and economic radicalism, it is today clear that those who held power to structure the national institutions of Revolutionary Mexico were not primarily the radical intellectuals or the agrarian caciques in arms. It is true that the Revolution created new political forces in Mexico. The success of the "generals" and "chiefs" of the Revolution in making good their claims to economic and political prerogative has been part of the flavor of public life in Mexico ever since. The demands for labor and social reform measures on the part of the agrarian reformers, the "Red Battalions," and the radical intelligentsia were backed with power that could not be ignored in Revolutionary Mexico. But the holders of this power were not the ones who would decide the manner in which these claims would be honored.

The early post-Revolutionary presidents did not emerge from the radical sectors of Revolutionary support. Madero saw the cause of Revolution as merely that of bringing effective liberal democracy to Mexico. Carranza, Obregón, and Calles were essentially moderate in their approach to reform. They seemed primarily concerned with bringing unity and stability to a nation torn by violence and factionalism. As such, they sought to satisfy the personal and policy demands of the new Revolutionary elites, but this was done within an over-all policy which was, on the whole, cautious.

The Querétaro Constitution of 1917 is often said to embody the basic principles of the Mexican Revolution. Articles of the fundamental law provide for extensive land reform, an advanced type of labor regulation, and a radical diminution of the Church's secular power. But taken as a whole it is a most unremarkable document. It provides Mexico with a quite conventional system of liberal democracy along federal lines. This is not surprising, for those who drafted the document were in large measure urbane men of law and letters rather than the immediate leaders of an agrarian revolt. They assumed the legitimacy of the political system they provided and probably would have had difficulty visualizing an alternative to it. Politically, they had to recognize the new demands that had arisen out of the Revolution, but it was they who were to determine the framework within which these demands would be met.

The work of the Querétaro delegates in drafting the new constitution has a parallel in the activities of the economic advisers to the Revolutionary governments in the years from 1917 to 1934. Led by Secretary of Hacienda (Treasury) Alfredo Pani, this group saw their mission as that of reconstructing the institutional machinery of the Mexican national economy, which had been devastated by the Revolution. They sought to re-establish the nation's foreign-trade position, restore confidence in the monetary system, and get channels of domestic trade and commerce operating once more.

These economic advisers had not emerged from the new Revolutionary elites. Rather, they were largely products of the rudimentary capitalistic structure of Mexico City which had been developing during the long regime of Porfirio Díaz. The first real impetus to modernization of Mexico's economy had come during the *Porfiriato,* which began in 1876 and was ended by the Revolution in 1910. During this period of "no-nonsense" politics, an attempt was made to pull Mexico up by its bootstraps. Díaz surrounded himself with a group of advisers, the *científicos,* who would point the way to the "scientific" development of Mexico, which is to say, the way in which Mexico could link itself to the processes of transformation at work in the advanced nations and emulate the process of their growth. Largely through the investment of foreign capital, a facade of modernity was superimposed on the traditional structure of the Mexican economy. Accompanying this development, a Mexican economic elite of administrators, financiers, and entrepreneurs emerged in the nation's capital. It was from this group that most of the economic policy makers of the new Revolutionary governments were drawn.[7]

Nurtured on the economics of the Díaz period, these latter day *científicos* largely accepted the legitimacy of the intricate and many-faceted institutions of the modern economic system as it had been elaborated and developed in the advanced nations of Europe and North America. To attempt to measure their economic proclivities against the conventional strictures of socialist or capitalist thought would seem to be to ask the wrong question, for by the era in which these men worked, actual Western economic practice was far too intricate to be circumscribed by one or the other of these theoretical designs. One might say they had an "orthodox" approach to economics, in the context of their times, in that they anticipated no radical departure in their planning from the economic institutions and practices prevailing in the industrialized nations. Accepting this model for the economic modernization of Mexico, they conceived their mission, in a sense, as that of implementing programs that were the unfinished business of the *Porfiriato*.

The Revolution did not carry with it a doctrine of the radical restructuring of the total economic system. In fact, the Mexican Revolution was accompanied by no coherent ideology or doctrine. Rather, the leaders of the insurrection, the agrarian reformers, the labor agitators, the socialist intelligentsia, assumed a set of quite specific reforms. They were dependent on the experts in the total mechanics of modern economic society to guide their programs and make them effective.

That the banking device, and the financial mechanisms of modern capitalistic society, would appear to the policy makers of post-Revolutionary Mexico as natural means to be used to stimulate economic modernization is obvious. What is not so apparent is the legitimacy of banking as a tool of public policy, enabling government to give direction to the processes of economic change. Yet the exceptional role permitted for public economic activity in a system which assumed the legitimacy of orthodox economic principles is not so surprising when one takes account of certain key facets in the economic evolution of modern Mexico.

The need for financial reconstruction after the Revolution. The re-established Revolutionary government of Venustiano Carranza in 1917 was confronted by a Mexico near financial breakdown. The nation's position in the international financial system was in jeopardy, as foreign creditors became convinced that Mexico would not meet the obligations on the huge external debt contracted during the Revolution. Furthermore, by 1917 Mexico had virtually returned to a metallic standard, and paper money was for all real purposes worthless. The rudimentary private banking system of Mexico had, in 1912, come to the support of the counter-Revolutionary Huerta government, funding this regime through loans which far exceeded the resources of the banks. As reserves and deposits decreased, paper money was issued to cover these extensive credits. The inflationary effect caused by the issue of paper money in support of Huerta was intensified by the practices of the Revolutionary armies in the field. Lacking resources to pay for food, arms, and supplies, they made legitimate their acquisitions by the issue of paper money against the future success of the Revolution. Financial technique was subordinated to the ends of the political conflict. Those who funded the rival factions saw their investment as contingent on the success or failure of the military operations, thus upsetting the normal expectations of the economic system.

If the key to the realization of the Revolutionary program was to be the evolution of a modern economic system in Mexico, an imperative first step must be the financial reconstruction of the system. The twenty-four private banks which had controlled the issue of paper currency prior to 1910 were discredited in the eyes of the Revolutionaries for their collaboration with the Huerta government. Furthermore, they were in ruins and could hardly serve as a basis for rebuilding the Mexican economy. The only alternative seemed to be to establish a central bank, under public auspices, to control currency issue. This measure, suggested first by Carranza in 1913, was made part of the Querétaro Constitution. As conceived by its proponents, however, the function of the central bank was not to replace private banking but to reestablish it on a sound basis, within an effective monetary system, so that it could contribute to the mobilization of capital resources required for the fulfillment of the Revolutionary program.

The central bank—the Bank of Mexico—did not come into existence until 1925. In the interim it was necessary to liquidate the discredited banks of issue (a task made difficult by the government's inability to meet its obligations on the substantial public debt held by the banks) and to acquire sufficient capital to fund the new central bank. The "austerity" economic policies of the Obregón and Calles governments, in large measure inspired by Hacienda Secretary Pani, were in large part linked to these aspirations. During these years, the government bureaucracy was reduced in size, Revolutionary programs were postponed or reduced in scope, and international confidence was restored through Mexico's willingness to assume payment on her large foreign debt. Again, one notes the effective dominance of those who saw Revolutionary reform as one facet of the construction of a modern economic system, as the regimes of the 1920's were able to keep the Revolutionary coalition [8] intact though giving second priority to the agrarian and social reform measures which were the primary interest of many Revolutionary elites.

The confidence restored in the financial system through the success of the central bank after 1925 itself gave rise to conditions permitting the elaboration of the development banking system in the 1930's. In the private sector, the banking system was developing rapidly, deposits and instruments of capitalization were increasing in volume, and mortgage paper, which for years had been almost absent from the market, began to reappear. The monetary reforms of 1931–32, and Mexico's abandonment of the gold standard, aided the development of credit and gave the financial system greater flexibility. In short, the increasing legitimacy of the financial structure itself permitted a wider range of financial innovation.[9]

The evolution of a modern, capitalistic economic structure in Mexico was itself an objective of public policy. In understanding the willingness of the orthodox economic policy makers of the Revolutionary governments to support substantial public financial activity through development banking, one must see through their eyes the Mexican economic system as it existed after the Revolution. The capitalistic structure of Mexico at that time was quite embryonic. These policy makers were not acting in defense of an established order but were advocating, as an element of public policy, the development of a specific economic system. Furthermore, in nations like Mexico, the understanding of the interrelatedness of the many facets of a complex economy preceeded the deed, rather than appearing as a *fait accompli* after a long period of evolution as in the advanced nations.[10] Thus, Mexico's economists conceived of a total network of economic institutions and processes necesssary to complete the structure they were creating, and if the private sector could not supply these, it seemed the obligation of the state to do so, in the interest of the development of the private sector itself.

Simply put, the whole economic setting had to be changed so that investment would begin to flow toward those activities that would bring about the modernization of the economy. The Mexican investor had to be weaned away from his traditional preference for land, urban real estate, jewelry, and short-term commercial credit, and toward long-term capital investment in industry and other fields.[11] The public financial institutions were to play a role which was a mixture of tutelage and stimulation of the private sector.

Substantial precedent, both in Mexico's colonial and independent history, and in the experience of the advanced nations which Mexico sought to emulate, existed for the type of state financial intervention which Mexico was to undertake. Mexico's economic heritage was simply different from that of England or the United States. The Spanish colonial system was one which included substantial economic activity and direction by the state. Something of this tradition was carried over into Mexico's period of independence. There are few programs of the Mexican Revolution for which historic precedent cannot be found. Public development banking has roots in the industrial development bank founded by Lucas Alamán in the 1830's, in the Monte de Piedad, which dates from 1774, and in the agricultural development banks and bank projects which appear throughout the nineteenth-century and early twentieth-century history of Mexico. However, in the midst of the chaos of nineteenth-century public affairs, none of these institutions ever achieved a permanent basis for existence.[12] Attempts had been made in the 1890's to centralize the issue of paper money, though opposition of the private banking system defeated the effort.

Furthermore, by the time of the post-Revolutionary evolution of development banking in Mexico, such institutions were well-established in many of the advanced nations that were to serve as models for Mexico's economic evolution. Central banking was in existence in the industrialized nations, and the progress of the industrial revolution on the Continent had been accompanied by the establishment of institutions which were, in effect, development banks. As the Querétaro constitutional convention debated Article 28 of the new constitution, which provided for a monopoly of currency issue in the hands of the state, the increasing importance of central banking in the advanced nations was often noted. Furthermore, the rapid elaboration of the development banking system in the 1930's in Mexico parallels a similar development in the United States, as the establishment of institutions such as the Reconstruction Finance Corporation and the Federal Housing Authority added weight to the acceptability of similar undertakings in Mexico.

The public-credit mechanism was deemed to be reciprocally beneficial to the development of a modern, capitalistic economy and to the achievement of Revolutionary reforms. Through the credit mechanism, government could direct the economy toward the fulfillment of programs specified by the Revolutionary power structure. Yet most of these programs could, through the assumption of a modern, "national" economy, be demonstrated as essential to the stimulation of the private sector. For example, land redistribution is a backward step in the achievement of a modern economy unless connected with facilities for raising the levels of production and consumption of the small farmer, of moving him out of the traditional subsistence economy into the modern world of markets and cash crops—from a local economy to a national one. This requires capital investment in the agricultural sector. Use of the credit mechanism for this purpose not only instructed the small farmer in economic technique appropriate to modern agriculture, but also, through reinvestment of returns on loans, served to further stimulate the entire economic system.

And the "mixed form" of Mexican development banking (soon to be discussed), in which both private and public capital participates, in theory provides a return on private investment in support of public policy that can be reinvested once again in the private sector.

The desire to create a total modern economy has a political coefficient in the phenomenon of Mexican nationalism. To a great extent, the support of the Revolutionary coalition for the development banks harks back to Revolutionary "anti-imperialism." Reaction to the power of foreign economic interests is usually given as a major cause of the insurrection of 1910. Ever since, policies designed to reduce the scope of foreign economic activity have had great popular appeal in Mexico, an appeal which serves to unify the always divisive components of the Revolutionary coalition. Thus, while Mexico's stress on capitalistic industrialization, with its attendant effect of creating a new class of wealth, may seem a betrayal of the radical aspirations of the Revolution, it is also consistent with one of the primary consensus values of the Revolutionary elites. Public policies which promote economic self-sufficiency in Mexico, then, may be supported both by the radical intellectual and by the conservative entrepreneur, though each for his own reasons.

The impact of Keynesian thought and Cárdenas' leadership provided the basis for a vigorous extension of the banking system in the early 1930's. The emergence of several of these banks specifically, and all of them in general, is related to major shifts in the political and economic structure of Mexico that occurred at this time. In the economic realm, we have already commented on the success of the central bank and the conservative monetary policies of the 1930's in bringing greater confidence in the usefulness of the credit device both in the private and public sectors.

Coupled with this was the rise to power of Lázaro Cárdenas. Cárdenas successfully shifted his basis of support from the Revolutionary inner circle led by Plutarco Calles and rebuilt the official party, the government-linked labor movement, and the government bureaucracy to his own specifications. As part of this restructuring of Revolutionary elites, Cárdenas brought to positions of influence economic advisers of a more liberal stripe, many of them oriented toward Keynesian principles, whose conflict with the "orthodox" economists of the Revolution has continued to the present day.[13] The changes in the top leadership of the *Secretaría de Hacienda,* of the Banking Commission, and of the Bank of Mexico all are illustrative of the transition and have become part of the lore of financial controversy in Mexico.

While Cárdenas continues to be the hero of those who interpret the Mexican Revolution as an experiment in radicalism, his administration does not really represent a drastic shift in the aspirations of Mexican policy makers. The policies he promoted were those assumed to be part of the Revolution all along. But Cárdenas did quicken the pace of the Revolution. Programs long postponed came to fruition during his administration. While Cárdenas is remembered for his extension of the agrarian reform, his nationalization of the petroleum industry, it is evident that the link which related his various programs was the assumption of the desirability of constructing the total structure of a modern economic system. In retrospect, his administration closely resembles the "New Deal" in the United States, which it paralleled in time.

The Mexican development banks emerge out of such a broad framework which accounts for the legitimacy of the public credit device as a whole. Yet, each individual bank is the product of a specific set of economic and political circumstances. The present day development banking system of Mexico corresponds to no plan for economic development. One would have difficulty finding a relationship between these institutions in terms of any overall theory of economic growth. Rather, it is to the political system that we must look to explain the emergence of this hodge podge set of institutions, which is a system only insofar as it reflects a reconciliation of the policy demands which had to be met in order to maintain the cohesion of the Revolutionary coalition while achieving economic development through the creation of a modern economy.

Agrarian reform was a product of the specific aspirations of groups which had won power in the Revolution. As the ideology of the Revolution developed, support for such policies had extended beyond the particular champions of these reforms, and they had come to be accepted by an increasingly broad audience, including the growing middle-sector government and official party bureaucracy. Furthermore, the factor of nationalism must not be neglected, for many of the lands to be expropriated were in the hands of foreign owners. Hence, the establishment of the Agrarian Credit Bank early in the Revolutionary period (1926) was a logical outcome of the pattern of politics that was developing.

Cárdenas' emphasis on agrarian reform, a product of the political and financial factors discussed earlier, led to the establishment of the Ejido Bank in 1935, separating the credit operations connected with the agrarian reform from the elder Agrarian Credit Bank and establishing two institutions in this field. In broad outline, of course, this move served to underline the government's concern for agrarian reform and especially for the extension of the *ejido* system.

Yet more specific considerations were also involved. The advocates of agrarian reform had considerable distaste for the older Agrarian Credit Bank. It represented the less reform-minded credit policies of the conservative era of the Revolution. Operating on "pure" banking principles, the senior bank was unprepared to reconcile the conventional needs for agricultural credit with the particular requirements of the *ejido* system, where conventional guarantees were not available due to the legal inalienability of *ejido* lands, and the peculiar requirements of social reconstruction that went with land redistribution. The outcome was that the bank had favored safer, more conventional credits to private landowners. From 1926 to 1931, the bank averaged annual authorized credits of M$57,854,870 annually, but *ejido* loans only averaged M$5,334,160 annually.[14] Furthermore, the corruption surrounding many Revolutionary institutions had discredited the Agrarian Credit Bank in the eyes of the new reformers. Revolutionary favorites had dipped deeply into the funds of the bank for large sums, sometimes only vaguely related to agricultural purposes.[15] As has happened many times in Mexican history, new policies imply new institutions—to separate the new departure from past failures, to create the image of a "fresh start."

Cárdenas' strategy of appealing to the "popular" sectors as a means of breaking dependence on the political structure of the older Revolutionary elites required implementation in fields other than agrarian reform. While large-scale industry, commerce, and finance was growing in Mexico in the 1930's, impelled by government policy, the Revolutionary left which supported Cárdenas was becoming increasingly uneasy about the growing strength of this prosperous sector of the economy. As part of their program to redress the balance in the industrial and commercial field, the *Banco Nacional Obrero y de Fomento Industrial* (Workers' and Industrial Development Bank) was established in 1939. Designed to foster grass-roots industrial and commercial development, it was to provide credit for small productive enterprises. Never achieving a secure financial foothold, this bank was eventually allowed to die, perhaps once its symbolic function of demonstrating policy concern for a vital political interest had been demonstrated. However, the Cooperative Development Bank of the 1950's is the lineal descendent of this institution.

The two pairs of banks that appeared in the 1930's, the Agrarian Credit and Ejido banks and the Nacional Financiera and the Workers' Bank, indicate the consistent Mexican effort to structure the development banking system so as to satisfy the interests of distinct political forces operating in the same sector of the economy. Although agrarian reform was the symbol of the Cárdenas years, the unreformed landowners found, in the continued activity of the Agrarian Credit Bank, an indication that the official agrarian policy was more intricate and more sensitive to their interests and political power than official propaganda revealed. Although Mexican industrial development has always been based on the large productive unit, the Workers' Bank seemed to indicate policy attention to the demands of the small producers, and could be used to counter the charges of hypocrisy which were to be leveled against the "reformist" Cárdenas government.

The consistent devotion of Mexican policy makers to the goals of large-scale industrialization and economic nationalism is evident in the establishment of Nacional Financiera and the Foreign Commerce Bank. Many see in the creation of these banks the direct influence of the economic elites, be they the "new rich" of the Revolution or the older upper class. While it is true these groups, at the general policy level, would support the stimulation of capitalistic enterprise in Mexico, it seems unlikely that they have received undue financial benefit from these institutions.

The influence of entrepreneurial groups is more evident in the extension of Nacional Financiera's activity in the early 1940's than in the creation of the institution. The New Group of Mexican industrialists which emerged in the 1930's and 1940's have been among the leading supporters of the official policy of stimulation of a modern economy. Largely organized around small firms using Mexican rather than foreign capital, these enterprises developed rapidly in meeting wartime demands for articles no longer available through foreign trade. Operating outside of the "inner circle" of Mexican wealth, they have often felt insecure in their economic position and have sought government support for their activities. Through their interest organization, the *Confederación Nacional de Industrias de Transformación* (the National Confederation of Manufacturing Industries), they have been vigorous in their efforts to influence public policy.[16]

In general, however, Revolutionary nationalism probably accounts more for the creation of Nacional Financiera and the Foreign Commerce Bank and their support by the various components of the Revolutionary coalition than the direct activity of any specific interest groups. In a sense, Nacional Financiera had as much to do with the creation of the New Group itself as the activities of that group had to do with buttressing and defending the role of that development bank.

The presence of two development banks operating primarily in Mexico City, the Small Merchants' Bank and the Transport Bank, would seem to reflect the urban bias of Mexican politics. The tendency for political decision making to be concentrated among the small, articulate elites of the capital is characteristic of underdeveloped regions. Mexico is no exception to the type. Slight, subtle shifts of interest and opinion in Mexico City are apt to have many times more influence on national policy than a gross change in rural areas.

Both of these banks seem to have been created to satisfy the aspirations of specific groups of producers in the capital. While it seems demonstrable that there was a demand for adequate credit facilities to provide for the needs of these small entrepreneurs, the selection of these two groups for preferred treatment would seem to demand further explanation.

In the case of the Transport Bank, there is a situational explanation which partially accounts for the creation of this institution. The origins of this bank date to 1927, when a cooperative was established among the taxi drivers of Mexico City. The cooperative eventually became the Banco Latino. During the 1940's, the Banco Latino fell under the control of a small group of "mobsters" who controlled the taxi industry through the bank.[17] In 1953, the National Banking Commission intervened the bank for irregular practices. Given the role of the Banking Commission, and the fact that the Social Security Administration owned a substantial interest in the Banco Latino, the decision to establish a development bank in this area does not seem surprising.

A further factor in explaining the creation of these two banks in Mexico City would seem to be the personal influence of Pedro Ugarteche, the city's "reform mayor." Ugarteche's personal influence within the inner circle of policy makers and his program of development for the capital seem reflected in the Transport and the Small Merchants' banks.

However, a thorough explanation of the emergence of these banks must take into account the increasingly strategic political power of the Mexican middle sectors.[18] These groups, concentrated in the capital, administer the industries, staff the public bureaucracies, edit the newspapers, provide professional services, exercise the skilled trades, and run the larger businesses. They provide leadership for other political forces. They are the most articulate sector of public opinion.

One notes that the Small Merchants' Bank was established in 1942, when inflationary conditions and shortages of consumers goods had caused the cost of living in Mexico City to skyrocket and the black market to flourish. Attempts to provide low-cost credit for the small merchants of the capital city and to assist them in forming associations to reduce purchasing costs, the two basic functions of this bank, both bear directly on the interests of that influential sector of the population that was most sensitive to the effects of the rising costs of living.[19]

Similarly, the function of the Transport Bank, to modernize Mexico City's transport system, shows again the particular influence of the urban population on national policy making, and is not unrelated to the middle-sector desire, in Mexico as throughout the newly emerging world, to surround itself with a facade of modernity, in the form of both consumer goods and the urban facilities that are similar to the environment of their counterparts in the advanced nations.

The political complex that lies behind the establishment of the Armed Forces Bank will be familiar to every student of Latin American affairs. Although by the time of the bank's establishment in 1946 the direct political power of the military was on the wane, even today, in a nation where the military does not intervene directly in politics, it remains a considerable influence, capable of defending and implementing its own prerogatives. Here again, the Mexican view of the banking device as an instrument to serve a related system of political and economic functions may be seen. While overtly structured to filter part of the savings of the military into productive channels, and thus to advance the development effort, it also served to add to the emoluments of the military establishment, thus providing it, like other politically significant sectors of Mexican society, with the favor of a public bank designed specifically in terms of its economic interest.

After examining the diverse origins and characteristics of these banks, it might be concluded that we are not here talking about development banking at all, but about the total structure of government credit institutions in a society. The conclusion is worth discussing. For to have defined "development banking" in such a way as to exclude those institutions which are not demonstrably related to the assumed problems of developmental economics would have been to have eliminated the political problem of development banking altogether. What is significant about this analysis is that it illustrates the diverse images of what is entailed by "modernization" in an underdeveloped society, and the varied demands that are placed on public capitalization agencies by different interests in the society. Except in a highly authoritarian situation, it seems unlikely that development banking institutions, be they in the form of a single development authority, or multiple in character, as in Mexico, will be able to restrict their operations to a formula of capitalization required for economic growth as prescribed in any of the more simple theories of developmental economics.

Yet it is clear that those models of economic development which take into account the interrelatedness of all of the institutions of a modern economy serve a remarkable political purpose as well as describe an approach to economic understanding. For such theories may become virtually a political ideology, to bring accommodation between diverse sectors of a political system. One has only to examine the intricate justifications for the establishment of the Mexican development banks to see the impact of modern, but orthodox, developmental economics on the political theory of the leaders of modern Mexico. Agrarian reform, which might be opposed by the economic elites, is interpreted to stress the bringing of small landowners into the market economy with beneficial effect on domestic industry, an effort further justified in terms of the consensus value of nationalism. A bank supporting the direct interests of the armed forces is justified as a means of channeling these seemingly wasted resources into productive outlets. Industrialization is assumed to be a prerequisite to effective labor reform. It is clear that public policy in Mexico has arisen out of the specific demands of conflicting interests. It is evident that the reciprocal dependence of economic factors and interests in the theory of economic growth of the total modern economy may make legitimate public policy which requires the accommodation of political interests which might be in conflict if the development effort were cast in different terms. It would seem that development banking serves to supplement other techniques of demonstrating and enhancing the interdependence of public policies whose legitimacy lies in their assumed reciprocal benefit to the coalition of interests essential to political stability. The content of that vague, ephemeral, but so important notion of "The Revolution" in Mexico may be more a vision of the complex interdependence of a total modern economy than any of the specific reforms which the Revolution is conventionally believed to represent.

The legitimacy of development banking in Mexico, then, seems to rest on the following set of factors. (1) The assumption that the financial institutions and processes of modern capitalistic society were appropriate to the realization of the objectives of the Revolution. (2) The acceptance of the propriety of these institutions and processes being used as instruments of public policy, which grew out of the needs for financial reconstruction of the nation after the Revolution, historic precedent, the experience of the advanced nations, nationalism, and the assumption that the creation of a modern economy was itself to be an objective of public policy. (3) The ability of development banking to cope with the specific aspirations of important power factors that had emerged from the Revolution. (4) The presumption that these specific programs were mutually interdependent in the fulfillment of the aspirations of the various members of the Revolutionary coalition.

The Development Banks and the Political System

In describing the political characteristics of the Mexican development banks, it is first necessary to locate them within the Mexican governmental system, briefly noting their relationship to major political institutions and processes. The stability achieved by modern Mexico, in marked contrast to most of Latin America, is a product, for better or worse, of the distinctive political system developed in that nation. In part the effectiveness of this political system is due to the success of leadership in shaping a policy maintaining the intricate dynamic balance of the political forces contained within the Revolutionary coalition. In part it is due to the persistence of hierarchical assumptions concerning the nature of political authority. Many interpreters of Mexican politics base their analyses predominantly on one or the other of these facets of the Mexican political experience.[20] However, an adequate understanding must rest on both of these phenomena, and on the relationship between them.

The tradition of presidential authority. To an extraordinary extent, decision-making authority in Mexico over problems large and small is concentrated in the person of the chief executive, along with the powerful inner core of ministers of the traditionally powerful government ministries (*Gobierno, Hacienda, Relaciones Exteriores,* etc.) and a small coterie of individually important political leaders. A prime characteristic of the system of executive supremacy is that it is virtually self-perpetuating.

Although "no re-election" is one of the most sacrosanct principles of the Mexican Revolution, succession to the presidency has inevitably been determined by the incumbent chief executive and his immediate advisers. Also characteristic is the political impotence of the Mexican Congress, which is little more than a ratifying agency for executive decisions.

Formally, executive control derives from the dominance of the single, official party and its attendant elites. At a deeper level, such concentration of political authority in the executive has been attributed to the Spanish colonial heritage of authoritarian government, the "personalism" that has long been an outstanding facet of Mexican public and private life, the patron-peon relationship writ large, a pattern usually identified with the historic landholding system which has actually been an all-pervasive aspect of Mexican life—in short, to the total substance of an hierarchically organized, traditional society in which paternalism, public and private, has been an essential component of the social structure. That Mexico is breaking from this tradition is of course obvious, but the past has left important residues which are very much a part of the "transitional mix" of contemporary Mexican politics.[21]

The official party. In its various incarnations, known as the Party of the National Revolution (PNR), the Party of the Mexican Revolution (PRM), and the Party of the Institutionalized Revolution (PRI), this organization has, since the early 1920's, served as the instrument of consolidation and mobilization of the more numerous sectors of the Revolutionary coalition. Dependably, the official party wins each election.[22] Inevitably, electoral skullduggery is charged. In recent years, however, given PRI's relation to the Revolutionary mystique, its financial assets, its elaborate campaigning organization, and its patronage capabilities, it sometimes appears that to maintain democratic appearances connivance is necessary in order to permit adequate minor party representation.

The party's internal structure is formally democratic in nature.

Its organization is of the functional or corporate type, the party being composed of agrarian, labor, and "popular" sectors, the latter including the military, the public bureaucracy, and the middle-sector activists not otherwise affiliated. Theoretically, representation flows upward from the local party unit through a variety of intermediate levels to the national party organization. This flow of communication through the hierarchy, and the interest accommodation and reconciliation which seems to take place within the party organization, has led many interpreters to classify Mexico as a democratic one-party system.

While there is a measure of truth in this assertion, it must be balanced against other facets of the Mexican political scene. While the aggregation of interests that takes place within the party is important, it is only one aspect of the broader pattern of consensus building through public policy which takes place in Mexico. For example, the business, financial, and industrial interests which have by no means been excluded, in terms of policy advantage, from the Revolutionary coalition, are explicitly eliminated from participation in the PRI organization. Furthermore, there would seem to be a considerable rift of interest identification between intermediate level party leaders and their mass followings. Increasingly, labor and agrarian leaders are becoming men of middle-sector tastes, aspirations, and values. Also, the interlocking character of government and party bureaucracies, a factor whose importance is enhanced by the tendency of middle-class Mexicans simultaneously to pursue several careers, makes it difficult to ascertain whether party leaders feel their primary responsibility to be representation of their followers, or their unification in support of official policy. Finally the influence which the party per se has on policy making is a subject of some controversy. While Scott feels that its importance is paramount, stating that "the political process [is] centered in the machinery of the Revolutionary party," [23] others are inclined to see the party as an instrument for implementing and consolidating political support behind decisions made in the

inner circles that surround the president.[24] Brandenburg suggests
that accent on the PRI has distorted our understanding of Mexican politics, and that it is precisely those groups which have
been excluded from the PRI (industry, commerce, etc.) which
have gained most since World War II.[25] To this problem we
will shortly return.

Interest groups. The modernization of Mexico has been accompanied by the proliferation of interest groups of all types. Most
of these possess a semiofficial status, or they utilize secondary
relationships with such semiofficial groups as means of achieving
access to policy makers. The mass interest group organizations,
in labor and agriculture, are apt to be components of the sector
organization of the official party. Such is true of the official labor
organization, the Mexican Confederation of Labor (*Confederación de Trabajadores Mexicanos,* or CTM) and the National
Peasant's Confederation (*Confederación Nacional Campesina,*
or CNC). A dominant factor in the popular sector of the party
is the Federation of State Workers Unions (*Federación de
Sindicatos de Trabajadores al Servicio del Estado,* or FSTSE).

Major groups outside the official party, such as the Confederation of Industrial Chambers (*Confederación de Cámaras Industriales de los Estados Unidos Mexicanos,* or CONCAMIN)
and the Confederation of Chambers of Commerce (*Confederación de Cámaras Nacionales de Comercio,* or CONCANACO),
also possess a semiofficial status. All but the very smallest commercial and manufacturing units are required by law to affiliate
with one of the member chambers of these organizations. The
Secretary of Economy has considerable power over the organization and activities of these groups. Consultation with such
groups by government officials in the decision-making process
has become more or less institutionalized. In such organizations
as the Production Council (*Consejo de Producción*) one sees
efforts to develop more formal organs of interest group consultation, integrating the groups more closely with the governmental apparatus. Representatives of the Mexican Bankers' As-

sociation (*Asociación Mexicano de Banqueros*) now sit on the National Securities Commission and the National Banking Commission.[26]

A recent study by Kling indicates that those interest groups which have grown up outside of this semiofficial apparatus of representation seem, as an element in their strategy, to attempt to influence the policies of such semiofficial groups as CONCAMIN and CONCANACO.[27]

The political process. A brief account of the interaction of political forces in a society as complex as Mexico can only lead to gross oversimplification. Yet a sketch of certain characteristics of this system is essential if we are to understand the politics of development banking.

A comparison of the role of the chief executive in the United States and Mexico would seem a fruitful approach to such a problem. In neither nation is the president independent of the component political forces that are the base of his power. Yet Neustadt's [28] description of the U.S. president as chief bargainer and creator of agreement among numerous power centers does not seem to fit closely the Mexican experience. Rather, the Mexican chief executive would seem to have considerably more autonomy in decision making. He need not be as immediately responsive to pressures from below; for the decision of a group (and here we include the components of the PRI as interest groups), feeling itself mistreated, to bolt the Revolutionary coalition is far more perilous than would be a comparable decision of a United States group to utilize the ultimate bargaining sanction and withdraw into opposition. The Mexican president must be constantly aware of the margins of toleration of the components of the Revolutionary coalition, for his power is ultimately dependent on the maintenance of that coalition; but in comparison to his United States counterpart, he can count on greater leeway for independent decision making before a group will confront, as a real question, the fateful choice of whether to endure or to oppose.

Institutionally, the difference between the two political systems is fundamentally the distinction between a one-party and a two-party system, and, as a corollary to this, the reduced number of independent access points for interest group activity in Mexico. Yet the system is buttressed by the traditional mystique that surrounds the presidential office in Mexico. The characteristic style of the Mexican interest group is "petitionary" rather than "bargaining." The manifestos of Mexican interest groups sound far more like requests for favor to be dispensed than like threats of retaliation if demands are not met. The statement by Mexican journalists in celebration of the Day of Freedom of the Press in 1961, thanking President López Mateos for permitting freedom of the press to exist, appears quite strange to North Americans accustomed to a quite different understanding of the nature of such freedoms. While the modernization of Mexico, and the eagerness of interest groups in this nation to learn from their United States counterparts, is changing the nature of interest group activity, and attempts to influence public opinion and "lobbying" are becoming more frequent, a strong flavor of a more traditional approach to such activity continues to prevail.

The decentralized agencies.[29] The development banks, along with other of the most important agencies of Mexican government, do not pertain to the classic structure of the state. Nominally within the executive establishment are some one hundred and seventy decentralized agencies and some seventy state participation enterprises. The largest number of them have been created since 1940. Today, their total operations, both in terms of expenditures and personnel, exceed that of the regular government ministries and departments.

The distinction between the two forms of organization noted above is established by law. Decentralized agencies (*organismos decentralizados*) are created by law or decree, performing specialized public or social service functions. State participation enterprises (*empresas de participación estatal*) are created in the usual form of a private corporation, but are controlled by the state either through majority stock ownership, by a charter which establishes a series of stock to which only government can subscribe, or by a requirement that government select a majority of the board of directors.[30]

Outstanding examples of the former include the Mexican Social Security Institute and *Petróleos Mexicanos,* the petroleum monopoly; and of the latter, the *Altos Hornos* steel complex and the development banks.

The rationale for the establishment of such agencies follows a course by now familiar. The decentralized agency permits activities deemed to be primarily technical, administrative, or entrepreneurial in nature to be protected from direct political influence. Furthermore, the autonomous institution was seen as a more appropriate organization form for many of the welfare and economic functions that the state was to undertake than would have been their inclusion in regular ministries. However, such justifications, and the "mixed enterprise" form which such autonomous agencies have taken, reflect again the desire to reconcile policies calling for extensive state activity in economic development with the assumptions and reservations concerning such public activity entertained by the Mexican economic elites. As Castellanos Coutiño of the Mexican Public Administration Institute has observed:

> With reference to decentralized organizations, in trying to develop an explanation of their origin, the hypothesis is suggested that they came forth precisely as a consequence of the conflict between state intervention and private initiative, since in this type of institution, government combines with private individuals to provide a public service . . . and through the collective use of public and private capital, with the stimulus of profit, the economic development of the community is enhanced.[31]

Mexican commentators on the decentralized agencies are quick to point out, however, that the notion of "mixed enterprise" suggests considerably more private control than is in fact the case. The autonomous status of such agencies is legally quite circum-

scribed, and control by political authority seems structurally to
be insured. As one authority on Mexican administration has
stated:

> In reality, the decentralized organism in Mexico does not corre-
> spond to the European type, because it maintains an intimate relation
> with the central government, and except for the National University,
> all the rest are managed by councils or boards of directors composed
> of administrators of the executive branch.[32]

In addition to exercising almost total control over the boards
of directors, since 1947 consistent efforts have been made to
strengthen the power of political authorities over these agencies.
By the aforementioned Law of Decentralized Agencies, the Secretary of Hacienda (one of the "inner circle" cabinet posts) and
the Secretary of National Property were empowered to supervise closely the activities of these institutions.[33]

Nonetheless, it is clear that one of the primary political problems of Mexico continues to lie in the control of these agencies.
There are continual suggestions that in this area presidential
control has broken down, and that the decentralized agencies
have become a web of competing and overlapping institutions,
poorly managed, registering unexplained losses—in short, quite
removed from political responsibility. As Lic. Eduardo Busta-
mente, Secretary of the National Patrimony, recently said:

> The government is often accused of an economic centralism that
> doesn't exist. The decentralized agencies are practicing feudalism.
> Each one manages its own affairs for its own account and risk, only
> occasionally giving notice of its activities. This has to stop.[34]

In retrospect, the legislation of 1947 concerning administrative agencies of this type appears as one in a series of recurrent
efforts to consolidate political control over these agencies. Every
recent presidential administration has attempted new measures
to bring a measure of coordination and responsibility to these
institutions. In most instances, all that seems to be accomplished
is that old institutions are supplemented or replaced by new ones
having virtually the same powers.[35]

The structure of the development banks. This discussion of
the decentralized agencies locates the development banks within
the Mexican political system and reveals their general characteristics. As state participation agencies they are formally structured
so that the state will control a majority of the voting stock. Following a conventional financial pattern, ownership of stock issues is specified in the charter. Generally, series A stock, constituting fifty-one per cent of the total, may be subscribed only
by the national government.[36] Series B stock is generally reserved for bank subscription, and subsequent series for clientele
groups or for other interests related to the bank's activities.

In most cases, the bulk of series B stock, intended primarily
for the private banking community, has been subscribed by other
development banks, particularly the Bank of Mexico, although
Nacional Financiera, the Foreign Commerce Bank, and others
have also been active investors.[37] This pattern is characteristic
not only of the development banks but of the entire structure
of the decentralized agencies. A chart of capital flow between the
decentralized agencies would reveal a fantastically complex web
of government capital inbreeding. It is quite improbable that this
was designed to strengthen government control of these institutions, which was in any event guaranteed in their charters. Rather,
it would seem to represent a financial technique to substitute for
the lack of receptivity in the private sector to the legally anticipated provisions for their participation in these enterprises. This
is reflected in the progressive concentration of capital in government hands over time. For example, in the case of the Agrarian
Credit Bank, between 1926 and 1950, series A capital increased
tenfold, series B capital was cut in half (the state governments, for
whom this block of stock was specified, were more or less coerced
into participation in the first place), and series C capital quad-
rupled.[38]

It would appear that the mobilization of capital through series
specified for supplementary investors was only a secondary purpose of this design for capitalization. More important, perhaps,

was the desire to enhance the banks' legitimacy by provisions for participation by their prospective clientele, the banking community, and groups deemed to have an interest in the activity of the bank; to satisfy aspirations that bank organization reflect democratic forms; and a desire to provide a form of tutelage in investment activity for groups at the margin of the modern economy. The last is particularly evident in the case of series C stock in the Small Merchants' Bank, which is structured along credit union lines, purchase of a share of stock being requisite for all bank clients.[39]

It is quite clear that these capitalization schemes have little to do with providing for a mixed enterprise form of corporate government. While owners of supplementary series of stock usually have more than a proportionate number of representatives on the governing boards of the banks,[40] charter provisions usually make it possible for a minority of series A stockholders (i.e., representatives of the executive branch of the federal government) to veto decisions of the board. For example, three representatives of series A stock can veto board actions in the Ejido Bank, two in the Bank of Cooperative Development. In the case of the Bank of Mexico and the Public Works Bank, the representative of the Secretary of Hacienda has exclusive veto power over many policy questions.

Government representation on the boards of directors is structured around those national ministries and departments most closely related to the work of the bank. Thus, the board of the Ejido Bank includes representatives of Hacienda, Agriculture, and the Department of Agrarian Affairs (charged with the agrarian reform program). In addition, through ownership of supplementary stock series, the Agrarian Credit Bank, the Foreign Commerce Bank, the Bank of Mexico, and the *Almacenes Nacionales de Depósito* (National Warehouses) are also represented. Such a structure is almost duplicated in the Agrarian Credit Bank, with a representative of the Secretary of Industry and Commerce and of the Ejido Bank included. The Public

Works Bank includes on its board representatives of Hacienda, the Secretaries of Public Works and Water Resources (*Obras Públicas and Recursos Hidráulicos*), the Federal District, and the Bank of Mexico. The board of the Cooperative Development Bank includes representatives from the Secretaries of Economy and Labor and, since 1955, of Maritime Affairs (*Marina*), an outcome of the bank's important relations with cooperatives in the fishing industry.

Thus, the governing boards of the banks become, in effect, forums for the coordination of the activities of executive and decentralized agencies, as they come to focus on particular policy areas in which the credit instrument may be used as a technique of government.

Representatives of private interests on the bank boards, far from being coequal holders of decision-making authority as in a true mixed enterprise, would seem to possess a role more in keeping with the tradition of semiofficial interest group representation in Mexico. Such interests as are represented on bank boards have structured access for consultation and advice in the banks, but such representation does not involve an actual share in decision-making authority. Even this limited form of participation in bank decision-making authority has been defaulted through the unwillingness of private interests to participate as anticipated in the capitalization of the banks. Their places filled by representatives of other decentralized agencies, the boards, while serving to coordinate public agencies, are hardly instruments for accommodating public and private interests concerned with the banks' activities.

In essence, formal power over bank policy would seem to derive from the chief executive and his immediate circle of inner cabinet ministers. Although power to appoint the director and top administrators of the banks is usually formally vested in the board of directors, it seems probable that such choices are in fact made by the president and his immediate advisers. As reports were issued concerning administrative appointments after

the inauguration of López Mateos in 1958, frequently announcement of the board of directors and the top bank administrative
personnel were made at the same time, in a presidential announcement.[41]

The formal control of cabinet officials and the interlocking
web of representatives of other development banks and decentralized agencies is supplemented by other administrative
arrangements for supervision and coordination of the development banking system. The National Banking Commission performs conventional inspection functions for both public and
private banks. This agency is directly under the control of the
Secretary of Hacienda. The Bank of Mexico, on which the other
development banks either directly or indirectly are highly dependent for a great part of their financial survival, has institutionalized part of its influence over these banks in the Credit
Coordinating Committee (*Comité Coordinador de Crédito*),
bringing together representatives of the development banks to
avoid duplication of activities and to direct credit programs to
the most appropriate institutions.

The Committee on Public Sector Importations (*Comité de
Importaciones del Sector Público*), presided over by the Foreign Commerce Bank, attempts to regulate and conserve foreign
exchange used by public agencies, including the development
banks. Finally, the direct financial control of Hacienda, the
planning functions of the new Secretary of the Presidency, and
the regulation of the Secretary of National Patrimony all constitute devices of coordination and control of the development
banking system.[42]

Given these substantial limitations on bank autonomy, it may
be that the primary problems of control and responsibility are
not to be found in the linkage of the banks to political authorities
but in the internal administration of the institutions themselves.
And in surveying the extensive literature on bank mismanagement, corruption, and malpractice, one point comes clear.
Charges of irresponsible conduct are predominately leveled

against those banks which, by the nature of their function, have adopted a decentralized form of administration. Such institutions as Nacional Financiera, the Bank of Mexico, and the Public Works Bank, whose operations are concentrated in a limited number of offices, and which deal with a relatively sophisticated clientele, have been remarkably free from criticism. On the other hand, those banks which deal in a high volume of small transactions, which serve an economically and socially disadvantaged clientele, and which operate through a large number of small agencies, have been the target of criticism for failures ranging from excessive red tape to outright theft, graft, and larceny on the part of bank officials.

The agrarian banks have borne the brunt of this criticism. The form of organization adopted by these institutions, in which credit cooperatives were to distribute credit granted by local bank agencies to individual clients, has not generally been successful. Since the great majority of members of these cooperatives are unprepared to understand or to cope with the responsibilities of cooperative membership, these organizations have generally been an ineffective way both of administering credit and of organizing an interest group which could demand honest, efficient performance by bank personnel. Unscrupulous bank agents and cooperative leaders may conspire to defraud both the clients and the bank itself. Attempts by the central bank office to insure honest performance through detailed rules and regulations and a centralization of decision making have more often resulted in binding the functions of the bank in a maze of red tape than in correcting administrative ills.

In recent years, efforts have been made to correct some of these administrative deficiencies. Since 1958, the Agrarian Credit Bank has been severely restricting its business with inefficient agricultural cooperatives, concentrating its activities on a limited number of better credit risks. In that same year, a system of regional banks was established, now numbering six, in order to achieve the benefits of decentralization without losing control through fragmentation of responsibility. These banks are tied to the central organization through financial techniques. Although each regional bank has its own capital, the central institution is the majority stockholder and is empowered to rediscount the paper of the regional banks. The central institution must approve plans of agricultural development or industrialization made by the regional banks, approve their warehousing programs, and authorize their annual plan of operation and budget. The regional banks cannot contract liabilities without authorization from the central office. However, the regional banks are free to fix limits on credit within their district and to adopt a form of organization and operation appropriate to the needs of the region. As part of this reorganization of 1958, local agents were empowered to select clients and make loans without previous consultation with the central office.[43] In 1961, the Ejido Bank similarly undertook a program of rapid decentralization of its activities, moving important functions to a system of regional banks. Many Mexicans have seen in these measures a program to reunite the two agrarian banks in a central institution, operating through a system of common regional banks and local agencies. At present, it is pointed out, inefficiency and wastage of resources results from the overlapping functions of these two institutions.

Yet the agrarian banks have not been the only victims of the perils of credit decentralization in a society where levels of economic sophistication are low. The Small Merchants' Bank in its early years was also the target of criticism. In 1949, it was reported that leaders of the *Federación Nacional de Comerciantes en Pequeño* (National Federation of Small Merchants), acting as agents of the bank, in the markets of the Federal District, were exploiting the merchants behind the back of the bank, using "gangster" tactics to keep the small vendors from joining credit unions and to prevent them from protesting against the extortionary practices of federation leaders. Members of the federation threatened businessmen with death or kidnapping and at times destroyed their booths in the market place when they ventured to protest. Largely as an outcome of this situation, the Bank abolished the agency system and replaced it with its famous "banks on wheels," mobile banking institutions, staffed by employees of the bank, which make the rounds of the markets of Mexico City.[44]

Financial technique as an administrative device. The increasing use of the autonomous government corporation around the world gives testimony to the usefulness of financial devices as a means of structuring administrative and political relationships. There is a flexibility and adaptability in the political use of the capitalization techniques of the modern corporation which often serves purposes not fully met by conventional designs of administrative organization, relying more directly on political sanctions for support. In Mexico, the use of such devices has had a peculiar fascination, as illustrated by the structure of the development banking system, in which such techniques have been used not merely as the means of strengthening the relationship of decentralized agencies to political authorities, but as an instrument of internal administration as well—as seen in the structure of the regional agencies of the agrarian banks.

It is clear that the formal structure of the development banks has not worked out as expected. The mixed enterprise form of capitalization seemed to anticipate a system of bank government in which private investors and client groups would have a structured right of consultation, though ultimate authority would continue to rest in government hands. Due to the unwillingness of private investment to join in this process, bank government has become largely a means of coordinating diverse administrative agencies with an interest in the policy of a specific bank.

The Political Process and Policy Making in the Development Banks

Description of formal institutional arrangements is not adequate for the purposes of political analysis. It is necessary to look more closely at the role of the development banks within the Mexican political process—to assess their character as actors within a political system. To do so, we must examine the conflicts that have emerged over development bank policy and the manner in which such conflicts are resolved. We must look to the institutions and processes which influence the policies of the development banks and to the reciprocal power of the banks to shape the economic programs of which they are a part.

In seeking to grasp the political character of these development banks, we shall ultimately come to ask whether they may be said to correspond to one of the following ideal types of political organization: (1) Are they in fact primarily administrative instruments of political leadership, in a sense "dummy corporations" which represent merely a convenient organizational device for carrying out politically determined public credit policies? (2) Are they, to some extent, "private governments," providing services specified by a particular clientele? (3) May they in any way be characterized as "autonomous centers of power" where a managerial elite prescribes and carries out policies within a self-defined sphere of competence?

Conflict over the appropriate economic role of the public sector. In ascertaining the political character of the development banks, we must look first to the conflicts that have arisen over bank policy in Mexico, and then to the manner in which these conflicts have been resolved through the political process.

It has already been noted that the economic advisers of the early Revolutionary governments anticipated a total modern economy in which private industrial and commercial enterprise would play a substantial if not a preponderant role. Public policy was, in a sense, directed toward the creation of such private economic activity. This was deemed to be the best way to achieve rapid economic development and the "decolonization" of the nation from foreign economic exploitation. The very success of this policy is to be seen in the creation of the new economic elites in the fields of industry, commerce, and agriculture. Their growing economic power, particularly during the past two-and-one-half decades, has been paralleled by an increase in their political influence. In a pattern familiar to Western observers, with their increasing power they have come more and more to act as a "countervailing force," as prime critics of public economic policy.

Much of their criticism is directed at the decentralized agencies. Through such institutions, the state is accused of exercising monopoly control over the most important and productive facets of the economy, notably in the fields of petroleum, steel, other heavy industry, and finance. Their critique of the decentralized agencies is based on a number of specific arguments. Perhaps their least important approach has been to raise the constitutional issue, citing Article 28—outlawing monopolies—and seeking to apply this to the public as well as to the private realm.[45]

A second approach has been to attempt to define the legitimate boundary between public and private enterprise in the Mexican economy. It is argued that government may act to create the infrastructure for economic development and to provide basic public services, but that it should not enter the field of "productive enterprise" on a permanent basis. Where it is legitimate for government to enter into productive activity, because of the imperative nature of the enterprise in the total economic development effort and the unwillingness or inability of private entrepreneurs to do the job, government should act to liquidate its holdings in the enterprise, and should place them in the hands of private owners as soon as its "transitional purposes" have been served. Only in this way can government avoid competing or excluding private capital from the most profitable enterprises. Furthermore, by liquidating its holdings in firms satisfactorily "on their feet," the public sector will have more capital to invest in works which private enterprise cannot undertake.[46]

The third, and perhaps most pertinent, critique made by these economic elites decries the "financial disequilibrium" which they charge results from public economic activity. Government capital support for decentralized agencies which "cannot pay their own way" results in deficit financing, and in the inflationary conditions which have been the most widely recognized blemish on Mexico's economic progress during the past twenty-five years.[47]

These criticisms reflect beliefs about the corporate form adopted for Mexico's decentralized agencies. The continued legitimacy of these institutions in the eyes of the economic elites is dependent on their ability to fulfill the norms deemed applicable to this form of organization—to break even or to show a profit on capital investment. At times, the inability of state enterprises to fulfill these expectations brings forth the classic argument that public enterprise is intrinsically inefficient in productive activity, due to excessive bureaucratization and to exemption from the normal conditions of market competition and the profit motive deemed applicable under private management.[48]

This public controversy over the legitimate economic role of government, which is certainly one of the crucial public issues of contemporary Mexico, constitutes a primary pressure on policy formulation in the development banks. Insofar as such agencies as Nacional Financiera and the Bank of Mexico are the prime sources of capital for state enterprise, the criticisms applicable to the conditions and scope of such enterprise reflect directly on the policies of such banks. Insofar as the development banks are themselves subject to the criteria of self-sufficiency believed pertinent to such forms of economic organization, they share the criticisms leveled against the decentralized agencies generally when their capital must be replenished by the state. To this latter point we shall first direct our attention.

Institutional criteria of banking effectiveness and the political conflict. The expectations concerning what a bank is and does are well known and understood in the modern world—on both sides of the Iron Curtain. Banks loan money, with the expectation of repayment at interest. The "skill" of banking, highly respected as a profession throughout the Western world, consists precisely in assessing the optimum possibilities for return among alternative investments. Such expectations apply to development banks and their managers as well. But in addition, such banks are expected to carry out their operations in a specific sphere of public or community interest. Frequently, the sphere of competence of a development bank lies in an area where private bankers, in the exercise of their skill, have determined that extensive investment would be injudicious. The inherent conflict between the two sets of expectations is obvious.

In Mexico, the historic tension between the desire to create a total modern economy and to implement the specific reforms pledged by the Revolution is a further problem which often must be resolved in the arena of development-bank policy making.

No clearer illustration is available than the problem of agricultural credit in Mexico. As has been noted, land redistribution alone has never been considered adequate for the purposes of agrarian reform. Assistance to the new small landowner was essential were he to become an effective producer and his way of life actually to be bettered. That agrarian credit should be the principal means to this end was dictated by the belief that this represented the most efficient use of scarce resources, and that credit provided a form of tutelage to the small farmer essential to his integration into the modern economy.

Yet agricultural credit is at best a risky business. Natural hazards make the assessment of loan security a much more difficult task than assessment in industry. In addition, the agricultural development banks were charged with the extension of credit to the traditionally submarginal, "economically irresponsible" sector of agriculture, to assist them through a daring but quite unsettling transformation in customary technique.

The outcome has been a cyclical pattern of emphasis in agricultural banking policy. During some presidential administrations, under some types of bank leadership, notably in the Cárdenas years, sound banking policy was sublimated to the social-service objectives of the agrarian reform. Prior to and, in varying degrees of emphasis, since that time, stress has been placed on fulfilling the institutional criteria of the banks qua banks.[49]

Although contemporary official propaganda protests loudly that large landholding has ceased to exist in Mexico, it is clear that the large farm or ranch is as characteristic of Mexican agriculture today as it was during earlier periods. In part, this apparent ambiguity—some would say hypocrisy—in agrarian policy is due to official policies of dramatically increasing agricultural production for reasons unrelated to or in conflict with agrarian reform, such as to improve the nation's balance-of-payment position or to feed the growing urban population. Yet such a trend has been effectively implemented by the preference given by the Agrarian Credit Bank to better credit risks and to generally large, efficient, mechanized farmers, so that the criteria of sound bank management might be fulfilled.

This policy has been particularly apparent in recent years. In 1958, the Agrarian Credit Bank announced that it was cutting the number of clients served in half while doubling the value of credits authorized. Primarily this was due to the bank's decision to stop dealing with poorly organized cooperative credit societies. The bank was the target of much criticism as a result of the corruption and inefficiency of the cooperative system. Furthermore, many continued to receive credit though badly in arrears on previous debts. However, the bank's decision to cease operations with ineffective cooperatives apparently had the effect of strengthening the position of the more efficient farmers and of excluding the weaker producers.[50]

For Mexican advocates of agrarian reform, the ultimate irony of this conflict between bank technique and land reform came during the early land program of the López Mateos administration, when some 179,000 hectares to be redistributed were acquired from the Agrarian Credit Bank through a transfer to the

Department of Agrarian Affairs, these lands having come into the bank's possession because the former tenants were unable to pay their debts to the bank.[51]

The Ejido Bank, established originally to bypass the Agrarian Credit Bank's preferential treatment of better credit risks, thus neglecting newly created *ejidos,* has been subjected to similar criticisms. Placed in a highly enigmatic position, due to the inalienability of *ejido* lands and the lower sophistication of its clientele, it too has failed to meet the criteria of banking performance, registering large losses. Following in the footsteps of its companion institution, it has come more and more to favor credit extension to more successful *ejidos.* In fact, both banks seem condemned to operate in a storm center of criticism. Their inability to "succeed" is a source of complaint for the private banking community and the economic elites. Their efforts to succeed, by rigorous selection of credit investments, and stern—at times arbitrary and occasionally strong-arm [52]—efforts to collect debts, have won no sympathy from their clientele or from those who see them as existing primarily to fulfill a social function.

While the dilemma of the Mexican development bank is most apparent in the case of agricultural credit, this is in fact a problem common to most of these institutions. The Foreign Commerce Bank, for example, is charged specifically with using the credit instrument to better the nation's foreign-trade position. When it operates in the agricultural field, however, advocates of agrarian reform feel that its effect, like that of the two agrarian banks, is to strengthen further the position of the large landowner at the expense of the small farmer. That such a feeling may be justified is evidenced by a recent statement by a spokesman for the bank, Lic. Ricardo J. Zeveda:

> The marginal producer has been disappearing. He or his creditors have absorbed the losses, but they have been eliminated, [for] in our export agriculture there is not room—and there hasn't been for a long time—for the inefficient and unprepared in the fields of cotton, coffee, tomatoes and [other products].[53]

Similarly, Nacional Financiera, the most successful of the development banks in terms of criteria of banking performance, has often been accused of supporting large enterprise and neglecting the small producer. Sanford Mosk, though generally favorable to this institution, did criticize this aspect of its operation:

> So far, Nacional Financiera has been of little help to the small manufacturer. Nacional Financiera has been chiefly occupied with financing the larger new industrial ventures, the types that the Mexican government has been especially anxious to encourage. Thus no one has attempted to meet the needs of small industry, although currently small industry as a rule is better adapted to the Mexican economic structure than big concerns.[54]

While Nacional Financiera's policy was largely a product of a general philosophy of stimulating enterprise through public investment in "basic" industries with assumed potential to create external economies, it would seem that its desire to meet the criteria of banking responsibility through investment in the "sounder" credit opportunities provided a supplementary impetus to such a policy.

There is, then, in Mexico as in all Western societies, an a priori case against the "irresponsible" use of the banking device as an instrument of public policy, a primary "rule of the game" limiting political control of these institutions. It is too simple to suggest that the case of Mexico represents, in terms of political influence, merely a victory of "economic conservatives" over "reformers." The fact seems to be that the institutional criteria of legitimate bank activity are accepted by virtually all political elites in Mexico. Those who criticize the antiagrarian reform effects of the agrarian banks suggest not that these banks emphasize the "social service" aspect of their mission, but that credit functions be separated from direct aid and technical assistance activities, both to strengthen the weaker elements in the agricultural sector and to enable the agrarian banks to operate on a sound financial basis.[55]

Fulfillment of the institutional criteria of banking also seems important to the bank managers themselves. Most of them emerge from or identify closely with the Mexican financial community. Their profession and training is apt to be in the field of financial management, and their success, measured both introspectively and by those who count, will come from responsible banking practice and not from any efforts to raise rural living standards through unrecovered loans. As Victor Thompson has recently noted,[56] contemporary emphasis on decision-making analysis should not lead us to neglect institutional determinants of administrative behavior. The Mexican development banks provide an excellent illustration of his point. Even the most "reform-minded" bank manager has a strong bias in favor of the institutional criteria of banking effectiveness.

Techniques of implementing presidential control over the banks. The institutional bias toward responsible banking conduct is reinforced by the attitude of important political forces within the Revolutionary coalition. Failure of the banks to meet these standards causes such groups to challenge their legitimacy as appropriate instruments of public policy. On the other hand, when adherence to such standards of financial responsibility diminishes the banks' ability to implement the specific public policy for which it was designed, criticism is heard from other members of the Revolutionary coalition.

Perhaps the prime political concern of top Mexican leadership, we have noted, is that of maintaining the Revolutionary coalition intact. The banking device itself originally seems to have been adopted in part as a means of reconciling the assumptions of both the economic elites and the advocates of specific reform policies concerning appropriate state economic activity. Techniques used by high political leadership, centered in the chief executive, to adjust banking policy to satisfy such criticism also seem designed to satisfy reciprocally the criteria of legitimate financial activity and the policy demands placed upon the banks. We note that such political adjustments of bank policy derive not from the banks as autonomous centers of power. Rather, in keeping with the character of the Mexican system of government, they generally represent a reassertion of the powers of the presidency and the cabinet.

Capital support for submarginal banks. The agrarian banks in particular have been kept alive by recurrent "bailing out" operations—by supplemental capital to offset their losses and to maintain their level of operations on a scale suitable to public policy—provided either directly by government appropriation or through credits from other development banks, predominantly the Bank of Mexico. This policy has satisfied neither the advocates of agrarian reform nor the advocates of banking responsibility. It has always been regarded as a temporary expedient, recurrently adopted in the belief that such capital infusions could put the banks on a sound financial basis.

Creation of new institutions. Rather than restrict the banks' power to select their own clients on the basis of risk calculations, political leadership has at times preferred to create new institutions to service those clients who had been given low-credit priority by existing banks. This was clearly the case with the separation of the Ejido Bank from the Agrarian Credit Bank in 1935, and it was implicit in the establishment of the Workers' Credit Bank in 1939, to supplement Nacional Financiera in the industrial field. Of course, the creation of such new institutions did nothing to make less preferred credit risks any better, and both institutions failed to meet the standards of banking success, the latter eventually passing from the scene, the former precariously maintained despite its losses, probably because of the greater political significance of its clientele.

The instrument of the trust fund. One of the more successful techniques used by political leadership to direct bank policy toward areas neglected by adherence to conventional banking practice has been the trust fund. Formally legitimate as a financial technique, this takes the form of a government appropriation for a specific purpose to be administered as a trust by a development bank. Thus, a financial technique rather than a more overt form of political direction is used to provide policy guidance.

Perhaps the best known of these trusts is the Fund for the Protection and Development of Medium and Small Industries (*Fondo de Garantía y Fomento de la Industria Mediana y Pequeña*), with an initial capital value of M$50,000,000. Nacional Financiera was empowered to act as a trustee for this fund, thereby directing its operations to those smaller enterprises it had been criticized for neglecting.

Examples of similar efforts to encourage activity in specific areas through trust funds could be cited for virtually all the development banks. To mention a few relevant examples, the Foreign Commerce Bank administers funds for the development of cacao, the administration of government-owned coffee fincas in Chiapas state, development of a national merchant marine, the production and refining of candelaria wax grown on *ejidos*, the provision of credit for henequin growers in Yucután, and the provision of meat refrigeration facilities in the Federal District, among others.[57]

The Cooperative Development Bank administers a fund of roughly M$10,000,000 for the development of the Mexican fishing industry, which has become one of the most prominent activities of the bank. Among the various trusts administered by the Agrarian Credit Bank are funds for the construction of warehouses and poultry-raising installations. (Here the Secretary of Agriculture plans and constructs the facilities with the bank only acting as a financial agent, though trust funds are often used to empower banks to act directly in substantive public activities.) Other funds are designated for the improvement of corn and bean production in impoverished regions or during poor harvest years. The bank also, from 1935 to 1942, acted as trustee for the government in the development of irrigation and colonization projects in the North of Mexico, particularly in the famous cotton growing Laguna Region.[58] Similarly, following the enormously destructive hurricane of 1957, the Small Merchants' Bank was granted a special trust to extend its operations to the hard-hit cities of

Tampico and Manzanilla, the first break in the bank's policy of operating exclusively within the Federal District.

Coordination of the banks within a special presidential program. The use of interagency commissions or committees, in which relevant ministries and decentralized agencies are fitted to particular tasks in carrying out a general program demanded by top political leadership, is a prominent characteristic of Mexican political organization. In surveying the changing patterns of priority activities within the development banks, one frequently notices the impact of such special programs on bank policy. Here again the techniques of reconciling expectations concerning responsible banking conduct with politically motivated policy functions are to be noted.

One striking example of the use of this technique in recent years was President Ruiz Cortines' plan to make Mexico self-sufficient in basic foodstuff production. Initiated in 1953, the over-all program was formulated by the President and the Secretary of Agriculture, while the relevant banks and other agencies were called on to direct their policies to the ends of the plan. Emphasis was placed on attaining self-sufficiency in such products as corn, wheat, beans, meat, and milk. The agrarian banks established differential interest rates in favor of these products, the Ejido Bank cutting its rate on corn and beans to 7 per cent from a normal 9 per cent. The Agrarian Credit Bank announced that it would provide intermediate term credit only for the irrigation works, land clearing, and capital equipment that was necessary for basic foodstuffs production. (Then in a conservative policy cycle, this bank was generally cutting back on the range of its activities. Its emphasis on support of the presidential program was balanced by a reduction of activity in other fields, primarily cotton.[59]) The Foreign Commerce Bank provided large credits for price stabilization in the basic commodities. It took a particular interest in the development of the poultry industry, providing both credit and technical assistance to poultry raisers and advancing credit to rural normal schools to expand their programs in poultry husbandry.[60]

In a similar fashion, the cotton crisis of 1959 was met by the formation of an interministerial board whose program implied specific activities on the part of the banks. The Secretary of the Treasury, with the Foreign Commerce Bank, was to seek further foreign markets. The Secretary of Agriculture was to require fertilizer and insecticide-producing factories to sell directly to farmers, avoiding middleman charges. Many of these factories are controlled by development banks, predominantly Nacional Financiera. The Secretary of Industry and Commerce was to set about developing cotton marketing cooperatives, a policy sure to involve the agrarian banks. The Bank of Mexico was to "intervene" between cotton growers and bankers so that sufficient credit might be made available.[61]

Such interagency coordination also takes place at the local level. Here again bank and ministerial policy is coordinated, usually, it would seem, with ministerial initiative to which the banks fit relevant credit policies insofar as their capacities permit. For example, the local water boards (Juntas de Aguas) now being established in various localities are composed of representatives of the ministries of Agriculture and Water Resources, the Ejido and Agrarian Credit banks, the local irrigation system, and farmers.[62]

Direct administrative control. One must not underestimate the potential of relevant ministries or of the president to influence bank policy directly. In case of conflict between bank management and ministerial control, resignation of the bank officer as a last resort is the rule. No case of a bank attempting to mobilize political support against a ministry has come to my attention. Generally it may be said that the banks are seldom capable of formulating policy apart from ministerial supervision and that they are quite responsive to such supervision.

Interest group activity and the banks. Further evidence that conflicts over bank policy are resolved at the ministerial or presidential level and not within the banks themselves is to be seen in the pattern of interest group activity as it affects bank policy. Although one could cite many instances of interest group representation which is presented directly to bank management, it seems more common that demands and complaints are directed to a relevant minister or to the president himself. Again, the "petitionary" character of interest group activity is evident. There would seem to be something of an inverse relationship between the influence of the group and the level to which it carries its plea. For example, grievances of rural credit cooperatives and other farmers' groups are usually directed to the president and/or ministerial level officials.[63]

Organized clientele groups, such as the Cooperative Federation in the case of the Cooperative Development Bank or the General Federation of Autotransport Workers in relation to the Transport Bank, may request an appropriate ministry (perhaps Economy in the former case and the Federal District in the latter) to "intervene" before the bank in its behalf.[64]

During presidential campaigns, and in presidential "audiences," interest groups are apt to present petitions describing a total program of government action in support of their economic position, which often includes proposals for bank policy. Frequently, these become the basis for special presidential programs of the type noted above. In a recent statement, Ing. Guillermo Guymán, economist for the Foreign Commerce Bank, noted that the bank's program of commercial aid to guayaba producers came about at the suggestion of the Secretary of Agriculture, and that the program itself emerged directly out of the visit of President López Mateos to the Calvillo region where guayaba is grown, and the petitions which were presented to him at that time.[65] In the 1958 presidential campaign, many chambers of commerce in provincial cities requested an extension of the activity of the Small Merchants' Bank to their localities. This was usually done through petitions presented to the candidate during his campaign tours. At present, this bank is making plans to develop its operations in other parts of the country.[66]

In contrast to this style of interest-group activity, an organization such as the Bankers' Association, though of course having access at many levels, is apt to work quite directly with the Bank of Mexico, which in a sense represents the private banks before political leadership.

Characteristic of interest-group activity in Mexico, access in terms of bank policy seems primarily to be sought within the executive branch. Although some of its component organizations, notably the National Peasant Confederation (CNC), have been vigorous critics of bank policy, the official party organization itself does not appear to be an important forum for interest-group activity concerning bank policy. No notable efforts by the Congress to oversee bank activity have occurred since a senatorial investigation of the Ejido Bank in 1942 and a short-lived inquiry into the operations of Nacional Financiera by the Chamber of Deputies in 1947.[67] Litigation seems to play little part in interest-group efforts to influence public banking.

The power of the banks: Reciprocal influence in the political process. While it would seem that political control is generally effective in resolving conflicts over bank policy in Mexico, and that the fear of irresponsible development bank autonomy is not particularly applicable in this case, our consideration of the political character of these institutions cannot be dismissed at this point. Power is best understood as a reciprocal relationship. Hence, we must look also to the ways in which the development banks exert influence in the formulation and execution of economic policy in the Mexican political process.

The differential prestige of the banks. The ability of the banks to influence public policy in Mexico is in large part a function of the respect for the institutions among the more influential and articulate political elite. This varies considerably among the development banks. The Bank of Mexico and Nacional Financiera, quite deservedly esteemed for their efficiency, integrity, and successful financial practices, are heard with respect when their leaders comment on economic policy. Within its sphere of competence, the Foreign Commerce Bank also enjoys considerable prestige. In contrast, the agrarian banks are constant targets of criticism, their historic problems of corruption, mismanagement, and financial loss bringing attack both from their agrarian clientele and from the economic elites.

Interesting conventions concerning the appropriate scope of public criticism seem to exist in Mexico. It is considered poor form to attack the president directly in the public forum. Criticism should be directed instead at a cabinet official or an executive agency. In a similar fashion, to criticize the nationalized petroleum industry or the *ejido* system is considered vaguely unpatriotic. Analogous conventions seem to exist with regard to the development banks. One may condemn the agrarian banks but not the policy of agrarian reform—which of course sets the conditions for the failure of the banks. However, while criticism of the government's extensive entrepreneurial role is acceptable, Nacional Financiera, the most prominent instrument of such economic intervention, is less frequently attacked. The reform of the bank's statute in 1955, permitting Nacional Financiera to double its capital, was unanimously supported in Congress, and the institution was praised and defended in debate by the conservative opposition party *Acción Nacional*.[68]

On several occasions press criticism of government economic activity has automatically absolved Nacional Financiera of blame and sought elsewhere for a scapegoat. One editorial, for example, after noting that "We know at the outset how extremely careful Nacional Financiera is in making its loans, with a consciousness of its responsibility that we applaud without reservation," goes on to request that the Secretary of the Treasury explain certain irregularities in the establishment of an industry supported by Nacional Financiera.[69]

The banks and economic expertise. It seems fairly clear that the more prestigious banks are influential as respected sources of economic opinion and advice. Their capacity to be heard in the arenas where economic policy is made is enhanced by the concentration of much of the outstanding professional economic talent in Mexico in the leading banks—the Bank of Mexico, Nacional Financiera, the Foreign Commerce Bank, and, to a lesser extent, the Public Works Bank.

One outstanding center of economic research and planning has long been the Department of Economic Studies of the Bank of Mexico. To an extraordinary extent, economic policy formulation is dependent on the statistical and analytical resources of this department, one of the few sources of reliable economic information in the nation. A similar dependence for economic *expertise* is to be seen in the case of the Foreign Commerce Bank. Within its own sphere of activity, its judgments on the trade requirements of the Mexican economy seem often to be accepted as authoritative in the formulation of public policy.

Simply put, these three or four banks are strong competitors for a commodity which is vital to policy formulation in a complex economy, yet is in extremely scarce supply in an underdeveloped area—that of skill in economic analysis. Few decentralized agencies or government ministries can rival the banks in this regard.

There are several reasons for this concentration of economic *expertise*. In the first place, success follows from success, and a young economist of talent considers a post in the Bank of Mexico or Nacional Financiera as the juiciest of plums. To his reference groups, the prestige of such an assignment is beyond question. The salary policies of these leading banks, not bound by the chaotic civil service requirements, permit the banks often to outbid the government ministries for first-rate talent. There is a feeling that one's achievements will not be so much limited by the demands of "politics" in the banks. Yet the door is not closed to political success and one's chances may even be enhanced by service in the banks, for there is a considerable exchange of personnel between top bank administrative posts and political positions. More than one cabinet official at one time or another in his career served with the banks.

Bank power and intragovernmental financing. Credit may serve as a sanction in the hands of political agencies and hence as a source of political power. We have already noted that development banks figure prominently in the capitalization of other decentralized agencies and state participation enterprises as well as in providing financing for conventional government services. Representatives of Nacional Financiera or the Bank of Mexico, and of other development banks, often sit on the boards of these agencies or on interagency commissions empowered to coordinate general government programs. Nacional Financiera reports that from 1946 to 1960 slightly over half of its credits were concentrated in efforts to develop the "infrastructure" of the Mexican economy, through investments in electric power, transportation, railroads, and communications.[70] In short, the bulk of this institution's activities in recent years has been directed to the public sector of the economy—through credits to decentralized agencies, such as the Mexican railroads—or to government ministries. Of the 14 per cent or so of Nacional Financiera's investments which have gone to "basic industry," a substantial proportion has gone to enterprises in which Nacional Financiera has a controlling interest. These industries, about sixteen in number in 1960, are formally designated as state participation enterprises, integrated, through a variety of procedures, into the governmental process.[71] Such institutions as the Bank of Mexico, the Public Works Bank, and others have also directed a large proportion of their investments to such public agencies.

The question is, of course, whether investment implies control. May a development bank extend or deny credit in such a way as to influence authoritatively the policies of public agencies which are dependent upon it for capital?

In the area of over-all policy, there would seem to be no record of a situation in which a bank was able to overrule a political (i.e., presidential) decision to implement a policy by depriving the relevant agency of credit. The banks rather seem predisposed to invest in a program or agency at political request even though such an investment may represent a poor credit risk. In fact, what occasionally seems to happen is that development banks offset obligatory losses in "political" investments by stricter requirements and higher interest rates in other areas. In short, the representative of a development bank who sits on the board of a decentralized agency in recognition of that bank's investment has but limited real power. He may encourage certain policies on behalf of his institution, but he is powerless to do more unless his position is supported by the political representatives on the board.

Yet at a lower level of policy making the rigorous investigatory practices of such institutions at Nacional Financiera and the Bank of Mexico prior to extending credit, and the inspection and technical assistance services provided in some instances after investment, probably constitute some degree of control in cases where political considerations are not paramount.[72] At best this power of technical advice and investigation, derivative as a source of power from the economic *expertise* concentrated in the banks, constitutes no more than a bargaining device, representing but one facet in the complex of considerations which influence intra-governmental investment.

Similarly, Nacional Financiera's majority control of certain nationalized industries does not seem to constitute a basis for the day-to-day control of these enterprises by the bank. While the bank plays a major role in selecting the top managerial personnel of these enterprises (and there has been some exchange of personnel between Nacional Financiera and these industries), once selected, they seem to be permitted considerable autonomy in their operation of the industries. In fact, Nacional Financiera's reticence in exercising administrative control in these cases may constitute the missing administrative link that has led to persistent official agitation over the "irresponsible autonomy" of such enterprises, an agitation which led most recently to the authorization of the secretaries of National Patrimony and Presidency to exercise general planning and supervisory powers over state participation enterprises. This move, if successful, will further restrict Nacional Financiera's power in this area. In general, the relationship of Nacional Financiera with the firms it controls would seem to bear considerable resemblance to the model described by James Burnham and others of the relation of the North American corporate board of directors to its top management.

The power of the banks and the private sector of the economy. Increasingly, in recent years, the Mexican economic elites have expressed fears concerning the extent of government intervention in economic activity. Revolutionary governments have favored policies of considerable regulation of private economic activity, particularly in such fields as labor-management relations. Furthermore, actual government participation in the economy, in which the development banks figure prominently, seems to them to be extending at a rapid rate, threatening the role of private enterprise which such public activity was ostensibly designed to enhance.

The manifestations of this problem, insofar as it concerns the banks, of course include the obvious prominence of the Bank of Mexico and Nacional Financiera in the financial field, and the intervention of the latter in the industrial arena. Some suggest that the Bank of Mexico's "selective intervention" in the securities market, to strengthen and stabilize this form of investment and as a byproduct of rediscounting activity, actually has come to give the bank a controlling interest in a good number of private firms. The bank itself tends to discount this as a source of control of private enterprise. Its purchases and sales of securities are in constant flux and possession of a controlling interest in a firm seems to be temporary and incidental. Furthermore, for the bank actually to exercise control on the basis of stock ownership derived in this manner would probably be deemed illegitimate in terms of the rules of the game of contemporary Mexican economic life. However, the entrance of development banks other than the Bank of Mexico and Nacional Financiera into extensive economic activity has also been noteworthy. The agrarian banks and others engage to a considerable degree in the ownership and regulation of productive enterprise, in activities not strictly subsumed under the generally recognized functions of a bank.

Agitation for a larger role for private investment has increased markedly in recent years. Such heightened criticism of the public role in economic development reflects the changing nature of the Mexican economy and poses a dilemma for the development banks.

As we have noted, the extent of public capitalization of productive enterprise in Mexico was to a certain extent unintentional. The entire structure of public financial activity reflects expectations of a role for private investment that was not fulfilled. Hence, the inbred public capitalization of the development banks was in a sense improvised when the private banking community failed to participate to the extent anticipated in the capitalization of these institutions. The issue of securities on its own holdings by Nacional Financiera was itself a response to this institution's inability to stimulate a private stock exchange of adequate proportions, and its desire to mobilize private investment for the economic development effort. The extensive entrepreneurial activities of Nacional Financiera and other development banks generally represent areas of investment deemed essential to the creation of a total modern economy, to provide the necessary base for the efforts of private enterprise, in areas where private investment was unwilling or unable to play the leading role.

The very success of the development banks in stimulating private investment has been instrumental in creating the current mood of agitation. As private enterprise has increased in strength and become more attuned to modern investment psychology, it has waxed impatient in confronting the vistas that seem closed to it by reason of their inclusion in the public sector.

Hence, the private banking community has begun to agitate for more liberal banking regulations, which will permit it greater participation in economic growth, and it seeks to enter such pre-empted investment areas as the petroleum industry.[73] Industrial groups, such as CONCAMIN, protest that Nacional Financiera dominates the most profitable investment activities, and seek to have that institution divest itself of its holdings in favor of private investors as soon as it has placed the assisted enterprise on a firm financial basis.[74]

The response of the development banks to this pressure has been mixed. In the first place, required as they were in the early part of the López Mateos administration to respond to agitation from the left for the "Mexicanization" of certain outstanding private activities, primarily foreign-owned, they have increased their industrial participation considerably, notably in the field of electric power. However, the Bank of Mexico, Nacional Financiera, and other development banks have been trying to reduce their portfolios so as to put a greater quantity of securities in private hands. During 1958–59, the Bank of Mexico reduced its holdings by 26.3 per cent, and the other development banks by 5.6 per cent, while private banks raised theirs by 16.7 per cent.[75]

On the other hand, Nacional Financiera seems loath to surrender its present industrial empire. It formally announced as an article of policy five years ago that it would turn these industries over to private enterprise "once their economy is absolutely healthy." [76] Yet in early 1961 the working capital of Nacional Financiera was doubled, this in an effort to bring state participation in the enterprise down from 92 to 51 per cent, through sales of securities to private investors to cover the new capitalization.[77] Throughout this recent period, a slogan that has frequently accompanied Nacional Financiera's public statements is, "The fruitful association of public and private capital." It would seem that, rather than divesting itself of its industrial holdings, Nacional Financiera has been attempting to reconcile the interests of pronationalization and antinationalization groups in the classic tradition of the development banks. It has played from its particular source of strength among the economic elites, which consider Nacional Financiera securities extremely attractive, and has promoted the idea of mixed enterprise.

In short, extensive public supervision, regulation, and participation in the economy continue to be an abiding facet of Mexican life. Yet such institutions as the development banks do not exert unchecked power. A strong countervailing force has emerged, and is growing in strength, which sets conditions for the activity of public economic operations—a force which was itself to some extent the product of public economic intervention. But the power of these economic elites is also conditioned by the demands of interest accommodation within the entire Revolutionary coalition.

It is now time to characterize the banks as political institutions, to present a portrait of them as they stand in relations of influence and power to the processes and institutions of the Mexican political system. In so doing, let us ask to what extent the development banks are described by the categories suggested at the beginning of this section.

The banks as administrative instruments of political leadership. This is to ask the extent to which the banks are in a sense "dummy corporations," existing primarily for a legally recognized institutional capacity, which may be fitted at will by political leaders to various public policy purposes. There would seem to be considerable evidence that such a conception of the banks' function looms large in the Mexican understanding of the role of these institutions.

It is evident that a large part of the activity of these banks represents specific financial operations within more generally conceived public policies. The banks, with their unique characteristics, are to be fitted through coordination with other agencies in an over-all attack on a specific problem. Examples include the integration of the Agrarian Credit, Ejido, and Foreign Commerce banks with the ministries of Agriculture, Agrarian Affairs, and others in the basic foodstuffs program; the cooperation of the Public Works and Armed Forces Banks with the Social Security Institute, the Institute for Civil Service Welfare (*Instituto de Seguro Social al Servicio de los Trabajadores del Estado,* or INSSSTE), and various government ministries in public housing; and the Commodity Regulation Corporation (*Compañía Exportadora-Importadora Mexicana,* S.A., or CEIMSA*) with the agricultural banks and the *Almacenes Nacionales de Depósito* in commodity price control.

Furthermore, it is apparent that the banks are often regarded as appropriate repositories of a wide variety of administrative responsibilities, ranging from technical assistance and research to the supervision of government enterprises, the promotion of Mexican products abroad, and the administration of trust funds for an extremely wide variety of purposes. Especially in the case of the more prestigious institutions, or those operating in fields of special public concern, such as agriculture, these institutions have been called upon to undertake functions quite remote from their basic banking responsibilities.

Finally, there seems to exist a generally understood chain-of-command relationship between relevant ministries and top bank leadership. Rather than conceiving of himself as the possessor of policy-making competence within the sphere of activity allocated by the legislation that constituted his agency, the typical bank manager seems to feel himself as part of an administrative relationship with the line agencies, responsible to them for continuing over-all policy supervision.

The banks as autonomous centers of power. It is often suggested that development authorities or banks may become autonomous centers of power in the newly emerging nations, removed from responsibility to political leadership. Perhaps the most vivid statement of this idea, in relation to Latin America, is that of

---

* Later known as *Compañía Nacional de Subsistencias Populares,* or CONASUPO. See footnote on p. 65, above.

Harold Seidman. He notes the widespread use of public corporations in Latin America as a "panacea for inefficient or even corrupt government." But the separation of such agencies from political control may be carried to extremes. Ministries may become "hollow shells." It is suggested that "In some parts of Latin America, public corporations can be said literally to constitute a headless and irresponsible fourth branch of government." [78]

Such autonomy as the Mexican development banks possess would seem to be derived primarily from prevailing assumptions concerning legitimate banking behavior, assumptions reinforced by the power of the economic elite within the Revolutionary coalition and by the attitudes of economic policy makers and the bank managers themselves. Hence, dedication to agrarian reform programs has to some extent been thwarted as the agrarian banks, to reduce consistent losses, have come more and more to deal with better credit risks—and also insofar as more funds have been available for industrial than agricultural credit due to the greater success of banks operating in the industrial sector.

On the whole, however, rather than checking the power of political leaders over the banks, assumptions concerning legitimate banking activity have led policy makers to devise financial techniques to reconcile demands for proper banking conduct with politically determined public policies, such as the creation of new banks—when existing institutions acting according to norms of banking conduct are unable to meet public policy expectations—and the trust fund device.

However, given the expectations concerning legitimate banking conduct, the concentration of economic *expertise* in the staffs of some development banks does provide them with a bargaining tool, a reciprocal form of influence of admittedly undetermined significance, in economic policy making.

The banks as private governments. There is little evidence to suggest that policy making in the development banks is dominated by their clientele groups. Rather, the more general pattern is for the development banks to be used to encourage performances by their clientele deemed desirable in terms of general economic policy considerations. The relationship of the banks to their clientele is more apt to be tutelary or directive than responsive.

Nor does it seem that the more prestigious development banks have in recent years been used to any great extent as a source of illicit enrichment by the more influential economic elites. For example, in the case of Nacional Financiera, it does not appear that the so-called "Revolutionary families" exert undue influence in credit decisions. Generally, this group has adequate access to private sources of credit, and Nacional Financiera appears consistent in its general requirement that private sources of credit be thoroughly explored before it will participate in an undertaking.

The most evident exception to this generalization concerning the role of clientele groups in bank policy is that of the Armed Forces Bank. Established originally as a means of diverting military resources into productive activities, it has become increasingly a means of providing a wide range of fringe benefits for the armed forces. In recent years the bank seems to have abandoned even the pretext of making loans for entrepreneurial activities. The bulk of its operations now include direct consumers credit, mortgage loans for military housing, commercial activities (including low-cost pharmacies, and commissaries), educational loans for cadets and administrative and financial activities in connection with the military pension plan.[79]

The activities of the bank reflect its organization. Seldom do more than one or two civilians sit on the eight-man board of directors. The ministries of Agriculture and Economy generally appoint military men as their representatives on the board, as did Treasury until quite recently. In recent years, an army officer has always served as director and as assistant director of the bank.[80]

In summary, while Seidman's fear that development banks might become an "irresponsible fourth branch of government" does not seem applicable in the Mexican case, it is clear that even in this system, where political control is generally effective, the development banks are not merely passive recipients of political power but stand in an active and dynamic relationship to the totality of the political process.

Development Bank Credit as Political Sanction

Most policies of the modern state are not self-enforcing. In addition to possessing means for resolving conflicts over public purposes, an effective political organization must be able to assure that decisions taken on public purposes may in fact be carried out. To a large extent, this capacity of government normally rests on the assent or acquiescence of citizens to the decisions of political leaders. Yet such authority is always supplemented by other means, more so in societies where less consensus exists concerning the legitimate ends and techniques of political life. Sanctions derive in part from the primordial power of government as possessor of a legitimate monopoly of force. But the modern state, acting as a participant within a complex web of economic and social systems, has at its disposal a wide range of rewards and deprivations which may be imaginatively fitted to the demands of policy. Public credit and investment, in an expanding and changing economy, may effectively be used as a carrot and a stick to bring about behavior deemed appropriate to certain public purposes.[81]

To illustrate this point in relation to development policy and the activities of development banks, we turn again to the case of Mexico. Here the use of credit as a means of effecting public policy is revealed most clearly in the field of agriculture.

Agrarian credit as sanction. Producer autonomy must be regarded as a basic underlying principle of the Mexican agrarian reform. While this cold, analytic term may seem to some to do an injustice to the many emotional connotations that surround the quest of the *campesino* for "land," it does sum up what was at issue when the Revolutionists insisted that "the land belongs to him who works it." The demand for agrarian reform, which for many epitomizes the Mexican Revolution, must be seen in the context of the then-prevailing landholding system.

The latifundia, or great estate, in essence represented a largely self-contained political, economic, and social system, sanctioned by tradition and reinforced by the power of the state. The technique used to buttress legally the stability of this institution is usually referred to as peonage, or debt slavery. As the semifeudal structure derived from the *encomienda* system of the colonial period came to be regarded as inappropriate to a nineteenth-century liberal ideology, the formal controls of the patron over his workers were shifted to practices deemed more consistent with orthodox economic practice. The peon became a wage earner rather than a serf. Yet the low wage structure combined with the resistant paternal expectations concerning the patron's role resulted in the use of credit or advances on wages to meet the expenses of festivals, illness, and funerals, or simply to meet consumption necessities. Given the prevailing conceptions of contract, a worker could not cease his employment until his obligations to his employer had been met—which could rarely be achieved—and the power of government, in the form of a rural police force, could be used to enforce these contractual obligations. In short, credit became an appropriate sanction in squaring the existing landholding system with the strictures of liberal economics.

For many, the Revolution was fought to replace the latifundia either with the small freeholding or with a "return" to the semi-communal system of community agriculture. Land redistribution as a dominant theme in agrarian policy became the technique appropriate to this end. However, this principle had to be reconciled with demands coming from other sectors of the society. Land redistribution alone did not define an agrarian policy. The ideal of the total modern economy required that the reformed farmers be brought into the national marketplace. The industrial superstructure to be constructed demanded an agricultural base producing far beyond subsistence requirements. Again, the credit mechanism became an appropriate means of reconciling the ideal of producer autonomy with the development of a new economic system.

In many regions where land reform was carried out, due to the urgent credit needs of the farmers both for capital improvements and, more pervasively, for day-to-day financial assistance, the agrarian banks became a powerful means of channeling the efforts of the small landholders toward over-all agrarian policy. One effect of their activity is to be seen in the place of the agrarian credit society in the life of the small farmer. By requiring that clients organize into such credit cooperatives, the Agrarian Credit and Ejido banks hoped to simplify their administrative problems and to encourage the cooperative spirit. Ideologically, cooperation was deeply imbedded in the Revolutionary tradition, which placed great trust in grass-roots communitarianism. In theory, cooperatives would emerge from below out of the needs of the farmers, such voluntary enthusiasm being implemented by technical advice and assistance. In fact, the credit sanction was used to create an institution that was not in general spontaneously accepted or understood. Ideally, credit cooperatives would be controlled democratically, grants of credit from bank to cooperatives being allocated by representatives of the members. In fact, the politically unsophisticated small farmer was usually unable to control the society. Power fell into the hands of the better-prepared, upwardly mobile farmers, who often exploited their opportunities to the full. As the banks came more and more to employ the credit sanction to encourage performances deemed desirable in terms of over-all agrarian policy, a coalition of bank personnel and the cooperative cacique often appeared which, viewed from below, seemed to represent arbitrary power based on the imperative need for credit. Perhaps overstating the case a bit, but hitting at an important dimension of the problem, the Mexican social scientist, Dr. Lucio Mendieta y Núñez, writes as follows:

In Mexico, the ejidal cooperatives are a farce. There are no co-operatives of this type. The Bank does everything. The Bank decides how much they can make, a correct approach in that the great mass of the Indians have absolutely no background for understanding what a cooperative is all about. In many instances, the so-called members of the group don't even speak Spanish. And between the leader, a friend of the Bank, and the Bank itself, they have in ten years lost M$ 130,000,000, no matter what the Secretary of Agriculture says to the contrary.[82]

In addition to supporting the cooperative organizations, the credit sanction as used by the agrarian banks serves other purposes. It is used to enforce programs of technical assistance and advice. Short-term *ejido* credit is given on the succeeding harvest. Credit grants are based on a production plan submitted by the farmer covering the agricultural cycle. Credit may be made contingent on the adoption of specific techniques by the producer, the purchase of quality seeds or fertilizers through the bank, and the satisfactory performance of work outlined in the plan. Usually credit is given only after specific activities have been completed according to the plan, allotments from the total credit made after such processes as planting, fertilization, cultivation, and harvesting have been successfully completed. As a result of this pattern, the banks have become central to the whole process of agricultural technical assistance in Mexico. Much technical assistance work is carried out under their own auspices. In other undertakings, they coordinate their work with that of the Ministry of Agriculture. In both instances, linking technical assistance to the supply of credit has seemed a far more effective way of creating acceptance of new techniques than could be achieved through efforts to induce voluntary cooperation.

The dominant role which the banks have come to play in agricultural marketing is also derived from the technique of using credit as a basis for other policy purposes. Since harvests are generally the only effective collateral on loans, the banks maintain an interest in their disposition. As a by-product of the pressure on the banks to protect themselves against loss, they have become deeply involved in regulating the conditions of sale of agricultural products, both to assure that their security "does not fly," to use the Mexican phrase, and to find markets at a price that covers both the banks' investment and the farmers' needs.

The banks have become a direct part of government price-support programs. The present structure of commodity price regulation is based on coordination of the banks, CEIMSA, and the *Almacenes Nacionales de Depósito.* The banks act as purchasing agents for the public commodity corporation, the warehousing company's facilities being used for storage. Given the desires of the banks to meet the criteria of responsible performance by minimizing their risks, considerable pressure seems to be applied in many cases to get the farmer to sell at the guaranteed price— pressure which in view of the role of public credit in the economic and political life of many small farmers may be highly effective.[83]

In addition to its role as agent for CEIMSA, the banks are often empowered by the farmer to serve as agent. The result is that in many regions anything resembling an open market for agricultural commodities has all but disappeared. The banks' deep involvement in marketing has led them to engage in supplementary activities, which further serve to "routinize" their dominance in this aspect of the agricultural economy. They own and operate processing plants, cotton storage facilities, and coffee *beneficias,* or drying operations, to cite but a few examples. Thus, Mexico has been able to construct a fairly effective distribution system and a means of effecting policies of price stabilization for both producers and consumers, using development banking as a primary administrative instrument.

A third sanctionary use of credit has already been noted in another context. Through the establishment of differential interest rates, or by allocating the credit supply among various crops, the banks have a relatively effective means of fitting agricultural production to national needs as determined by policy makers. The policy of foodstuff self-sufficiency of recent years was largely effected by reducing credit supply for fiber crops and increasing it for corn, beans, and wheat. The agricultural pattern of entire regions was successfully shifted by this technique.

Since alternative sources of credit are so often undesirable, and since the banks' clients are so completely without resources or any real ability to form capital, they are more or less tied to the public sources of credit and, as such, are responsive to requirements attached to the provision of credit. Through this mechanism, Mexico seems to have found a fairly effective means of reconciling the formal structure of producer autonomy with other agricultural policy demands.

Yet the legal fiction thus engendered has not been overlooked by the small farmer. There is a considerable body of evidence to indicate that the agrarian banks loom large in the perceptions of political power held by the *ejiditarios* or small freeholders.[84] The web of peripheral functions performed by the bank, from seeds and insecticides to operating tractor stations, seems further to envelop the small farmer in a virtually complete economic dependence on the agrarian bank. The parallel between the use of the credit sanction in this context and in the old latifundia system is not infrequently made. However, it should not be overdrawn. Without the public banks, the small farmers would have had to look elsewhere for capital, with results that would probably not have been far different and with the additional danger of an actual reconcentration of landholding. The most prominent alternative to the credit device, the use of more direct sanctions to fit agrarian behavior to policy expectations along the Russian or Chinese models, has drawbacks so apparent they need not be discussed here.

Usually the agrarian banks have acted out of the best of motives, though they often misunderstood or were helpless to correct the real problems they were confronting. The failure of the banks to create cooperative solidarity through the credit sanction is illustrative. Seldom has this form of organization been effective despite its intimate association with the total program of agrarian reform, and the banks are now gradually seeking to bypass or eliminate ineffective local credit societies from their operations.

Again, the reciprocal nature of power is evident. Agrarian credit was indeed an appropriate sanction as the threads of producer autonomy and the creation of a total modern economy were interwoven in Mexican agrarian policy. Yet it was not an absolute or compelling sanction, as the failures of the cooperatives and the inability of the banks to recover losses indicate. In an underdeveloped society, where conventional political analysis might assume that the unassimilated masses possess no relevant power base and source of influence, their real potential for noncooperation with policy expectations and resistance to change may be the most forceful determinant of public policy of all.

The credit sanction and the federal system. It is well known that the real political system of Mexico is quite different from the constitutionally prescribed federal structure. Robert Scott, whose doctoral dissertation was devoted to federalism in Mexico, dismisses the subject in a footnote of his work on the political process of that nation.[85] Yet it is something of a pity that discussion of this subject usually ends in a disquisition on its irrelevance, for one of the more interesting aspects of such institutional fictions is that the techniques used to breach the formal structure generally must be consistent with expectations concerning the processes appropriate to the operation of the formal system. Thus, the centralization of power that has taken place in Mexico is in large part due to the control of state and local party offices by the official party, formally consistent with the liberal democratic tenets held by the authors of the Constitution of 1917.

Similarly, public credit, largely administered by the Public Works Bank, has become a technique for enforcing compliance to national policy by state and municipal governments without abandoning the forms of federalism or the formal autonomy of local units to make decisions on such matters as public utilities and services. By prescribing and regulating the conditions of credit for the financially weak state and municipal units of government, the Public Works Bank is capable of directing local activity toward purposes consistent with national policy, and enforcing compliance with national standards of performance and administration. The effect of Public Works Bank credit is quite similar to that of the grant-in-aid device as employed in the United States. Again, in Mexico the president can effectively control the bank's power in this field. Among his weapons is the legal power to cancel debts of local governmental units, a power occasionally employed for political reasons.[86]

About one sixth of all Public Works Bank credits are invested in local governments. In 1957, some M$85,288,000 went for state projects and M$75,326,000 to local governments. The remainder of the bank's credits were invested in federal works or public housing.[87] The bank sets conditions of priority for local works, specifying projects of "first necessity" and requiring that the projects strengthen the financial structure of the local unit. On all credits over M$500,000 the bank must oversee and inspect the project and supervise bidding for contracts. Since 1939, the bank has supervised the work of the *Juntas de Mejoras Materiales* (Boards of Public Improvements) which were established to administer water, sanitation, and electric power services in provincial areas. The bank also provides technical assistance and advice in support of its investments.

The sanction of industrial credit. There is little point in describing again the work of Nacional Financiera in attempting to direct investment capital toward outlets consistent with economic development policies. The battery of techniques used by this institution, ranging from stimulation and direction of a stock exchange and the issue of highly attractive securities on its own holdings backed by the pledge of repurchase by the Bank of Mexico, to capital credit for industrial investment strategically placed to encourage further entrepreneurship, all define a central purpose—to induce behavior by investors deemed appropriate to the construction of a total modern economy. The selection of strategies to this end is pre-eminently a political act, the effort being to find a set of programs that will effectively elicit responses from those with entrepreneurial talent or investment capital appropriate to carrying out public policy decisions.

We have said that credit may represent either a carrot or a stick when used as a political sanction. This double representation is certainly evident in the case of agricultural credit. Yet in the field of industry the power of credit deprivation is muted and the reward component dominant. The reason for this difference is clear. The small farmer, given the economic system within which he operates, is dependent on credit for survival. Generally, he first assumed debt to undertake production at all, and this situation is self-generating. Each year he must be supported until harvest, when (theoretically) he pays off his loans and the process begins all over again. The potential entrepreneur or investor, on the other hand, is more apt to be economically autonomous. The problem is to encourage him to perform differently, rather than one of enabling him to perform at all. Furthermore, the entrepreneur or investor is more apt to have a plurality of sources of financial assistance. While access to private credit under favorable terms may be difficult for the "outsider" in Mexican financial circles, his situation is in no way comparable to the *ejiditario* who may not legally mortgage his lands and who generally has recourse only to the local money lender should he choose to oppose the direction of the agrarian bank.

In general, Nacional Financiera and other institutions operating in the field of industrial credit have acted on orthodox economic assumptions concerning the motivations of "economic man" in the financial marketplace. In a sense, they were working to structure a situation in which the expected "laws" of investment activity would begin to act automatically. Many of the policy innovations which Nacional Financiera has adopted to stimulate investment (including the famous Nacional Financiera bonds and the extensive state ownership of productive enterprise through bank investment) seem to be adaptations to the fact that they found the "threshold" of inducement—which had to be offered to the Mexican investor to bring him to act in ways relevant to economic development—higher than anticipated in economic theory. From this point of view, policy making in Nacional Financiera often appears as a search for strategies adequate to goad the reticent investor into activities desirable in terms of a specific theory of the process of economic development.

Conclusions

Perspective on the politics of development banking in modern Mexico must come within an understanding of the recent course of economic evolution in that nation. Hence, it is to the nature of economic development in Mexico and to the place of the development banks within that process that we now turn.

Mexican Economic Growth: Basic indices

	Population (thousands)	Real per capita income (1939 pesos)	Industrial production (1945 = 100)	Agricultural production (1945 = 100)
1939	19,413	350	79.6	83.3
1941	20,332	380	82.9	89.8
1943	21,418	424	91.3	94.2
1945	22,576	469	100.0	100.0
1947	23,810	481	103.2	113.2
1949	25,132	496	111.3	136.5
1951	26,540	556	130.1	161.0
1953	28,052	525	131.4	169.2
1955	29,675	587	155.8	219.2
1957	31,426	612	183.6	217.4

Sources: Dirección de Estadística, Banco de México, Nacional Financiera.

Many observers feel that Mexico may no longer be numbered among the underdeveloped nations. Through a process of rapid, dynamic industrial growth it has achieved the status, as some would say, of a "middle developed" or transitional nation. For W. W. Rostow, Mexico must be counted among those nations which have achieved take off into self-sustained economic growth.[88] Certainly, most of the standard indicators of economic progress when applied to Mexico sweep upward in a graph plotted over time, some at a dizzying rate. As the preceding table indicates, in the years since 1939, Mexico's population has increased by half, per capita real income and industrial production have doubled, while agricultural production has increased about two and one-half times.

The public face that Mexico turns to the world is one filled with economic optimism. The press, the statements of political and business leaders, and public and private economic studies all reflect the same preoccupation with record-breaking productive accomplishment and self-congratulation over the achievement of economic stability.

Distribution of National Income: Mexican Families by Deciles

10 per cent of families	Per cent of income	
	1950	*1957*
1	2.7	1.7
2	3.4	2.7
3	3.8	3.1
4	4.4	3.8
5	4.8	4.3
6	5.5	5.6
7	7.0	7.4
8	8.6	10.0
9	10.8	14.7
10	49.0	46.7

Source: Dr. Ifigenia M. de Navarrete, *La distribución del ingreso y el desarrollo económico de México,* Universidad de Mexico, 1960, p. 85.

Yet this state of economic euphoria is not without its detractors. One need only read Oscar Lewis's *Five Families* or *The Children of Sánchez* [89]—essays, as they are called, in the culture of poverty—to understand how far Mexican economic development is from fulfillment. As is apparent to even the most casual tourist, a substantial part of the Mexican population continues to live in poverty. Some authoritative reporters even claim that the real standard of living of the lower-class Mexican has actually declined since the Revolution. As the recent study by Dr. Ifigenia Navarrete demonstrates, the real point at issue in assessing Mexico's economic development is not growth of income alone but the distribution of that income among the Mexican population. As the preceding table indicates, while the group benefiting from economic change is to some extent broadening and prosperity is filtering down to a new upper-middle class, the poorest half of the Mexican population is becoming increasingly poorer.

The implication, according to Daniel Seligman, writing in *Fortune,* is clear: "Indeed, it might correctly be said that the true hero of the Mexican investment boom is the ordinary Mexican worker, whose acceptance of a declining real income has in effect 'subsidized' much of the nation's building." [90]

Not only are the gains of economic development poorly distributed within the Mexican class structure, but they also are concentrated within certain regions of the nation. Navarrete points out that the average income in Mexico as a whole is M$693 per month, while in the Federal District it reaches M$1282, and descends to an average of M$689 in the Gulf of Mexico region, M$675 in the North of the country, and M$447 in the Pacific-South. [91]

What Mexico seems to have achieved is a "dual" economy, a modern, dynamic economy of prosperity set side by side with a traditional economy of poverty. In the early 1950's, Sanford Mosk had already wondered whether the rapid pace of Mexican industrialization was not passing by the total development of the society. [92] Even more critical of Mexico's industrialization program was Frank Tannenbaum, who suggested that the nation should satisfy itself with a philosophy of "little things," seek to develop its rural, agrarian potential, and not attempt industrial greatness. [93]

In any event, what seems to have occurred is that the "filtering down" effect, which was assumed to follow upon rapid industrialization, has not yet been sufficiently realized.

It is perhaps too early to pass judgment on the distinctive route which Mexico has taken in her efforts to achieve economic development. The "Mexican experiment" is not yet complete, and the problems reported above constitute but a cross section of a continuous process. That adjustments will have to be made so as to provide a more propitious distribution of the fruits of accomplishments realized so far is apparent. One may find reason for cautious optimism in the demonstrated capacity of the Mexican political system to reflect and cope with demands for modification of the course pursued.

The problematic nature of Mexican economic development is of course important as it reflects on the policies of the development banks. What is of greater interest, however, is that the banks themselves were the products of a broader political process which guided the pattern of development seen in modern Mexico.

For the Mexican, the concept of the "Revolution" defines the meaning of that process of social transformation which is both the problem and the product of twentieth-century Mexico. But the idea of the Revolution remains vague and unclear, without precise definition, for its significance is itself the product of a process of political reconciliation of diverse groups and interests, each seeing in the Revolution the opportunity for fulfillment of its own aspirations for change.

The emergence of an extensive system of development banks may in part be understood as the product of the accommodation of these differing interpretations of the Revolution. The public-credit institutions provided an obvious and appropriate mechanism which could resolve certain problems inherent in simultaneously responding to competing demands. The specific aspirations for reform which were the product of the Revolution were to be honored, but they would be met within the context of the institutional framework appropriate to the construction of a total modern economy, based on the ideas, standards, conventions, rules, processes, and structures which were the heritage of the industrial revolution in Europe and North America.

However, the use of the development banking device in such circumstances often left the institutions themselves to cope with an irreconcilable policy conflict. Designed to assist in the implementation of certain policy objectives, they were also expected to perform according to the economic standards appropriate to their institutional form. Depending, to a large extent, on the sector of the economy in which they were expected to operate, the banks achieved different levels of success in fulfilling these expectations. In agriculture, they fell between the two stools and failed to satisfy the advocates either of responsible financial practice or of agrarian reform. In industry, they were remarkably effective. The over-all effect was that the differential performance of the banks naturally supplemented other pressures within the society, tending to give policy priority to the industrialization effort.

It is often suggested that Mexico's economic development took place in an "unplanned" manner. This is true to the extent that it was not based on any set of explicitly formulated periodic "plans" for development. As we have noted, however, there has been a remarkable consistency in the objectives of economic policy makers. The Mexican political process—the efforts to maximize the accommodation of divergent interests within the Revolutionary coalition—provided a basis for the concentration of effective political and economic power in the president and cabinet, a pattern sanctioned by a long tradition of strong executive authority. The cabinet in a sense became an agency for the planning and coordination of economic development programs, yet a planning agency not alone concerned with structuring an economic process, but responsive as well to political demands. Although Mexican leaders have evinced concern about the lack of responsibility of decentralized agencies to central control, and constant attempts to strengthen lines of authority and coordination have been made, the development banks, both formally and effectively, seem capable of being fitted by policy makers into coordinated programs for the implementation of policy decisions.

It is apparent that the extensive use of the public-credit mechanism has set a distinctive pattern for the economic development of Mexico. The use of credit as a political sanction has enabled government to provide regulation and direction to the development effort without seeming to betray the spirit or the forms of liberal society. When Mexicans proclaim that they have found a "middle way" between communism and capitalism, they may perhaps in part be suggesting that the route they have taken to economic development reflects a minimum of overt coercion and yet includes effective public direction and control. However, some will suggest that in some areas, notably in the *ejido* system, the results of the use of bank power to implement public policies are only marginally different from harsher measures of social control.

What are the implications of the Mexican experience for other nations in which development banks or authorities are assuming a prominent place in the political and economic system? The classic problem always posed with regard to autonomous agencies, that they will come to exert irresponsible power, does not seem to be particularly applicable in the case of Mexico. Yet we have observed a second classic tendency, that such agencies extend their sphere of activities to embrace economic functions quite unrelated to those of banking itself. What is the source of Mexico's ability to keep this potential power relatively well checked? It may lie in the legal formula of strictly limited autonomy. It may have something to do with the use of multiple banks rather than a single development authority. But it is more likely that the answer lies in the nature of the political system of which the development banks are a part. The ability of the Revolutionary coalition to bring together potentially conflicting groups, and the pervasiveness of the Revolutionary mystique, dampens the desire of dissatisfied groups to find an alternative to the state as an outlet for political demands. The degree of political consensus achieved by a society would seem to bear some relation to the danger that the state itself may spawn the monster that will lead to its undoing.

However, it is possible that the potential power of development banks is not the real problem at all. Perhaps the real lesson of the Mexican experience lies in the implications of the desires of "modernizing elites" to emulate the institutions and practices of advanced nations, and their ability to impose these standards as the context within which problems indigenous to their own societies will be met. The impact of the criteria of responsible banking performance demanded by these elites on the Mexican agrarian program is illustrative. The problem of the adaptation of institutions in alien cultures will long be with us. To date, economists have been far less suspicious of the transferability of structures and processes than have political scientists. The Mexican experience with development banking is abundant in examples of creative and imaginative applications of the public-credit device. It also is illustrative of efforts to force a pattern on seemingly inappropriate situations.

Furthermore, as the heterogeneous purposes to which development banking has been put in Mexico reveal, only in the economist's notebook or in a highly authoritarian situation is the marshaling of public investment apt to be "rationally" directed toward those areas where it will theoretically have the greatest impact on raising levels of productivity. The images of desirable economic change are many in underdeveloped societies and do not always correspond to the dictates of economic science. Insofar as political stability and the achievement of "open societies" are also desired goods for most of the participants in the present process of world-wide change, the achievement of these goals may require an allocation of capital resources not always consistent with the theoretical imperatives of economic development. Political considerations will require that some seemingly peripheral demands placed on scarce capital resources be honored, though a strictly economic view of the development process will consider them wasted.

Finally, it would be worth while to be constantly aware of the political character of the economic processes involved in the achievement of development. The great diversity of man's economic inventions provides tools for the creative statesman to use in devising policies that embrace divergent interests, and result in that "creation of agreement" which is the political art at its best. Development banking is one device that may be used to this end, but it is merely an example of a theme with infinite ramifications and possibilities.

Appendix
THE MEXICAN DEVELOPMENT BANKS

Banco de México, S.A. (*The Bank of Mexico*)   *1925*

Although not a development bank as such, the importance of this institution derives from its position as the cornerstone on which the development banking system was built, from its central role in the entire Mexican banking system, and from the manner in which it has used its powers to stimulate economic growth.

Its functions are similar to those of central banks generally: (1) control of the supply of money through control of the rediscount rate, the foreign exchange reserves, and the direct purchase of securities by the bank; (2) control of the supply of credit through manipulation of the obligatory deposit requirements of private banks; (3) treasury and agency functions for the national government; (4) stimulation of the nation's embryonic securities market through pledges to buy at par bonds of the government and other public credit institutions, use of its obligatory deposit power to make it advantageous for private banks to use stocks and bonds as part of their required deposit, and marginal intervention in the stock market to prevent sudden shifts in prices. The Bank of Mexico through its economic studies department also serves as a prominent source of economic intelligence in the formulation of public policy.[1]

Nacional Financiera, S.A.   *1933*

Nacional Financiera is Mexico's archetypal development bank. Its function would seem to be that of providing the nation, through

1. Evangelina Aguilera Schaufelberger, "El banco central en la política de desarrollo" (University of Mexico, 1958), unpublished Ph.D. thesis; Banco de México, S.A., *Informe Anual: 1960* (Mexico, 1960), pp. 59–60.

government participation in the economy, with that network of financial operations which mobilize the capital savings of a nation and bring them to bear on productive activity.

Originally established to supervise and regulate the securities market, to act as a savings bank and investment company, and, since 1941 particularly, to advise the government in financial transactions, it has played a central role in implementing the government's policy of rapid industrialization.

Deriving resources from the issue of its own securities, credits from abroad,[2] and reinvestment of profits, Nacional Financiera finances Mexican industrialization either through loans or through direct investment in private and public enterprises. The bank has come to control a number of basic industries and, with private capital, participates in the ownership of many others. Its criteria of investment give precedence to industries that will result in the greatest external economies for the national economy. It has also devoted substantial funds to the development of the economic infrastructure of the nation. As the institution states, ". . . Nacional Financiera carefully selects new projects according to their maximum potential for expansion, direct or indirect, on the national economy, and seeks forms of financing the new investments that tend to develop the national stock market, encourage private investment and use all available resources, with the careful protection of the public interest with which the operation is entrusted."[3]

2. Since 1942, Nacional Financiera received (US) $1,309,000,000 in foreign credits. Of thus sum, (US) $521,000,000 came from the Export-Import Bank, and (US) $195,800,000 from the International Bank for Reconstruction and Development. The remainder came from various sources, including (US) $100,000,000 from the Prudential Insurance Co. (*Excelsior*, February 18, 1961). During the Eisenhower administration, when preference was given to financing designed to bolster private enterprise, Nacional Financiera, with its policy of such private investement operations, became a preferred outlet for such funds.

3. Nacional Financiera, S.A., *Informe Anual: 1959* (Mexico, 1959), p. 56.

Banco Nacional de Comercio Exterior, S.A.
(*Foreign Commerce Bank*)   *1937*

The basic function if this bank is to act as the promoter, organizer, and developer of foreign commerce. Although many of the Mexican development banks engage in quite diverse operations, the Foreign Commerce Bank seems capable of entering virtually every area of financial activity that might be connected even remotely with the nation's foreign-trade position. It acts to support Mexico's primary export articles, to develop new ones, and to finance essential imports. Of the total credit authorized by the institution in 1960, 51 per cent went to price regulation, primarily for agricultural export commodities, 28 per cent to production loans, and 21 per cent for commercial purposes.[4]

Banco Hipotecario Urbano y de Obras Públicas, S.A.
(*Public Works Bank*)   *1933*

This bank is designed to serve as a financial instrument for the national government in public works construction. Until 1950, the bank stressed investment in highways, drinking water, and sewerage systems. Since that time, heavier emphasis has been put on public housing. The bank also provides credits to municipalities and states for public works projects consistent with national policy, and to contractors engaged in governmental projects.

Banco Nacional de Crédito Agrícola y Ganadero, S.A.
(*Agrarian Credit Bank*)   *1926*

This bank provides credit and other services for farmers not affected directly by the *ejido* reforms, which placed a substantial portion of Mexico's land in semicommunal small holdings. In addition to conventional agrarian credit operations, the bank is active in marketing and processing activities, as well as in the provision of technical assistance.

4. Banco Nacional de Comercio Exterior, *Informe: 1960* (Mexico, 1961).

Banco Nacional de Crédito Ejidal, S.A. (*Ejido Bank*) 1935

An agricultural credit bank which deals specifically with farmers organized in *ejidos*. Like the Agrarian Credit Bank, it engages in a wide variety of operations in connection with the organization of production within the *ejido* system.

Almacenes Nacionales de Depósito, S.A.
(*National Warehouses*) 1936

This agency provides warehousing and marketing facilities for agricultural commodities, as well as other middleman services. Closely related in its activities to the agrarian banks and to the state trading corporation (CEIMSA), this group of institutions provides a system for commodity price stabilization and marketing with substantial impact on the agricultural sector of the Mexican economy.

Banco Nacional de Fomento Cooperativo, S.A.
(*Bank of Cooperative Development*) 1941

The stimulation of the cooperative form of enterprise was a constant objective of the Mexican Revolution. Particularly in the 1930's, a number of cooperative societies were established in various fields. However, without financial support, they remained inactive or in an economically precarious situation. The Bank of Cooperative Development was designed to provide credit for such operations. The areas of economic activity which have received substantial support from this bank include fishing, truck transport, sugar processing, and salt production, as well as small manufacturing.

Banco del Pequeño Comercio del Distrito Federal, S.A.
(*Small Merchants' Bank*) 1942

Traditionally, the large number of small retailers who operate in Mexico City have been the victims of the money lender, whose rates of interest have contributed to the perpetual impoverishment of these merchants and to the high cost of living in the capital. The Small Merchants' Bank was established to provide inexpensive credit for this group. Termed "the bank with the least capital and the most business," this institution has been quite resourceful in meeting a high volume of demand for extremely small loans, primarily used to cover the day-to-day operating expenses of these merchants. Apart from its banking functions, this institution has been active in establishing purchaser's associations so as to save middleman expenses for these purchasers of extremely small quantities of merchandise.

Banco Nacional de Transportes, S.A. (*Transport Bank*)

1953

The Transport Bank was designed to assist the many small firms and individual proprietorships which operate the transportation facilities of Mexico City. It deals primarily in small individual loans to taxicab owner-operators and to bus line proprietors.

Banco Nacional del Ejército y de la Armada, S.A.
(*Armed Forces Bank*)   *1946*

Overtly structured to filter part of the savings of the military into productive enterprises through loans for such undertakings and the investment of savings deposits, the bulk of this bank's financing has gone to the military for direct consumption expenditures, and for mortgage loans for housing for members of the armed services. The bank is also charged with the administration of the military life insurance program and an obligatory savings fund for enlisted men.

Other Public Credit Institutions: This study was based on the activities of the institutions described above. However, a complete enumeration of the total public credit structure of contemporary Mexico would also include the following agencies: *Financiera Nacional Azucarera, S.A.; Nacional Monte de Piedad, S.A.; So-*

ciedad Obrera Vestuario y Equipo; Patronato del Ahorro Nacional;
Aseguradora Mexicana, S.A.; Uniones Nacionales de Crédito, S.A.;
Banco Nacional Cinematográfico, S.A.

Financial Summary: Mexican Development Banks
(figures in millions of pesos)

		Authorized financing	Capital	Reserves
Nacional Financiera	1942	146.1	9.5	2.1
	1948	874.4	100.0	10.0
	1955	6,321.7	200.0	74.4
	1959	9,902.6	200.0	425.0
Ejido Bank	1942	155.6	–	–
	1948	404.7	207.5	–
	1954	539.6	697.1	–
	1959	1,304.3	713.9	–
Public Works Bank	1934	12.4	10.4	–
	1946	162.8	30.8	5.9
	1949	337.4	28.2	17.3
	1959	1,826.1	200.0	14.6
Foreign Commerce Bank	1942	17.4	7.0	2.4
	1948	52.0	8.6	24.3
	1954	263.1	33.5	160.9
	1959	406.3	33.5	243.0
Armed Forces Bank	1947	11.8	5.2	–
	1954	28.9	24.4	4.0
	1959	44.9	42.2	4.9
Bank of Cooperative Development	1948	21.1	15.9	1.1
	1954	72.9	52.5	8.5
	1959	114.5	64.2	11.1
Small Merchants' Bank	1948	–	1.4	–
	1953	5.0	3.9	–
	1959	8.5	13.1	–
Transport Bank	1953	28.5	22.9	–
	1959	295.2	39.7	8.0

Source: Adapted from Octavio Campos Salas, "Las instituciones nacionales de crédito," in: Enrique Beltrán, et al., México: Cincuenta años de revolución I; La economía, Mexico, Fondo de Cultura Económica 1960. The Bank of Mexico was not included since its operations are not strictly comparable with the others. Figures for the Agrarian Credit Bank were not available.

Note: 1 U.S. dollar equals 12 Mexican pesos.

Selected Bibliography

I. GENERAL

Alatriste, Lic. Sealtiel. "El control de las entidades del sector público," *Sepanal*, num. 1, December, 1960.

Alba, Victor. "The Mexican Economy," *World Today*, 15, no. 11, November, 1959.

Alvarado, José. "El extraño caso de la Secretaría de Hacienda," *Problemas agrícolas e industriales de México*, V, num. 1 (January–March, 1953), 163–68.

Astudillo y Ursua, Lic. Pedro. "Banco de México, S.A.," *Revista de Administración Pública*, num. 6 (April–June, 1957), 5–16.

Banco Hipotecario Urbano y de Obras Públicas. *Informe Anual, 1956.* Mexico, 1957.

Banco de México, S.A. *Informe:* 1950–1960.

Banco Nacional de Comercio Exterior. *Informe:* 1954–1960. Mexico, 1955–61.

Banco Nacional del Ejército y de la Armada, S.A. de C.V. *Informe:* 1954–58.

Banco Nacional de Crédito Agrícola y Ganadero, S.A. *Informe:* 1950–58.

Banco Nacional de Crédito Agrícola y Ganadero, S.A. *25 años del Banco Nacional de Crédito Agrícola y Ganadero, S.A.: 1936–1951.* Mexico, 1951.

Banco Nacional de Fomento Cooperativo, S.A., su desarrollo en su campo de la economía nacional, Mexico, 1958.

Banco del Pequeño Comercio del Distrito Federal, S.A. *Informe: 1943.* Mexico, 1944.

Barros Sierra, Lic. Manuel. "Banco Nacional Hipotecario Urbano y de Obras Públicas, S.A.," *Revista de Administración Pública*, num. 6 (April–June, 1957), 49–53.

Bauer, Elizabeth L., ed. *Proceedings of the International Conference on Agricultural and Cooperative Credit.* vol. 5. Berkeley: University of California Press, 1952.

Beltrán, Enrique, *et al*. *México: Cincuenta años de revolución*, I: *La economía*. Mexico: Fondo de Cultura Económica, 1960.

Bett, Virgil. *Central Banking in Mexico*. Ann Arbor: University of Michigan Press, 1957.

Bermúdez, Antonio J. *Mis doce años al servicio de Pemex*. Mexico, 1960.

Bracho, José María. *Las jefaturas técnicas de zona del Banco Nacional de Crédito Ejidal*. Mexico, 1954.

Brandenburg, Frank. "Organized Business in Mexico," *Inter-American Economic Affairs*, 12, no. 4 (Winter), 1958.

Brandenburg, Frank. "Mexico: An Experiment in One-Party Democracy." Unpublished Ph.D. thesis, Pennsylvania, 1956.

Cárdenas, Felipe. "Comisión Nacional Bancaria," *Revista de Administración Pública*, num. 6 (April–June, 1957), 17–23.

Castellanos Coutiño, Lic. Horacio. "El estado y los organismos decentralizados." Manuscript in possession of Castellanos, 1961.

Chavez Hayhoe, Lic. Salvador. "El crédito agrícola en México," *Ciencias políticas y sociales*, año 2, num. 4 (April–June, 1956), pp. 25 ff.

Cropsey, Joseph. "On the Relation of Political Science and Economics," *American Political Science Review*, LIV, no. 1 (March 1960), 3–14.

Dahl, Robert A. and Charles Lindblom. *Politics, Economics and Welfare*. New York: Harper & Bros., 1953.

Diamond, William. *Development Banks*. Baltimore: Johns Hopkins University Press, 1957.

Economic Commission for Latin America. *Recent Developments and Trends in the Mexican Economy*. E/CN/12/217, March 26, 1951. UN, Mexico.

Escuela Nacional de Economía, Universidad Nacional Autónoma de México. *Nuevos aspectos de la política económica y de la administración pública en México*. Mexico, University of Mexico, 1960.

Fernández y Fernández, Ramón. "El crédito ejidal," *El Trimestre Económico*, 25, num. 2 (April–June, 1958), 157–88.

Fernández y Fernández, Ramón. "El difícil problema del crédito ejidal," *Revista de Economía*, 17, no. 8 (August 15, 1954), 23 ff.

Figueres, José. "Address to the Third Stanford Conference on Latin America," 1951 (mimeographed).

Fraustro, C. P. T., Oscar. "Nacional Financiera, S.A.," *Revista de Administración Pública*, num. 5 (January–March, 1957), 19–28.

Glade, William P., Jr. "Las empresas gubernamentales decentralizadas," *Problemas agrícolas e industriales de México*, XI, no. 1 (January–March, 1959).

Goodspeed, Stephen. *The Role of the Chief Executive in Mexico: Politics, Powers and Administration*. Berkeley: University of California, 1947.

Hoselitz, B. F. *Sociological Aspects of Economic Growth*. Glencoe: Free Press, 1960.

Kling, Merle. *A Mexican Interest Group in Action*. New York: Prentice-Hall, 1961.

Lewis, Oscar. *The Children of Sánchez*. New York: Random House, 1961.

Lewis, Oscar. *Five Families*. New York: Basic Books, 1959.

Lewis, W. Arthur. *The Theory of Economic Growth*. London: Allen & Unwin, 1955.

Limón, Gral. Gilberto R. "Banco Nacional del Ejército y de la Armada, S.A. de C.V.," *Revista de Adminstración Pública*, num. 6 (April–June, 1957), 61–65.

López Mateos, Adolfo. *Informe que rinde al H. Congreso de la Unión: 1959, 1960, 1961*. Mexico: Sria. de Gobernación, 1959, 1960, 1961.

López Rosado, Lic. Diego. "Banco del Pequeño Comercio del Distrito Federal, S.A.," *Revista de Administración Pública*, num. 6 (April–June, 1957), 41–48.

Luna Olmedo, Ing. Augustín. "Banco Nacional de Crédito Ejidal, S.A. de C.V.," *Revista de Administración Pública*, num. 6. (April–June, 1957), 33–40.

Manero, Antonio. *La revolución bancaria en México*. Mexico: Tall. Nacionales, 1957.

Mosk, Sanford. *The Industrial Revolution in Mexico*. Berkeley: University of California Press, 1950.

Myrdal, Gunnar. *The Political Element in Economic Theory*. Cambridge: Harvard University Press, 1953.

Myrdal, Gunnar. *Beyond the Welfare State*. New Haven: Yale University Press, 1960.

Myrdal, Gunnar. *Rich Lands and Poor*. New York: Harper & Bros., 1958.

Nacional Financiera, S.A. *Informe Anual 1945–1960*.

Padgett, Vincent L. "Mexico's One-Party System: A Re-evaluation," *American Political Science Review*, 51, No. 4 (December, 1957), 995–1008.

Pani, Alberto J. *El problema supremo de México*. Imp. de Manuel Casas, Mexico, 1955.

Reina Hermosillo, Lic. Praxedes. "Comisión Nacional de Valores," *Revista de Administración Pública*, num. 2 (April–June, 1956), 39–62.

Rodríguez Adame, Julián. *Reforma agraria y progreso agrícola*. Mexico, 1959.

Rostow, W. W. *The Politics of Economic Growth*. New York: Norton, 1952.

Rostow, W. W. *The Process of Economic Growth*. New York: Oxford, 1960.

Salas Villagomez, Manuel. "Problemas Financieros de la industrialización de México," *Revista de Economía*, 14, num. 1 (January, 1951), 455–62.

Schaufelberger, Evangelina, Aguilera. "El banco central en la política de desarrollo." Mexico: Universidad Nacional Autónomo de México, 1958 (thesis).

Scott, Robert. *Mexican Government in Transition*. Urbana: University of Illinois Press, 1959.

Senior, Clarence. *Land Reform and Democracy*. Gainesville: University of Florida Press, 1958.

Social Science Research on Business: Product and Potential. New York: Columbia University Press, 1959.

Solana Yañez, Delfino. "La Administración Pública en México," *Revista de Administración Pública*, num. 12 (July–August–September, 1959), 31–38.

Sria. de Gobernación. *Seis años del gobierno al servicio de México–1934–1940*. Mexico, 1940.

Sria. de Hacienda y Crédito Público. *Discursos pronunciados por los CC. Secretarios de Hacienda y Crédito Público en las convenciones bancarias celebradas del año 1934 a 1958*. Mexico, 1958.

Tannenbaum, Frank. *Mexico: The Struggle for Peace and Bread*. New York: Knopf, 1950.

Taylor, Philip. "The Mexican Elections of 1958: Affirmation of Authoritarianism?" *Western Political Quarterly*, 13, no. 3 (September, 1960), 277–94.

Tirado de Ruíz, Rosa Ma. "La hacienda pública y sus funciones económicas," *Revista de Administración Pública*, num. 11 (January–March, 1959).

Whetten, Nathan. *Rural Mexico*. Chicago: University of Chicago, 1948.

Wise, George. *El México de Alemán*. Mexico, 1949.

II. PERIODICALS: SELECTED REFERENCES FROM 1938–1961

Boletín Mensual de la Dirección de Economía Rural. August, 1944.
Carta de México.
Carta Semanal (Confederación de Cámaras Nacionales de Comercio).
Confederación (Confederación de Cámaras Industriales).
Diario Oficial.
Excelsior.
Hoy.
El Mercado de Valores (Nacional Financiera).
El Nacional.
Novedades.
El Popular.
Tiempo.
Transformación (Cámara Nacional de Industrias de Transformación).
Ultimas Noticias.
Universal.
El Universal Gráfico.

Notes
Index

Notes to Glade

1 New York: Knopf, 1951, especially chapters 11–13.
2 *La revolución mexicana en crisis,* Mexico. Cuadernos Americanos, 1944.
3 *The Industrial Revolution in Mexico,* Berkeley: University of California Press, 1950, especially pp. 304–11. This valuable study of the Mexican economy seems to have gone furthest astray in overestimating the constrictive effects of (1) bottlenecks, (2) market limitations, and (3) the degree of excessive industrial investment on the one hand, and in underestimating probable immediate future expansion in such critical fields as electric power, petroleum products, dry land farming, and siderurgical industry on the other. Errors of judgment regarding (2) and (3) appear attributable mainly to a somewhat foreshortened time horizon in the study, while the others flowed most likely from overemphasis on exogenous, as opposed to endogenous, factors. In retrospect, some of the imbalances of which Mosk spoke appear to have been Hirschmanesque "strategic imbalances" which were significant instrumentalities for eliciting supporting investment activity in the years following those included in the Mosk study.

To cite only one instance, Mosk stated (p. 145) that "The phase of expansion that got under way in Mexico's iron and steel industry in 1942 seems to be nearing an end. When all the new projects reach full-capacity operation, it is doubtful whether other developments of a substantial nature will be undertaken for some years thereafter." In 1951, Altos Hornos Steel Company launched the construction of a new blast furnace larger than any in the country at the time Mosk wrote, finished the project in 1954, and immediately started rebuilding its old furnace for larger capacity. Crude steel production in 1946 was 258,000 tons. In 1952 it was 537,000 tons, and by 1959 it was over 1,300,000 tons.

4   Interpretation of policy developments in terms of a sea change
    of direction circa 1940–1941 continues to play an important role
    in the analysis of U.S. scholars—see Oscar Lewis, "Mexico
    Since Cárdenas," *Social Research*, New York: 26, no. 1 (Spring
    1959), 18–30—but Mexican analysts have, more often, seen
    continuity of process as paramount: Edmundo Flores, "Dinámica
    de la economía mexicana: de la reforma agraria a la revolución
    industrial," *Combate*, San Jose, C.R.: no. 13 (November 1960),
    53–60; Jesús Reyes Heroles, "A propósito de 'La revolución in-
    dustrial en México,'" *Problemas agrícolas e industriales de Méx-
    ico*, Mexico: vol. III, no. 2 (1951), pp. 242–45; Vicente Lom-
    bardo Toledano, "Anotaciones al libro de Sanford A. Mosk: 'La
    revolución industrial en México,'" *op. cit.*, pp. 289–96; "México:
    1910–1960," *Comercio Exterior*, Mexico: vol. X, no. 11 (Novem-
    ber 1960), pp. 594–96; Manuel Germán Parra, *La industrializa-
    ción de México*, Mexico: Imprenta Universitaria, 1954, pp. 89–
    90, 133–34; Gonzalo Robles, "El desarrollo industrial," *México:
    Cincuenta años de revolución, I: La economía*, Mexico: Fondo
    de Cultura Económica, 1960, pp. 179–85. Writing from a soci-
    ologist's point of view, Lucio Mendieta y Núñez sees the Rev-
    olution as entering its constructive or creative phase in 1917 and
    views the Revolution as a continuing phenomenon with, thus
    far, forty-three years of development since that time: "Un bal-
    ance objetivo de la revolución mexicana," *Revista Mexicana de
    Sociología*, XXII, no. 2 (May–August 1960), 533.
5   Berkeley: University of California Press, 1956.
6   Contrast the Powell study, for example, with A. J. Bermúdez,
    *Doce años al servicio de la industria petrolera mexicana, 1947–
    1958*, Mexico: Editorial Comaval, 1960. It is hard to square
    Powell's patronizing diagnosis with the dramatic doubling of
    known crude reserves between 1947 and 1952 and the near
    tripling of crude production and refined output in the 1935–
    1956 period.
7   The biweekly news magazine *Visión* gave popular expression to
    these recurring fears in the title of its feature article for the issue
    of 29 July 1960, "Se ha estancado el país?"
8   International Bank for Reconstruction and Development
    (IBRD), Combined Mexican Working Party, *The Economic
    Development of Mexico*, Baltimore: The Johns Hopkins Press,
    1953.
9   "Mexico: Rapid Growth," in H. F. Williamson and J. A. But-

trick, eds., *Economic Development: Principles and Patterns,*
New Jersey: Prentice-Hall, Inc., 1954.

10 *The Stages of Economic Growth,* Cambridge, England: The University Press, 1960.

11 *New York Times,* 4 March 1961. According to Raúl Salinas Lozano, the minister, foreign capital has indicated a special interest in "the chemical, iron and steel, petrochemical, automotive and machinery industries manufacturing products normally imported."

12 Banco de México, *Informe anual a la asamblea general ordinaria de accionistas,* Mexico: 1958 and 1959. The years 1952 and 1953 were also notably bad years for agricultural production.

13 Dirección General de Estadística, *Anuario Estadística de México,* Mexico: various years. According to demographic projections made in a recent United Nations study, however, the rate of increase over the next two decades should drop somewhat from this high level—Louis J. Ducoff, *Los recursos humanos de Centroamérica, Panamá y México en 1950–1980, y sus relaciones con algunos aspectos del desarrollo económico,* document TAA/LAT/22, 25 June 1959.

14 Alfredo Navarrete R., "El financiamiento del desarrollo económico," in *México: Cincuenta años de revolución, I: La economía,* Mexico: Fondo de Cultura Económica, 1960, pp. 511–35.

15 D. Seligman, "The Maddening, Promising Mexican Market," *Fortune,* January 1956, pp. 103–105.

16 U.S. Department of Commerce, *U.S. Business Investments in Foreign Countries,* Washington: 1960, p. 89. Only Brazil, in Latin America, had received a larger amount of U.S. manufacturing investment, $438 million in 1959 (*idem*), and it, of course, has a population roughly twice that of Mexico, a far larger national territory and, probably, a more favorable and varied resource endowment to support industrialization. Additionally, the Brazilian national market is considerably less afflicted with the problems posed by cultural dualism in the Mexican scene.

17 It goes without saying that on this matter, at least, one hears no vetoes from the Marxian economists (see, e.g., Paul Baran's *The Political Economy of Growth,* New York: Monthly Review Press, 1957, particularly chapters 6 and 7), though the reasoning involved in their case is somewhat different, and the motivations and goals as well as the kind of revolution envisaged are

not the same. Non-Marxian analysts tend to employ a more flexible concept of revolution (and one probably more in accord with the historical record) which embraces such varied manifestations as a revolutionary change in orientation within an elite, as in the case of Japan and Germany, and "quiet" revolutions or accelerated evolution in social structure unaccompanied by the political developments normally associated with the term revolution (C. Wagley, "The Brazilian Revolution: Social Changes since 1930," in *Social Change in Latin America Today*, New York: Harper, 1960, pp. 177–230) as well as more "conventional" revolutions, e.g., the French Revolution, England's Glorious Revolution, and post-World War I Turkey.

18 *The Theory of Economic Growth*, Illinois: Richard D. Irwin, 1955, p. 87.

19 *The Economic Impact on Under-developed Societies*, Oxford: Blackwell, 1953, pp. 18–28.

20 *The Future of Underdeveloped Countries*, New York: Harper, 1954, pp. 201–27, and U.N. Department of Economic Affairs, *Measures for the Economic Development of Under-developed Countries*, New York: 1951, pp. 13–16.

21 G. M. Meier and R. E. Baldwin, *Economic Development: Theory, History, Policy*, New York: Wiley, 1959, pp. 334–59.

22 *México: Cincuenta años de revolución, I: La economía* (1960), *II: La vida social* (1961), *III: La política* (scheduled to appear in 1963), and *IV: La cultura* (scheduled for 1963), Mexico: Fondo de Cultura Económica. The economic analyst has been particularly favored by the voluminous outpouring, in the past two decades especially, of studies of the economic order—perhaps because, as Victor Alba has put it, "*México sufre una inflación de economistas*" (Victor Alba, *Las ideas sociales contemporaneas en México*, Mexico: Fondo de Cultura Económica, 1960, p. 271).

23 This point of view, which tends strongly to emphasize elements of discontinuity in both economic and political processes, receives its sharpest statement in the article by Oscar Lewis cited earlier (note 4) as well as in J. J. Johnson's chapter on Mexico in his *Political Change in Latin America* (Stanford: Stanford University Press, 1958, pp. 128–52), although a substantially similar notion is clearly implicit in the studies by Tannenbaum and Powell, and, rather less so, in Mosk.

24 Johnson, *op. cit.*, pp. 129–32.

25 Note, for example, the opening section in the cited article by Lewis.

26 *The Southwestern Social Science Quarterly,* XXXIX, no. 3 (December 1953). See also Lucio Mendieta y Núñez, "Un balance objetivo de la revolución mexicana," *op. cit.,* pp. 535–39; and W. P. Glade, *Las empresas gubernamentales descentralizadas,* Mexico: Problemas Agrícolas e Industriales de México, XI, no. 1 (January–March 1959), 28–34.

27 Octavio Paz, *El laberinto de la soledad,* Mexico: Fondo de Cultura Económica, 1959, pp. 141, 160–62. Octavio Paz—poet, essayist, playwright, diplomat—is himself an outstanding example of the "working intellectual" in Mexico. As Paz observes, however, the intellectuals have sacrificed a certain independence of position and the possibility of serving as an effective critical counterpoise to official policy by virtue of their close identification with the government. The well-known contemporary novelist, Carlos Fuentes, had this problem in mind when he wrote, in *La región más transparente* (Mexico: Fondo de Cultura Económica, 1958, p. 359), that "The Revolution was identified with the intellectual force which Mexico brought forth from its own resources in the same way that it was identified with the labor movement. But when the Revolution ceased to be revolution, the intellectual movement and the labor movement found that they were official movements." Incidentally, both Paz and Fuentes see the modern Mexican economy, which they call capitalism, as a direct product of the Revolution itself. Paz (*op. cit.,* pp. 161–62) states, "Nothing of that which has been accomplished would have been possible within the framework of classical capitalism. Even more, without the Revolution and its governments we should not even have had Mexican capitalists. In reality, our national capitalism is not only a natural consequence of the Revolution but is also, in large measure, the offspring, the creature of the Revolutionary State. Without the redistribution of lands, the large material works, the public and mixed enterprises, the policy of public investment, the direct and indirect subsidies to industry and, in general, without the intervention of the State in economic life, our bankers and our businessmen would not have had the chance to exercise their activity or would have formed part of the 'native personnel' of some foreign company." As he observes, intervention led to diversified development, not development built around one

isolated sector, as in the case of Venezuelan petroleum and Cuban sugar.

Emphasizing the continuity of Mexican development, Fuentes (*op. cit.*, pp. 112–13) sees Mexican capitalism as a product of both leftist and moderate governments. "Mexican capitalism owes a debt of gratitude to two men: Calles and Cárdenas. The first laid down the foundations. The second built upon the foundations actively, creating the possibility of a wide domestic market. He raised salaries and gave all kinds of guarantees to the working class, making them feel protected and eliminating the need to create disturbances, he definitively committed the government to a policy of spending on public works, he augmented credits, redistributed lands and, in all spheres, succeeded in letting loose a wide circulation of previously idle riches. These are the vital and permanent accomplishments. . . . If Cárdenas had not placed an official stamp on the worker movement, the subsequent governments would not have been able to work in peace and increase national production in such a fashion. And above all, with his policies, Cárdenas put an end to Mexican feudalism. After him, Mexico could become whatever it wanted except a country of latifundia ruled by a useless agrarian plutocracy. Plutocracy can still exist, but thanks to the growth of markets, it opens up new employment opportunities and pushes Mexico forward."

28 El Colegio de México, *Estadísticas económicas del Porfiriato. Comercio exterior de México* (1877–1911), Mexico: Fondo de Cultura Económica, 1960, pp. 75, 152–53.

29 G. Wythe, *Industry in Latin America,* New York: Columbia University Press, 1949, pp. 274–76.

30 E. Lobato López, *El crédito en México,* Mexico: Fondo de Cultura Económica, 1945, pp. 159–209.

31 From Secretaría de Comunicaciones, Mexico.

32 Emilio Vera Blanco, "La industria de transformación," *México: Cincuenta años de revolución, I: La economía,* pp. 262–64. According to statistical series developed by the Seminar on Modern Mexican History of the Colegio de México, and reproduced in Vera Blanco's article (p. 197), the level of production of manufacturing industry had risen by 50 per cent between 1899 and 1910.

33 See, e.g., D. M. Pletcher, *Rails, Mines and Progress,* Ithaca: Cornell University Press, 1958.

34 For the conventional picture of the Hispanic scheme of values,

see William Stokes' useful "The Drag of the Pensadores," in
J. W. Wiggins and H. Schoeck, eds., *Foreign Aid Re-examined*
(Washington: Public Affairs Press, 1958). That economic values
had long coexisted fairly strongly with noneconomic or even
antieconomic values is suggested by such early independence
period activity as the energetic efforts of conservatives led by
Lucas Alamán to promote industrialization (see R. Potash, *El
banco de avío de México*, Mexico: Fondo de Cultura Económica,
1960) and by the eighteenth-century Bourbon-directed reforms
to increase production in the kingdoms of the Indies (see, e.g.,
W. Howe, *The Mining Guild of New Spain and Its Tribunal General, 1770–1821*, Cambridge: Harvard University Press, 1949).

35 According to Richard Hancock in his *The Role of the Bracero
in the Economic and Cultural Dynamics of Mexico: A Case
Study of Chihuahua* (Stanford: Stanford University Press,
1959), by 1957 *bracero* earnings ranked third, after tourism and
cotton, as a foreign exchange earner, and an estimated 2.3 million persons derived much of their income from the 436,290
braceros working in the U.S. in that year.

36 Oscar Lewis, *op. cit.*, gives graphic portrayal of these elements
of culture change. See also pp. 55–67 of Paul S. Taylor, *A
Spanish-Mexican Peasant Community, Arandas in Jalisco, Mexico*, Berkeley: University of California Press, 1933.

37 Points (1) and (2) are elaborated in Alfredo Navarrete R., *op.
cit.*, pp. 512–17. See also, IBRD, Combined Mexican Working
Party, *The Economic Development of Mexico*, pp. 107, 110.
According to the Mexican economist, Victor L. Urquidi, about
one third of public investment has come from the excess of tax
receipts over current expenditures, another one third coming
from reinvested profits of state enterprises—"Problemas fundamentales de la economía mexicana," *Cuadernos Americanos*,
Mexico: Año XX, vol. CXIV, no. 1 (January–February 1961),
p. 87. Public investment outlays are particularly significant for
economic development as a sizable portion of private investment
goes into residential construction.

38 A concept essentially the same as that of "national integration,"
another recurrent phrase in the literature and policy pronouncements of the Revolution. Gunnar Myrdal has developed the international implications of this policy goal in both *An International Economy* (New York: Harper, 1956) and *Rich Lands
and Poor* (New York: Harper, 1957).

39 To refer to only one form of institutional control, property,

Alfredo Navarrete R. has estimated (*op. cit.*, p. 513) that by
the close of the *Porfiriato*, U.S. interests alone owned over one
half of the national wealth of Mexico.

40 Table 5, in Enrique Pérez López, "El producto nacional," *México: Cincuenta años de revolución, I: La economía*, p. 591.

41 Ifigenia M. de Navarrete, *La distribución del ingreso y el desarrollo económico de México*, Mexico: Escuela Nacional de Economía, Instituto de Investigaciones Económicas, 1960, p. 85. It is possible that the apparent worsening of the lower Mexican income group's position does not take fully into account the real income provided them by social welfare services (e.g., Asistencia Infantil, Seguro Social, school lunches, etc.) and the Compañía Exportadora e Importadora Mexicana, S.A. (CEIMSA) subsidies of food supplies for low income groups. Roughly a decade earlier, Diego G. López Rosado and Juan F. Noyola Vásquez ("Los salarios reales en México, 1939–1950," *El Trimestre Económico*, April–July 1951) had found statistical evidence of a decline in the purchasing power of certain groups which was a bit difficult to reconcile with other data indicating increased food consumption and increased purchases of clothing and some durable goods. They noted that while real wages for certain activities declined, there was an upward movement of the labor force on the occupational ladder.

42 Nacional Financiera, *Informe Anual: 1959*, Mexico: 1960, p. 38.

43 Carlos Fuentes, *op. cit.*, pp. 109–13.

44 B. F. Hoselitz, "Non-economic Factors in Economic Development," *American Economic Review*, vol. XLVII, no. 2 (May 1957), p. 29.

45 *Problemas agrícolas e industriales de México*, Mexico: vol. V, no. 1 (January–March 1953).

46 For a brief but informative description of revolutionary interest groups, see Johnson, *op. cit.*, pp. 128–35. Ideological and philosophical developments are well covered in Victor Alba, *op. cit.*

47 Mendieta y Núñez, *op. cit.*, p. 542.

48 *Ibid.*, pp. 530–31.

49 Edwin Lieuwen, *Arms and Politics in Latin America*, New York: Praeger, 1960, pp. 107–21.

50 José Vasconcelos, *Breve historia de México*, Mexico: Ediciones Botas, 1950, p. 483.

51 José Vasconcelos, *Conferencias del Ateneo de la Juventud*, Mexico: Imprenta Lacaud, 1910, p. 164.

52 P. Romanell, *Making of the Mexican Mind*, Lincoln: University of Nebraska Press, 1952, p. 56.

53 Leopoldo Zea, *Conciencia y posibilidad del Mexicano*, Mexico: Porrua y Obregón ("México y lo Mexicano" series), 1952, and other works in the same series, as well as the articles by S. Ramos, E. Uranga, and Zea in the May–June 1951 issue of *Cuadernos Americanos* and Abelardo Villegas, *La filosofía de lo Mexicano*, Mexico: Fondo de Cultura Económica, 1960.

54 For the structure and content of this elaborate study, see Antonio Carrillo Flores, Raul Ortiz Mena, and Alonso Aguilar M., *Estructura económica y social de México, presentación y introducción general*, Mexico; Fondo de Cultura Económica, 1951.

55 Secretaría de Educación Pública, *Estudio acerca de la educación fundamental en México*, Mexico: Edición de la Secretaría, 1947, pp. 73–79.

56 T. W. Schultz, "Latin American Economic Policy Lessons," *American Economic Review*, XLVI, no. 2 (May 1956), 425–32. Norman S. Hayner in "Differential Social Change in a Mexican Town," *Social Forces*, 26, no. 4 (May 1948), 386, observes that artisans in Oaxaca have sometimes been able to educate their children into middle-class occupations.

57 Wilbert E. Moore, *Industrialization and Labor*, Ithaca: Cornell University Press, 1951, p. 233. Ramón Beteta, in his *Pensamiento y dinámica de la revolución mexicana* (Mexico: Editorial México Nuevo, 1950, pp. 159–69), gives a concise but incisive account of the relation of this school program to larger national objectives, and more detailed information can be found in George I. Sanchez, *Mexico, A Revolution by Education*, New York: Viking, 1936; George C. Booth, *Mexico's School-made Society*, Stanford: Stanford University Press, 1941; Marjorie C. Johnson, *Education in Mexico*, Washington: U.S. Department of Health, Education, and Welfare, 1956; and George F. Kneller, *The Education of the Mexican Nation*, New York: Columbia University Press, 1951.

58 Katherine M. Cook, *La casa del pueblo*, Mexico (no publisher given), 1936, p. 145; and Oscar Lewis, *Life in a Mexican Village: Tepoztlan Restudied*, Urbana: University of Illinois Press, 1951, pp. 38–39.

59 *Ibid.*, pp. xxi, 221–52.

60 The description of recreational objectives is from Oscar Lewis,

Tepoztlan: Village in Mexico, New York: Henry Holt and Company, 1960, p. 76.

61 Mexico: Instituto Nacional Indigenista, 1958. For the following quote, see Alfonso Caso, "National Indigenous Institute of Mexico: A Report. Ideals of an Action Program," *Human Organization,* 17 (Spring 1958), 27–29.

62 George Foster, *Empire's Children, The People of Tzintzuntzan,* Mexico: Imprenta Nuevo Mundo, S.A., 1948, p. 34.

63 John Fayerweather, *Management of International Operations,* New York: McGraw-Hill Book Company, 1960, p. 30.

64 F. Rand Morton, *Los novelistas de la revolución mexicana,* Mexico: Editorial Cultura, 1949, pp. 16–22, 242, 246–51.

65 Mexico: Editorial Studium, 1953.

66 John Gillin, "Ethos Components of Modern Latin American Culture," *American Anthropologist,* vol. 57, no. 3, part 1 (June 1955), p. 495.

67 Chicago: University of Chicago Press, 1950.

68 Washington: Institute of Social Anthropology, 1953.

69 Allan R. Holmberg, "Changing Community Attitudes and Values in Peru: A Case Study in Guided Change," in *Social Change in Latin America Today,* New York: Harper and Brothers, 1960, p. 85.

70 Lewis, *Life in a Mexican Village* . . . , p. 300.

71 *Ibid.,* p. 177, 287–305. Foster's study (*op. cit.*) of Tzintzuntzan reaches somewhat similar conclusions on this point.

72 Charles M. Leslie, *Now We Are Civilized: A Study of the World View of the Zapotec Indians of Mitla, Oaxaca,* Detroit: Wayne State University Press, 1960, pp. 5, 11–12.

73 Lucio Mendieta y Núñez, "La clase media en México," *Revista Mexicana de Sociología,* XVII, nos. 2 and 3 (May–December 1955), 517–31. See also José E. Iturriaga, *La estructura social y cultural de México,* Mexico: Fondo de Cultura Económica, 1951, p. 76.

74 Fuentes, *op. cit.,* pp. 109, 105, and 111.

75 New York: Basic Books, 1959.

76 Merle E. Simmons, *The Mexican Corrido as a Source for Interpretive Study of Modern Mexico,* Bloomington: Indiana University Press, 1957, pp. 87–94. In this work, Simmons makes a convincing case for the use of the popular ballad as a valid indicator of public opinion among the lower, and largely rural, classes. His finding that (a) popular enthusiasm for Madero

was perhaps unequalled by any national figure before or since (with the possible exception of Cárdenas) and that (2) there was a notable public disinterest in the Constitution of 1917 (pp. 140 ff.) sheds interesting light on the conventional hypothesis that the Madero period was a middle-class phenomenon, the Revolution becoming a popular movement with the promulgation of the new constitution in response to the pressures of the Zapatistas.

77 *Ibid.*, pp. 224–35.
78 Redfield, *op. cit.*, pp. 1–13, 18–24, 46–66, 161–64.
79 Gainsville: University of Florida Press, 1958, especially pp. 195–97.
80 Leslie, *loc. cit.*
81 The activities of this financial innovation are described in the 1950 and 1951 *Informes Anuales* of the Bank and in Guillermo Martínez Domínguez, *Crédito al pequeño comercio: Banco sobre ruedas*, Mexico: Universidad Nacional, 1954.
82 Lewis, *Life in a Mexican Village* . . . , pp. 50–51. The previously cited pages in Redfield are also pertinent, as is Dan Stanislawski, *The Anatomy of Eleven Towns in Michoacan*, Austin: University of Texas Press, 1950, p. 50. Norman Hayner, *op. cit.*, pp. 384–86, notes the serious weakening of conservative upper class customs by the new middle class coming up from the lower social strata.
83 Lewis, *Life in a Mexican Village* . . . , p. xxvi; and Foster, *op. cit.*, p. 21.
84 See the annual reports of the Bank for the years 1936–1945.
85 John Gillin, "Some Signposts for Policy," in *Social Change in Latin America Today*, pp. 29–33.
86 Tomas R. Fillol, *Social Factors in Economic Development: The Argentine Case*, Cambridge: The MIT Press, 1961, p. 3. While the Mexican Revolution may have reduced the antisocial effects of Hispanic individualism, it has not, of course, eliminated them —see John Fayerweather, *The Executive Overseas*, Syracuse: Syracuse University Press, 1959.
87 U.S. Senate, Subcommittee on American Republics Affairs of the Committee on Foreign Relations, *Compilation of Studies of United States–Latin American Relations*, 86th Congress, 2nd Session, Senate Doc. no. 125, Washington: Government Printing Office, 1960, p. 556.
88 José Iturriaga, *op. cit.*, p. 67. See also N. L. Whetten, "The Rise

of a Middle Class in Mexico," in vol. II of *Materiales para el estudio de la clase media en la américa latina,* Washington: Union Panamericana, 1950.

89 See James G. Maddox, "Economic Growth and Revolution in Mexico," *Land Economics,* XXXVI, no. 3 (August 1960), 266–78, for what is probably the best short article on the economic dynamics of the Mexican Revolution.

90 Lewis, *Life in a Mexican Village* . . . , pp. xxvi, 54, 177. Norman Hayner, *op. cit.,* p. 384, observes that expropriation and violence drove many of the prerevolutionary Oaxacan elite to Puebla, Vera Cruz, and Mexico City where they often entered the middle class.

91 A. M. Carreño, "Las clases sociales de México," *Revista Mexicana de Sociología,* XII, no. 3 (September–December 1950), 333–50; Lucio Mendieta y Núñez, "La Clase Media en México," *op. cit.* Further details of these important shifts to a more open social structure are provided in *México: Cincuenta años de revolución, II: La vida social,* an invaluable reference on these matters.

92 José Iturriaga, *op. cit.,* pp. 66–67.

93 *Ibid.,* pp. 28–31.

94 Howard Cline, *Mexico: From Revolution to Evolution, 1940–1960,* London, Royal Institute of International Affairs, 1962, Chapter 11.

95 In terms of traditional social organization, these changes seem unquestionably a step in the direction of higher productivity even though recent analysis indicates that bureaucratization as it has operated in the past may itself give rise to contraproductive behavior patterns (Chris Argyris, *Understanding Organizational Behavior,* Homewood, Illinois: The Dorsey Press, 1960, Chapter 1). It is disturbing, however, that the organization-induced dysfunctional behavior described by Argyris might reinforce, through close resemblance, the poor interpersonal relations which Banfield suggests prevail in societies of Mediterranean origin.

96 Something of this collectivity-oriented ethos of the elite can be found in the prevailing philosophy of the state and its economic and social role. An attempt to describe the outlines of the concept of the tutelary state as well as to explore its possible derivation in Mexican cultural history and contemporary social structure is found in W. Glade, *op. cit.,* pp. 15–34. The book *La*

intervención del estado en la economía, by members of the
Escuela Nacional de Economía, Mexico: Instituto de Investigaciones Económicas, 1955, reproduces a group of lectures and
discussions relating to the rationale of interventionism which
are, for the most part, characteristic of dominant opinion. See
also the brief joint statement by the Ministers of Finance and
Industry on the "Posición del estado en materia económica,"
El Mercado de Valores, XX, no. 48 (28 November 1960), 593.

97 F. Tannenbaum, *The Mexican Agrarian Revolution,* New York:
Macmillan, 1929; Eyler Simpson, *The Ejido: Mexico's Way Out,*
Chapel Hill: University of North Carolina Press, 1937; Nathan
Whetten, *Rural Mexico,* Chicago: University of Chicago Press,
1948; Edmundo Flores, *op. cit.,* and "Agrarian Reform and
Economic Development" in K. Parsons, R. Penn, and P. Raup,
eds., *Land Tenure,* Madison: University of Wisconsin Press,
1956; Marco Antonio Durán, *Del agrarismo a la revolución
agrícola,* Mexico: Talleres Gráficos de la Nación, 1947; and
Joaquín Loredo Goytortúa, "Producción y productividad agrícolas," *México: Cincuenta años de revolución, I: La economía,*
pp. 99–164.

98 Loredo Goytortúa, *op. cit.,* p. 100.

99 Durán, *op. cit.,* pp. 27–28.

100 A brief but effective statement of the abiding continuity of Revolutionary goals and the tactics employed to further their realization was the speech of President López Mateos to the Confederación de Cámaras Industriales on 23 March 1961, reprinted in
El Mercado de Valores, semanario de Nacional Financiera, vol.
XXI, no. 13 (27 March 1961), pp. 145–46, 148.

101 Durán, *op. cit.,* p. 38.

102 Durán, "Condiciones y perspectivas de la agricultura mexicana,"
El Trimestre Económico, XXVIII, no. 109 (January–March
1961), 74.

103 *Ibid.,* p. 73.

104 Durán, *Del agrarismo a la revolución agrícola,* pp. 19–24.

105 Germán Parra, *op. cit.,* pp. 128–32, and Table 31.

106 Loredo Goytortúa, *op. cit.,* pp. 148–55.

107 The point is worth elaborating, if only briefly, for it bears on
the interrelations of saving, consumption, and output increases.
In less sophisticated models of development process, output increases appear to spring from savings-investment rather than
from consumption, so that the former appear as "means" to

ultimate realization of the latter as an "end." In this view, consumption increases tend to be self-limiting because of their diminishing effect on "means." The aim of economic development is, of course, a higher standard of living, and if the rural population raises its food intake, since it bulks so large in total population, this increase in consumption is, after all, a part of the accomplishment of the aim of economic development, in the short run. The crucial point, however, is that such immediate consumption increases are not necessarily self-limiting and, hence, not necessarily incompatible with further long-run increases in total output (and consumption). Indeed, in backward areas they may be, in some measure, prerequisite for the latter, providing energy-eliciting incentives, the nutritional basis for heightened work efficiency and a reduction in production-inhibiting behavioral friction (discontent, foot dragging, and the like). Therefore, at least some portion of the consumption increase may be taken as an investment in human capital, affecting positively the quality and quantity of this factor and, by paying off eventually in the form of higher output, the equivalent of other more conventional investment outlays. In short, consumption increments may appear not merely as an "end" of the economic process but rather, more appropriately, as part of an ends-means continuum of activity, having an instrumental value or character as well as a "final" value.

108 Germán Parra, *op. cit.*, pp. 136–38.

109 *Comercio Exterior* (international airmail edition), vol. VII, no. 2 (February 1961), p. 11.

110 *Mexico 1960: Facts, Figures, Trends,* Mexico: Banco Nacional de Comercio Exterior, 1960, pp. 299–300.

111 *Ibid.*, p. 108.

112 Manuel de la Lama, "L'Agriculture Mexicaine," in *L'Economie du Mexique d'Aujourd'hui,* Paris: Université de Paris, Institut des Hautes Etudes de l'Amérique Latine, 1957, pp. 37–38.

113 IBRD, Combined Mexican Working Party, *The Economic Development of Mexico,* p. 188.

114 *Ibid.*, p. 206. According to the Banco de México's *Informe* for 1959, total financing of agriculture and ranching by all financial institutions amounted to 5 billion pesos, of which 3.7 billion pesos came from government-operated credit institutions.

115 Durán, "Condiciones y Perspectivas . . . ," pp. 67–69. Even livestock population, hit hard by civil war and the *aftosa* epi-

demics of the 1940's, had begun to display noticeable progress in the 1950–1960 interval. During this time the numbers of cattle increased by an average annual rate of 3.12 per cent; horses, by 3.99 per cent; and mules, by 6.42 per cent. The rate for poultry was 9.3 per cent. *Ibid.*, p. 71.

116 Edmundo Flores, "La significación de los cambios del uso de la tierra en el desarrollo económico de México," *El Trimestre Económico*, XXVII (1), no. 105 (January–March 1960), 10 ff. In the Northern Zones, during 1944–54, some 41 per cent of the area was planted to cotton, largely for export; 22 per cent was in maize; 19 per cent in wheat; and the balance in fruits, vegetables, etc., much of which was for export.

117 *Ibid.*, pp. 12–14. According to Flores, the agricultural sector could support this change without lapsing into subsistence levels because aggregate earnings were increasing with the extension of cultivated acreage and more intensive land use, because export earnings were relatively high, and because the percentage of the economically active population in agriculture was reduced from around 90 per cent before the reform to around 52 per cent in recent times.

118 See also *ibid.*, pp. 13–14; and W. E. Moore, *op. cit.*, pp. 248–50.

119 Such, for example, is the general tenor of more recent interpretations of the agrarian reform. For an early statement of this point of view, see Ramón Fernández y Fernández, "Logros positivos de la reforma agraria mexicana," *El Trimestre Económico*, XIII (July–September 1946), 221–48. See also the cited works by Redfield, Oscar Lewis, Leslie, and Caso. It is interesting that experience elsewhere in Latin America tends to corroborate that of Mexico. Writing of Peru, Allan Holmberg finds "encouraging evidence that, where Indians live under conditions of greater independence and freedom as they do in indigenous nonhacienda communities, changes in attitudes, values, and behavior are occurring at a faster rate" (Holmberg, "Changing Community Attitudes and Values in Peru: A Case Study in Guided Change," in *Social Change in Latin America Today*, p. 74).

120 Individual agricultural entrepreneurs have been outstanding, but group entrepreneuring should not be overlooked as an additional important impetus to growth and change in the Revolutionary institutional framework. While firsthand modern social science studies of the Mexican hacienda system as it affected

these variables are, of course, lacking, there is no reason to believe that the conclusions of such studies of contemporary manifestations of Latin American *latifundismo* under essentially equivalent conditions cannot validly be used in appraising incentive-innovation-initiative changes in the Mexican case. Carl C .Taylor, in his *Rural Life in Argentina* (Baton Rouge: Louisiana State University Press, 1948, pp. 200–206), takes account of the strong negative consequences of a *latifundismo* in many ways more progressive or modern than that formerly prevailing in Mexico, while in the volume *Social Change in Latin America Today*, two noted cultural anthropologists, dealing with Peruvian and Bolivian conditions which probably correspond more closely with Mexican *latifundismo*, find disincentives, innovation-barring conservatism, and a stifling of initiative to be more or less built-in features of the system which Mexico moved to abolish in its Revolution (Allan Holmberg's previously cited article, pp. 74 ff.; and Richard W. Patch, "Bolivia: U.S. Assistance in a Revolutionary Setting," pp. 138–141).

121 There is some evidence that a somewhat similar effect may be emerging from the recent Bolivian agrarian reform, with expropriated *altiplano* landowners going into urban activity and trucking and moving to develop the new lands of the Bolivian Oriente area. See D. B. Heath, "Land Reform in Bolivia," *Inter-American Economic Affairs*, XII, no. 4, (Spring 1959), 3–27.

122 Edmundo Flores, "Dinámica de la economía mexicana: de la reforma agraria a la revolución industrial," *op. cit.*, p. 57. Gonzalo Robles, "El desarrollo industrial," *México: Cincuenta años de revolución, I: La economía*, p. 181, offers some corroboration on this point.

123 Alejandro Marroquín, in his *Tlaxiaco, una ciudad mercado,* Mexico: Instituto Nacional Indigenista, 1954, p. 85, observes relevantly to this point that the agrarian reform removed the hacienda as the "center of gravity" in the socioeconomic equilibrium of village life, and that the new center of gravity has tended to develop around merchants and mercantile activity.

124 Paralleling rural changes, "in the towns and cities the trend has been from adobe to cement, from clay pots to aluminium, from cooking with charcoal to cooking with gas, from eating with *tortillas* to eating with tableware, from the *metate* to the electric blender . . . from cotton to nylon . . ." Oscar Lewis, "Mexico Since Cárdenas," *op. cit.*, p. 20.

125   The relations indicated in this statement appear borne out rather
      markedly in the J. Walter Thomson Company's *The Mexican
      Markets* (Mexico: Walter Thompson de México, S.A., 1959),
      which study also suggests a strong correlation between urbani-
      zation, acculturation, new economic development, and income
      levels on the one hand and market demand on the other. Both
      new agricultural regions and growing urban centers have,
      therefore, been of special importance for the domestic market,
      because of their association with higher income levels and "mod-
      ern" patterns of taste. Of additional relevance in this respect
      are the findings of Ifigenia M. de Navarrete in her masterful
      La distribución del ingreso y el desarrollo económico de México,
      p. 85. Although between 1950 and 1957 the real income position
      of the bottom 20 per cent of Mexican families deteriorated
      both relatively and absolutely, as did that of the top 2.4 per
      cent, all intermediate sectors enjoyed at least some absolute
      increase in real income while the 6th–9th deciles and the bal-
      ance of the 10th decile—in other words, most of the consumers
      of the newer manufactured products—obtained relative in-
      creases as well. Between 1950 and 1957, these groups increased
      their share of national income from 48.6 per cent to 60.4 per
      cent. Señora de Navarrete quite properly concludes, however,
      that there was ample room for a beneficial downward redistri-
      bution of income. In 1957 the top 2.3 per cent of the families
      still appropriated 24 per cent of the total income, the top 4.9
      percent of the families garnering 36.6 per cent of the total.
126   Edmundo Flores, "La significación de los cambios . . . ," *op.
      cit.*, p. 2.
127   *Ibid.*, p. 14.
128   Some of the more important studies and appraisals of develop-
      ments in this field are: E. Lobato López, *op. cit.*; H. Dueñes,
      Los bancos y la revolución, Mexico: Editorial Cultura, 1945;
      J. Gurza, *Las funciones monetarias del Banco de México*. Mex-
      ico: Private edition, 1941; Antonio Manero, *La revolución ban-
      caria en México, 1865–1955*, Mexico: Talleres Gráficos de la
      Nácion, 1957; two articles in *México: Cincuenta años de revo-
      lución, I: La economía*, "Moneda y Crédito," by Raúl Ortiz
      Mena, and "Las instituciones nacionales de crédito," by Octa-
      viano Campos Salas; E. Lobato López, "La política monetaria
      mexicana," *Investigación Económica*, XVIII, no. 72 (4th quar-
      ter, 1958), 557–81 and Virgil M. Bett, *Central Banking in*

Mexico, Ann Arbor: University of Michigan, Bureau of Business Research, 1957.

129 *El Mercado de Valores,* XX, no. 50 (12 December 1960), 617, 623.

130 In all probability the modernization of the whole banking system has reduced the relative amount of hoarded funds and thereby channeled private savings increasingly into productive uses. At the same time, abandonment of the gold standard in 1931 and any metallic standard in 1935–1936, together with the abandonment of the real bills doctrine around the same time, permitted the adoption of a flexible monetary policy by which hoarding was reduced to relative economic insignificance. The Cárdenas administration chose to make national development the prime goal of monetary policy and used monetary ease to finance public works programs and encourage industrial expansion (Lobato López, "La política monetaria mexicana," *op. cit.,* pp. 572–74).

131 Fourth meeting of Technicians of Central Banks of the American Continent, May 1954, "Relación y operaciones entre el Banco Central y las instituciones de crédito a mediano y largo plazo," *Proceedings,* vol. I (Washington: Federal Reserve Bank, 1955), p. 331.

132 This "direction" of national investment outlays has also been accomplished by public spending programs and other policies noted below. As a factor making for economic growth, it may have been as important as the steps taken to increase aggregate capital accumulation. Such, for example, is the clear meaning of the analysis of Latin American economic development in "Problems of Latin American Economic Development," Study No. 6 in *Compilation of Studies of United States–Latin American Relations,* pp. 574–79. The Banco Nacional Hipotecario Urbano y de Obras Públicas, as its name indicates, has been a basic source of financing for local public works programs; several banks have increased the flow of financing to agricultural production; and Nacional Financiera has concentrated its huge investments in basic industries: electric energy, iron and steel, coal, transport, and communications, with additional funds placed in such critical areas as fertilizers and cement.

133 This is not to imply that Mexicanization itself has been thought of as an end in any ultimate or final sense. Rather, all along it has appeared as more of an end-in-view or intermediate end,

constituting, through its effect on the pattern of resource organization and utilization, a means of approaching the goal of diversified, balanced, and socially beneficial economic development.

134 Such a view was widespread during the 1930's, but it has persisted as a retrospective interpretation well into the 1950's. Thus, in a book published in 1956 J. R. Powell, *op. cit.*, p. 18, saw the Cárdenas era as a triumph of socialism and Marxism. While it is perfectly true that much of the language of the time, official and otherwise, was a rather florid mixture of European philosophical notions and nationalistic exhortations, in his thoughtful review of Mexican social philosophy, Victor Alba, *op. cit.*, pp. 249–56, concludes that in the 1930's Cárdenas was far more a Mexican than a socialist or communist, a man, along with many, for whom "socialism" really meant "social justice" or the use of state action to protect the position of weaker social elements. In a revealing quotation from Cárdenas' speech of 30 November 1936, the alleged exponent of Marxism states that "El hecho mismo de que exista, bajo el control oficial, un sistema de crédito para ejidatarios y otro para agricultores en pequeña escala, demuestra que no se gobierna en interés de una sola clase sino que tienen presentes los derechos de todas ellas." And as an interesting commentary on the conventional interpretation of the oil expropriation, Alba quotes Cárdenas' statement that "el espiritú nacionalista de nuestra filosofía política no debe significar una actitud de puerta cerrada o de hostilidad hacia el capital, nacional o extranjero, que tienda a consegrar sus esfuerzos a engrandecer nuestra patria, respetando las leyes, estableciendo su residencia en México y gastando en México su riqueza."

135 For three of several such recent "reassurances," see the story by Paul P. Kennedy, "Mexico's Regime Assures Business" in the *New York Times* of Monday, 6 February 1961—also noted in *Visión*, vol. 20, no. 6 (13 January 1961), p. II, "Noticias de México" section; the address by Antonio Ortiz Mena, Secretary of Finance and Public Credit, to the 27th National Banking Convention, in *El Mercado de Valores*, XXI, no. 18 (1 May 1961), 205–10; and the speech of President Adolfo López Mateos to the General Assembly of the Confederation of Industrial Chambers, 23 March 1961, in *El Mercado de Valores*, XXI, no. 13 (27 March 1961), 145–46 ff.

136   The concept of "benefit" as used in this context implies a rela-
       tion to political and social considerations as well as to economic
       criteria so that manufacturing enterprises, for example, by ini-
       tiating new forms of economic activity, by substituting for
       imports, and by providing employment and training opportuni-
       ties for the domestic industrial labor force are viewed as being
       of service to the nation and compatible with Mexicanization
       in a way that export-oriented, primary-product enclaves are not.

137   For a brief but effective appraisal of the investment climate for
       foreign capital see pp. 17–22 of *Investment in Mexico,* Wash-
       ington: U.S. Department of Commerce, 1955.

138   The complex process of ruination has been analyzed in a num-
       ber of studies; A. B. Cuellar, *La situación financiera de los
       ferrocarriles nacionales de México,* Mexico: Universidad Na-
       cional Autónoma de México, 1935; V. Fuentes Díaz, *El prob-
       lema ferrocarrilero de México,* Mexico: Edición del Autor,
       1951; Servando Alzati, *Historia de la mexicanización de los
       ferrocarriles nacionales de México,* Mexico: La Empresa Edi-
       torial "Beatríz de Silva," 1946; Gustavo Molina Font, *El desastre
       de los ferrocarriles nacionales de México,* Mexico: Biblioteca de
       "Acción Nacional," 1940.

139   As Evelyn Waugh put it in his *Mexico, An Object Lesson* (Bos-
       ton: Little, Brown, 1939, p. 46), the Mexican railways had
       come to embody "in their most aggravated form all the jokes
       people have ever made about railways."

140   In several obvious ways, summarized as factors contributing to
       raising the marginal efficiency of capital, such developments have
       increased the attractiveness of investment in these newer forms
       of production. Even where the element of subsidy has resulted
       in a mere shifting of firm costs to the social-cost category, the
       investment-inducing effect would still obtain, implying a higher
       rate of capital formation, entrepreneurial expansion, and labor
       training (through shifts in labor to the expanding industries
       stimulated by this policy)—that is, a "forcing" of the rate of
       investment in capital equipment, modern marketing structure,
       and upgrading of human resources at the expense of some forms
       of consumption, given the nature of the fiscal system.

141   The importance of this "closing out" of certain investment al-
       ternatives has been developed by Charles Rollins in an article
       entitled "Mineral Development and Economic Growth," *Social
       Research,* October 1956, pp. 253–80. Arguing from the basis of

Bolivian experience, Rollins suggests (p. 277) that positive
incentives such as the creation of external economies, the provision of low interest rate loans, and rising market demand are
apt to be insufficient for inducing an adequate investment level
in the private sectors of the less developed economies. Therefore, to assist in breaking the traditional pattern of spending
and investment preferences, negative measures are needed to
block the flow of funds (and energies) into customary paths. As
indicated, Mexican policy has attended to both aspects.

It could be added that in terms of prerevolutionary conditions
the traditional patterns of expenditure were probably rational to
a large degree. That is to say, the reluctance to innovate by
investing in new industry and agriculture was probably at least
as much an accurate reflection of high risk levels and the low
marginal efficiency of capital in such fields (together with
institutionally-based factor supply inelasticities) as it was a
function of an aristocratic or archaic cultural preference for
nonindustrial pursuits. The situation is essentially like the
one described with reference to prerevolutionary achievement
motivation. Taken together, the two sets of prerevolutionary
conditions noted describe the inadequacy or insufficiency of
market-induced marginal changes in inaugurating economic
development in pre-1910 Mexico. They also imply the major
contribution of the Revolution to economic development: its
role as an agent of structural change.

142   As most of the actions for which the oil companies were criti-
      cized were rational in terms of market-directed economic be-
      havior from the perspective of the firms involved, it is evident
      that extra-economic, or at least extra-microeconomic, factors
      weighed heavily in the dispute. The concept of countervailing
      power is relevant to this and to certain other instances of inter-
      vention, for in weaker economies the state may frequently ap-
      pear to be the only available counterpoise to large foreign in-
      terests.

143   The oil company's position was well set forth in D. Richberg's,
      The Mexican Oil Seizure, New York: Arrow Press, 1940; that
      of the Mexican government, in J. Silva Herzog, *Petróleo Mexi-
      cano*, Mexico: Fondo de Cultura Económica, 1941; Government
      of Mexico, *Mexico's Oil*, Mexico: 1940; and José Domingo
      Lavín, *Petróleo, pasado, presente y futuro de una industria
      mexicana*, Mexico: E.D.I.A.P.S.A., 1950. W. Gordon (*The Ex-

propriation of Foreign-owned Property in Mexico, Washington: American Council on Public Affairs, 1941) assesses both sides in an objective fashion.

144 For postexpropriation developments, see the cited works by Lavín, Powell, and Bermúdez, along with annual reports of Pemex and George K. Lewis, "An Analysis of the Institutional Status and Role of the Petroleum Industry in Mexico's Evolving System of Political Economy," unpublished Ph.D. thesis, University of Texas, 1959.

145 *Comercio Exterior* (international airmail edition), vol. VII, no. 2 (February 1961), p. 10.

146 In the latter year, two other government-owned companies, the Chapala concern and a smaller one, accounted for something over 120,000 kw. of installed capacity. An additional amount approximating 600,000 kw. of installed capacity was privately owned but generated for internal uses rather than for public service. To some extent, this rather sizable bloc of generating capacity indicates the degree to which traditional public utility arrangements failed, for whatever reasons, to provide external economies to other firms in the nation.

147 For developments in this field, the following are useful sources of information: Comisión Federal de Electricidad, *Qué es la comisión federal de electricidad?,* Mexico: C.F.E., 1948; *ibid., Electricidad para el progreso de México,* Mexico: C.F.E., 1950; C. Lara Beautell, *La industria de energía eléctrica,* Mexico: Fondo de Cultura Económica, 1953; and *ibid.,* "La industria de energía eléctria," *México: Cincuenta años de revolución, I: La economía,* pp. 243–58.

148 *Comercio Exterior* (international airmail edition), vol. VI, no. 10 (October 1960), pp. 2, 4; and *ibid.,* vol. VII, no. 2 (February 1961), pp. 5–6.

149 This point has been developed at length by the eminent Cuban economist, Felipe Pazos. See his "Inversiones públicas versus inversiones privadas extranjeras en las regiones subdesarrolladas," *Revista Bimestre Cubana,* LXXV, segundo semestre (1958), 216–48.

150 See W. T. Easterbrook, "Uncertainty and Economic Change," *The Journal of Economic History,* XIV, no. 4 (Fall 1954), 346–60, for an analysis of the crucial importance of uncertainty factors in economic development. The term "specific uncertainties" refers, among other things, to the predictability of supply (or

cost) factors and demand (or price and profit) factors. Rising real incomes, the relatively wider distribution of that spending power, and population growth were a few of the trends favorably affecting the latter aspects of specific uncertainties. The external economies provided directly by government action— e.g., highway construction, energy provision, etc.—and indirectly—e.g., increase in the urban labor force, the public-works stimulated expansion of basic construction industries—had favorable repercussions on the former aspect.

151 In the early 1920's the Ley de Impuestos Sobre Sueldos y Utilidades laid the basis for a modern tax system, though in spite of repeated efforts to effect further modernization of the fiscal system it was not until 1946 that real changes began to be introduced (Beteta, *op. cit.,* pp. 473–78). For a comprehensive presentation of the evolution of fiscal and monetary policy in Mexico, see Manero, *op. cit.,* pp. 107–354. Alberto Pani's *El problema supremo de México,* Mexico: Imprenta de Manuel Casas, 1955 (segunda edición), furnishes a highly critical view of the general trend in this field. The relevant articles in *México: Cincuenta años de revolución I: La economía* are especially useful as well.

152 Rapid expansion in demand channels, it will be recalled, was a function of several more or less concurrent trends—population growth, urbanization, shifts in taste, increasing market participation on the part of the rural population, heightened geographical accessibility, rising real incomes, the somewhat wider distribution of purchasing power (to unionized labor and the emancipated peones), and increased money flows originating in government investment projects—acting upon an initially small base. For light industries in which the minimally significant aggregate market size is substantially less than that relevant to heavy industry, this rate of growth must have been a decisive factor from a fairly early period, governing anticipated profit yields on new investments and, thus, the marginal efficiency of capital and the rate of capital formation. In some instances, the market appears to have expanded to a greater extent than was at first realized. Sears, Roebuck, for example, opened its Mexico City store expecting to sell to the upper 5 or 10 per cent of the city's population. Within a relatively short time, however, it was tapping at least the upper 50 per cent of income groups in that city (Richardson Wood and Virginia Keyser, *Sears, Roebuck de*

México, S.A., Washington: National Planning Association, 1953, p. 11).

153   Further import duty relief and tax concessions were added in the 1946 Ley de Fomento de Industrias de Transformación and the 1955 Ley de Fomento de Industrias Nuevas y Necesarias.

154   In terms of specific (market) uncertainties alone, the import-substitution route to industrialization would appear to be particularly promising as the very existence of imports serves as a guide to the extent of the domestic market and its character. After 1944, tariff protection was supplemented by the imposition of quantitative import controls, on consumer goods especially. As a partial indicator of the relation of these controls to domestic industrialization, see Wood and Keyser, *op. cit.*

155   For a profile of industrial growth prior to 1941, see Germán Parra, *op. cit.;* Gonzalo Robles, *op. cit.;* and Emilio Vera Blanco, "La industria de transformación," *México: Cincuenta años de revolución, I: La economía,* pp. 261–87.

156   Index numbers computed by the Seminar of Modern Mexican History of the Colegio de México, the Office of Economic Barometers of the Secretaría de Economía, and the Combined Mexican Working Party are brought together in table I, p. 197, of Gonzalo Robles, *op. cit.*

157   John C. Shearer, *High-level Manpower in Overseas Subsidiaries: Experience in Brazil and Mexico,* Princeton: Industrial Relations Section, Department of Economics and Sociology, 1960, pp. 21–25, 91–114. The labor law of 1931 was, of course, a direct expression of the relation between industrialization and Mexicanization in the goals of Revolutionary policy.

158   The rapid growth of the "New Group" of industrialists clearly demands much more explanation than it has received in the past, for it is precisely the entrepreneurial factor that is generally observed to be in critically short supply in most backward areas. Furthermore, entrepreneurial development is customarily viewed as a rather long-term process—certainly longer than the brief period allotted to the rise of the "New Group" in Mexico in Mosk's work.

159   Of the several very good analyses of the economic dynamics of this impressive momentum, one of the best is Henry Aubrey's incisive "Structure and Balance in Rapid Economic Growth: The Example of Mexico," *Political Science Quarterly,* LXIX, no. 4 (December 1954) 517–40.

160 E. R. Barlow, *Management of Foreign Manufacturing Subsidiaries*, Boston: Division of Research, Harvard University Graduate School of Business Administration, 1953, pp. 118–27.

161 *Foreign Commerce Weekly*, vol. 65, no. 11 (13 March 1961), p. 7. In the view of officials of some of the foreign companies affected, the new law merely accelerates a development which would have come about eventually and by raising the net-after-tax profitability of mining should stimulate the long-term growth of the industry. *New York Times*, 19 April 1961, p. 47.

162 *Comercio Exterior* (international airmail edition), vol. VI, no. 12. (December 1960), pp. 4–5.

163 *Visión*, vol. 21, no. 1 (5 May 1961), pp. I–II, "Noticias de México" section.

164 Some two thirds of national industry is located in the Distrito Federal and the states of Mexico and Puebla. The reason for the appeal of closer links with the northern portion of the republic is suggested in the following table.

City	Per cent of total urban population	Per cent of total urban families with monthly incomes over 4,000 pesos	Per cent of total urban families with monthly incomes of 1,500–4,000 Pesos	Per cent of national sales
Ciudad Juarez	1.8	2.9	2.5	1.4
Tijuana	1.2	2.5	1.8	0.6
Nuevo Laredo	0.7	0.9	0.9	0.5
Reynosa	0.7	0.9	0.9	0.4
Matamoros	0.7	1.0	1.0	0.7
Totals	5.1	8.2	7.1	3.6

Source: J. Walter Thompson Co., *The Mexican Markets*, Mexico: Walter Thompson de México, S.A., 1959, pp. 87–89.

165 It is not necessarily true, for example, that individuals and groups in early twentieth-century Mexico were the best judges of their own interests, particularly over the long run. Given the arrested state of social development at the close of the *Porfiriato*, it seems a reasonable presumption that they were not. In any case, broad sectors of the population quite evidently lacked the knowledge and the wherewithall to act effectively to realize those interests.

166 A penetrating general statement of this interrelationship is found in Alexander Eckstein, "Individualism and The Role of the State

in Economic Growth," *Economic Development and Cultural Change*, VI, no. 2 (January 1958), 81–87.

167   As of June, 1960, 52 per cent of the financing provided by or through Nacional Financiera had been channeled into infrastructure (transport, communications, electric energy, irrigation, etc.); 18 per cent into basic industry (petroleum, coal, iron and steel, cement, and other construction materials); the balance into a variety of fields such as paper, fertilizers, chemicals, machinery and metal products, food processing, and textiles (Nacional Financiera, *Informe de Actividades*, 1960). In general, the policy of Nacional Financiera has been to abjure the arguments for investing initially in traditional labor-using processes or moderately modernized techniques in favor of introducing relatively advanced technology. In so doing, it might be argued that it has been able to realize not only that measure of increased output which derives from an increased stock of capital, but also that increment which appears to originate in the increased efficiency of modern technology. The validity of such a policy would seem to be confirmed by the studies of long-term growth in the U.S., which indicate that perhaps as much as one half of the growth since 1869 is attributable to technological advance, the balance deriving from increased resource inputs.

168   *El Mercado de Valores*, XXI, no. 11 (20 March 1961), 133–34. Though no studies of the subject are available, it would be significant to contrast the use of earnings in industrial enterprises sponsored by Nacional Financiera with that prevailing in domestically-controlled private concerns.

169   Frank R. Brandenburg in "Mexico, An Experiment in One-Party Democracy" (unpublished Ph.D. thesis, University of Pennsylvania, 1955); and Leon V. Padgett, in "Popular Participation in the Mexican One-Party System" (unpublished Ph.D. thesis, Northwestern University, 1955) trace the development of the party bureaucracy and organization, while Robert E. Scott (*Mexican Government in Transition*, Urbana: University of Illinois Press, 1959) and William P. Tucker (*The Mexican Government Today*, Minneapolis: University of Minnesota Press, 1957) present excellent studies of the apparatus of government.

170   Frank R. Brandenburg, "Organized Business in Mexico," *Inter-American Economic Affairs*, XII, no. 3 (Winter 1958), 26–50.

171   In relating "primary uncertainties" to political instability (in

which the possibility exists of drastic changes in asset values and their distribution through unforeseeable and arbitrary changes in policy), to property insecurity (through expropriation or physical damage), and the like, I am indulging in some license with Easterbrook's definition of the concept.

172   See John R. Commons, *Industrial Good Will*, New York: McGraw-Hill, 1919, for the initial statement of this key concept. In general, the importance of industrial good will has not been recognized explicitly in conventional economic theory—perhaps because the prevailing consensus in most mature Western societies, especially in England, the U.S., Scandanavia, and Holland, has enabled economists to take it for granted. Yet in many of the underdeveloped countries today, particularly those in which traditional patterns of social organization are disintegrating or are being called into question and rejected, it is precisely this factor which is most conspicuous by its absence. On the whole, this significant contribution of Commons to development economics has not received the attention it merits.

173   Moore, *op. cit.*, pp. 208, 293.
174   *Ibid.*, p. 239.
175   U.S. Department of Commerce, *Investment in Mexico*, p. 81.
176   Moore, *op. cit.*, pp. 239–40.

Notes to Anderson

1   For a partial index of such institutions, see William Diamond, *Development Banks* (Baltimore: Johns Hopkins University Press, 1957).

2   *Rich Lands and Poor* (New York: Harper & Bros., 1958).

3   Robert A. Dahl, "Business and Politics: A Critical Appraisal of Political Science," *Social Science Research on Business: Product and Potential* (New York: Columbia University Press, 1959), p. 3.

4   Joseph Cropsey, "On the Relation of Political Science and Economics," *American Political Science Review*, LIV, no. 1 (March 1960), 3.

5   See, for example, Gunnar Myrdal, *The Political Element in Eco-*

nomic Theory (Cambridge: Harvard University Press, 1953);
W. W. Rostow, *The Politics of Economic Growth* (New York:
Norton, 1952); W. Arthur Lewis, *The Theory of Economic
Growth* (London: George Allen & Unwin, 1955); Hugh G. J.
Aitken, *The State and Economic Growth* (Social Science Re-
search Council; New York, 1959); B. F. Hoselitz, *Sociological
Aspects of Economic Growth* (Glencoe: Free Press, 1960);
Ralph Braibranti and Joseph Swengler, eds., *Tradition, Values
and Socio-economic Development* (Durham: Duke University
Press, 1961).

6 José Figueres, "Address to the Third Stanford Conference on
Latin America" (Stanford: Stanford University Press, 1951),
mimeographed.

7 On the period in the history of Mexican banking, see Antonio
Manero, *La revolución bancaria en México* (Mexico: Tall. Nacionales, 1957); Virgil Bett, *Central Banking in Mexico* (Ann
Arbor: University of Michigan Press, 1957); Alberto Pani, *El
problema supremo de México* (Mexico: Imp. de Manuel Casas,
1955); José Alvarado, "El extraño caso de la Secretaría de
Hacienda," *Problemas agrícolas e industriales de México,* V,
no. 1 (January–March, 1953).

8 The term "Revolutionary coalition" will be used herein to refer
not only to the labor, agrarian, and popular sectors of the official
party, but to the total structure of the elites, including those
sectors of the military, business, and commercial interests, the
so-called "Revolutionary families," and political and intellectual
leaders who have generally supported the existing political system and leadership, and who have enjoyed consistent access to
policy makers.

9 Octavio Campos Salas, "Las instituciones nacionales de crédito,"
in Enrique Beltrán, *et al., México: Cincuenta años de revolución,
I: La economía* (Mexico: Fondo de Cultura Económica, 1960).

10 Gunnar Myrdal, *Beyond the Welfare State* (New Haven: Yale
University Press, 1960), p. 122.

11 Sanford Mosk, "Financing Industrial Development in Mexico,"
Inter-American Economic Affairs, V, no. 1 (June 1947), 5–50.

12 Victor Alba, "The Mexican Economy," *World Today,* 15, no. 11
(November 1959), 456; Antonio Manero, *La revolución bancaria
en Mexico;* Tannenbaum, *Mexico: The Struggle for Peace and
Bread* (New York: Alfred Knopf, Inc., 1950).

13 Alberto Pani, *El problema supremo de Mexico.*

14 Sria. de Gobierno, *Seis años de gobierno al servicio de México: 1934–1940* (Mexico, 1940), pp. 70–71.

15 Tannenbaum reports that leading politicians, among them Obregón and Calles, borrowed huge sums from the bank, some credits being in the neighborhood of M$12–15,000,000. Tannenbaum, *Mexico: The Struggle for Peace and Bread.*

16 Sanford Mosk, *The Industrial Revolution in Mexico* (Berkeley: University of California Press, 1950), pp. 21–22; Frank Brandenburg, "Organized Business in Mexico," *Inter-American Economic Affairs,* 12, no. 4 (Winter, 1958); *Transformación, passim.*

17 *El Nacional,* June 23–24, 1953.

18 John Johnson, *Political Change in Latin America: The Emergence of the Middle Sectors* (Stanford: Stanford University Press, 1960).

19 Banco del Pequeño Comercio del Distrito Federal, *Informe: 1943.* Wartime shortages of consumers goods also would seem to have influenced the industrialization boom of the 1940's, a phenomenon greatly stimulated by official policy, particularly through the expanded activity of Nacional Financiera. This bank, a rudimentary institution in the 1930's, became one of the most powerful organisms of Mexican Government in the years after 1941. Here again, if one bears in mind the consumption patterns of manufactured goods in Mexico, the influence of the urban middle sectors is to be seen.

20 The controversy engendered by these differences of interpretation is clearly revealed in a comparison of the writings of Robert Scott, *Mexican Government in Transition* (Urbana: University of Illinois Press, 1959); V. L. Padgett, "Mexico's One-Party System: A Re-evaluation," *American Political Science Review,* 51, no. 4 (December 1957), 995–1008; Philip Taylor, "The Mexican Elections of 1958: Affirmation of Authoritarianism?" *Western Political Quarterly,* 13, no. 3 (September 1960), 722–44; Tannenbaum, *Mexico: The Struggle for Peace and Bread;* Brandenburg, "Organized Business in Mexico," *op. cit.,* and "Mexico: An Experiment in One-Party Democracy," Pennsylvania, 1956, unpublished Ph.D. thesis; and Merle Kling, *A Mexican Interest Group in Action* (New York: Prentice-Hall, 1961). Also Martin Needler "The Political Development of Mexico," *American Political Science Review,* LV, no. 2 (June 1961).

21 The best single work on the role of the Mexican chief executive

is probably Stephen Goodspeed, *The Role of the Chief Executive in Mexico: Politics, Powers and Administration* (Berkeley: University of California Press, 1947).

22 The proportion of the popular vote won by PRI in recent presidential elections is as follows:

Year	Per cent	Year	Per cent
1940	93	1952	74
1946	79	1958	90

23 Robert Scott, *Mexican Government in Transition*, p. 32.

24 See Philip Taylor, "The Mexican Elections of 1958 . . . ," *op. cit.*

25 Frank Brandenburg, "Organized Business in Mexico," *op. cit.*, pp. 28–29.

26 Robert Scott, *Mexican Government in Transition*, pp. 278 ff; Brandenburg, "Organized Business in Mexico," *op. cit.*

27 Merle Kling, *A Mexican Interest Group in Action.*

28 Richard Neustadt, *Presidential Power* (New York: Wiley & Sons, Inc., 1960).

29 It is certainly requisite, at this point, to acknowledge the study by William P. Glade, Jr., "Las empresas gubernamentales decentralizadas," *Problemas agrícolas e industriales de México* (vol. XI, no. 1, January–March, 1959), which is vital for an understanding of the decentralized agencies of Mexico. Insofar as it deals with the development banks, this study, not known to me until near the end of my research, to some extent anticipates this one. Readers might be interested in comparing the approaches and emphases of an institutional economist and a political scientist in treating similar questions.

30 "Ley para el control de los organismos decentralizados y empresas de participación estatal," *Diario Oficial*, December 31, 1947.

31 Lic. Horacio Castellanos y Coutiño, "El estado y los organismos decentralizados," manuscript in possession of author, 1961.

32 Delfino Solana Yañez, "La administración pública en Mexico," *Revista de administración pública*, 12 (July–September, 1959), 35.

33 "Ley para el control de los organismos decentralizados . . . ," *Diario Oficial*, December 31, 1947.

34 *Novedades*, February 25, 1959.

35 On the reform of 1958–59, see "Ley de Secretarías y Departmentos de Estado," *Diario Oficial*, December 24, 1958, March

13, 1959, and April 1, 1959; Adolfo López Mateos, *Informe que rinde al H. Congreso de la Unión: 1959* (Mexico, 1959), pp. 8–9; Lic. Sealtiel Alatriste, "El control y las entidades del sector público," *Sepanal*, no. 1 (December 1960); Escuela Nacional de Economía, Universidad Nacional Autonoma de México, *Nuevos aspectos de la política económica y de la administración pública en México* (Mexico: University of Mexico, 1960); *Excelsior*, April 8 and June 11, 1959; *Universal*, April 1, 1959; *El Nacional*, April 23, 1961.

36 In the cases of the Small Merchants' Bank and the Transport Bank, it is held by the Department of the Federal District.

37 The following examples, drawn from three different periods in three quite different banks, are illustrative of conventional patterns of capitalization:

Agrarian Credit Bank (original capitalization: 1924)
    Series A   M$18,000,000—federal government
    Series B   M$ 55,000—state governments
    Series C   M$ 1,995,000—Bank of Mexico
               M$ 195,000—Banco de Londres
               M$ 66,400—others
Bank of Cooperative Development (original capitalization: 1944)
    Series A   M$8,882,000—federal government
    Series B   M$ 25,000—Banco Nacional de Mexico
               M$ 25,000—Banco Mexicano
    Series C   M$1,068,000—held by cooperative societies, all
                            but M$30,000 subscribed by one.
Small Merchants' Bank (capitalization in 1956)
    Series A   9,000,000 shares—Department of Federal District
    Series B   500,000 shares—Bank of Mexico, Foreign Com-
                            merce Bank, Nacional Finan-
                            ciera
    Series C   500,000 shares—held by clientele

38 Banco Nacional de Crédito Agrícola y Ganadero, S.A., *25 años del Banco Nacional de Crédito Agrícola y Ganadero, S.A.* (Mexico, 1951).

39 The bank usually provides considerable fanfare and pageantry for the meetings of the series C stockholders, at which time their representatives on the board of directors are selected, and payment of the guaranteed 6 per cent annual interest on these shares paid.

40 Typical structures of such boards of directors are:

	Series A	B	C	D
Bank of Mexico	5	4		
Nacional Financiera	3	4		
Ejido Bank	4	5		
Public Works Bank	2	2	1	2
Armed Forces Bank	8	2		

41 *Tiempo,* December 1958–March 1959. Although it is not usually the case, some of these appointments seem to be made purely for patronage reasons. Many eyebrows were lifted when the brother of López Mateos, with no previous experience in financial matters, was appointed director of the Almacenes Nacionales de Depósito.

42 These agencies, responsible generally for the control of decentralized institutions, were considerably restructured in the administrative reorganization carried out by President López Mateos in 1958. The old Secretary of National Property became the Secretary of the National Patrimony. Its Board of Governors has acquired most of the powers over the decentralized agencies formerly held by Hacienda, under the Law of Decentralized Agencies. With the National Banking Commission, it has the power to collect fiscal information, approve budgets and programs, carry out inspections, supervise contracting powers, and be represented on the boards of directors of the development banks.

The reform of 1958–1959 also led to the creation of Mexico's first planning agency, the Secretary of the Presidency, whose primary responsibility is that of planning, coordinating, and regulating the investment programs of the Mexican government and its decentralized agencies. Each government ministry and decentralized agency is required to submit an annual statement of projects to Presidency, where approval must be obtained before the project can be carried out. Essentially, Presidency's approach to planning has not been that of constructing a detailed program of action for the entire public sector, but rather that of acting as an instrument of control and guidance, with program initiation remaining in the hands of the individual agencies. One of the best discussions of these new agencies of coordination and control is contained in: Lic. Emilio Mujica, "Panorama económico nacional," *Nuevos aspectos de la política económica y de la administración pública en México* (Mexico: Universidad Nacional Autonoma de México, 1960).

43 Banco Nacional de Crédito Agrícola y Ganadero, S. A., *Informe: 1958; Excelsior*, May 24, 1958, June 30, 1958, July 4, 1958.
44 *Excelsior*, August 31, 1949.
45 Castellanos y Coutiño, "El estado y los organismos decentralizados"; Rodrigo García Treviño, *Precios, Salarios y Mordidas* (Mexico, 1953), pp. 29 ff.
46 *Confederación* (official organ of CONCAMIN), 11, num. 246 (March 1, 1959); Iñigo Laviada Arrigunaga, "Las empresas estatales," *Excelsior*, November 30, 1960, January 14, 1950.
47 *Confederación*, 11, num. 248 (April 1, 1959), num. 249 (April 16, 1959), num. 253 (June 30, 1959); *Bancos* (organ of banker's association), año 5, num. 4 (April, 1955); statement of Partido Acción Nacional leader Lic. Manuel Gómez Morín, *Universal*, September 1, 1950; statement of Eduardo Villaseñor, President of Bank of Mexico, 1940–46, *Universal*, September 1, 1950.
48 *Excelsior*, August 24, 1959, and *passim*.
49 *25 años del Banco Nacional de Crédito Agrícola, S.A.*
50 Number of clients of the Agrarian Credit Bank

Year	Total	Individuals	Cooperative societies	Credit institutions	Solidary groups
1953	34,719	6,284	876	9	1,139
1954	40,534	7,687	809	13	1,772
1955	37,000	5,006	894	14	3,022
1956	22,835	4,565	839	17	780
1957	31,707	8,633	1,057	18	1,096
1958	19,883	6,705	599	7	605

Source: Banco Nacional de Crédito Agrícola y Ganadero, S.A., *Informe: 1958*.

That the Agrarian Credit Bank has often broadly interpreted its legal grants of power to achieve banking effectiveness is admitted by the bank. Usually, such policies have later been recognized by changes in the bank's constitutive law. This has been particularly true of the extension of credit to farmers of large, mechanized farms. Originally, it was anticipated that the bank would extend credit only to farmers organized in cooperatives. However, the growth of larger agricultural units caused the bank to exempt them from this requirement. Similarly, the bank, in dealing with individuals, was required to limit its investment to one third of the mortgage value of the property. However, some new land opened by large operators had a low initial value. The real issue was to provide capital credit for irrigation and mechanization, to make the land productive. Hence, the bank interpreted its powers to apply the limitation of credit to private individuals to the potential value of the land after improvements, rather than to its initial value. *25 años del Banco Nacional de Crédito Agrícola, S.A.*

51 Ing. Julián Rodríguez Adame (Secretary of Agriculture under López Mateos), "Panorama de política agrícola," *Nuevos aspectos de la política y administración pública en México.*

52 Ramón Fernández y Fernández lists the following as means employed by the Ejido Bank to make good on loans:

1. Administration of marketing operations by the bank.

2. Purchase of harvests as part of government price-support programs. The bank frequently "pressures" farmers to sell at support prices to guarantee credits.

3. Pressure on private buyers to advise bank of operations with bank clients.

4. Blockade of roads and restriction of travel without permission to guarantee control of clients' economic transactions.

5. Calling out troops to collect harvest of remiss debtors.

6. Cutting off credit to clients, who are generally totally dependent on the Bank for financial support.

7. Judicial proceedings, resulting in embargos on goods of clients. Ramón Fernández y Fernández, "El crédito Ejidal," *El Trimestre Económico*, 25, num. 2 (April–June, 1958), 180–81.

53 *Nuevos aspectos de la política económica y la administración pública en Mexico*, p. 104.

54 *The Industrial Revolution in Mexico*, p. 254.

55 Ramón Fernández y Fernández, "El difícil problema del crédito ejidal," *Revista de Economía*, 17, no. 8 (August 15, 1954); *Universal*, February 1, 1945.

56 *The Theory of Human Organizations* (New York: Alfred Knopf, Inc., 1961).

57 Banco Nacional de Comercio Exterior, *Informe: 1954* (Mexico, 1955).

58 Sria. de Gobernación, *Seis años de gobierno;* Banco Nacional de Crédito Agrícola y Ganadero, S.A., *Informe: 1958; 25 años del Banco Nacional de Crédito Agrícola y Ganadero S.A.*

59 *Nacional*, February 4, 1953.

60 *Nacional,* January 23, 1955; *Excelsior,* September 6, 1955
61 *Tiempo,* January 19, 1959.
62 *Tiempo,* February 23, 1959.
63 Frequently, these appeals take the form of "open letters" and are hence designed to mobilize public opinion as well. Conservative newspapers, such as *Excelsior,* are quick to give space and attention to such criticisms of government banks. For examples of the format of such petitions, see *La Prensa,* June 12, 1941; *Universal,* September 8, 1950, October 11, 1957; *Excelsior,* November 14, 1952; *Novedades,* March 19, 1951.
64 *Excelsior,* June 16, 1955, April 17, 1957.
65 *Nacional,* March 16, 1961.
66 *Excelsior,* January 15, 1960.
67 *Excelsior,* October 27, 1947; *La Prensa,* November 13, 1942; *Nacional,* November 17, 1942, April 17, 1947, April 21, 1947.
68 *Nacional,* November 2, 1955.
69 *Novedades,* April 8, 1942.
70 Nacional Financiera, *Informe Anual: 1959* (Mexico, 1959).
71 The primary companies in which Nacional Financiera has a controlling interest are:
     Altos Hornos de Mexico, S.A. (steel)
     Montrose Mexicana, S.A. (insecticides)
     Fabricas de Papel Tuxtepec, S.A. (paper)
     Tubos de Acero de Mexico, S.A. (pipelines)
     Guanos y Fertilizantes de Mexico, S.A. (fertilizers)
     Ayotla Textil, S.A. (textiles)
     Celulosa de Chihuahua, S.A. (cellulose)
     Constructora Nacional de Carros de Ferrocarril, S.A. (railroad cars)
     Diesel Nacional, S.A. (engines, vehicles)
     Toyoda de Mexico, S.A. (textile machinery)
     Fertilizantes de Monclava, S.A. (fertilizers)
     Carbonífera Unida de Palau, S.A. (coal and derivatives)
     Cia. Mexicana de Coque y Derivados, S.A. (chemicals)
     Centro Industrial de Sahagun and Centro Industrial de Monclava (various industries)
     Nacional Financiera, *Informe Anual: 1960.*
72 However, one should not conclude that investments in "losing propositions" always constitute a political veto of financial advice from the banks. The leadership of Nacional Financiera, for example, defines its role more broadly than the simple criterion

of financial success. Hence, the institution's investment in the Mexican Toyoda works, criticized by CONCAMIN as a poorly conceived investment, was defended by Nacional Financiera as representing support for an industry necessary to Mexican economic growth—and that short-run financial success should not be the only criterion for judging the soundness of the investment (*Novedades,* March 16, 1959, August 29, 1959; *Universal,* May 26, 1956).

73 Agustín Legoretta (president of Mexican Bankers' Association), *Bancos,* año 5, num. 4 (April 1955), p. 5.

74 *Confederación,* 11, num. 246 (March 1, 1959).

75 Nacional Financiera, *Informe Anual: 1960,* p. 65.

76 *Novedades,* March 30, 1955.

77 *Excelsior,* February 21, 1961.

78 Harold Seidman, "The Theory of the Autonomous Government Corporation," *Public Administration Review,* 12, no. 2 (March 1952), 96.

79 Banco Nacional del Ejército y de la Armada, S.A., *Informe:* 1954–56; *El Popular,* April 18, 1958, May 11, 1958.

80 The bank has been amply capitalized. During the 1950's, the government increased the capitalization of the bank by about M$2,000,000 annually. The bank receives a specified amount from income-tax revenues. It has also been assisted by other development banks. In 1953, it received a M$1,000,000 loan from Nacional Financiera, and in 1955 the Public Works Bank absorbed the entirety of its bond issue of M$2,000,000 for mortgage-loan purposes. Banco Nacional del Ejercito y de la Armada, S.A., *Informe:* 1954 and 1956.

81 The reader will note the impact of Robert Dahl and Charles Lindblom, *Politics, Economics and Welfare* (New York: Harper & Bros., 1953), in suggesting this approach to development banking. This work is heartily commended to those who wish to study this problem in greater detail.

82 *Universal,* July 13, 1945.

83 See end note 52.

84 See, for example, Nathan Whetten, *Rural Mexico* (Chicago: University of Chicago Press, 1948); Clarence Senior, *Land Reform and Democracy* (Gainesville: University of Florida Press, 1958); Frank Tannenbaum, *Mexico: The Struggle for Peace and Bread.*

85 Compare Robert E. Scott, "Some Aspects of Mexican Federal-

ism, 1917–1948" (unpublished Ph.D. thesis, University of Wisconsin, 1949), and his *Mexican Government in Transition.*

86 Scott, "Some Aspects of Mexican Federalism. . . ."

87 Banco Hipotecario Urbano y de Obras Públicas, S.A., *Informe Anual: 1957.*

88 *The Process of Economic Growth* (New York, 1960).

89 *Five Families* (New York: Basic Books, 1959); *The Children of Sánchez* (New York: Random House, 1961).

90 *Fortune,* January, 1956. Cited in Oscar Lewis, "Mexico Since Cárdenas," *Social Research,* New York, 26, no. 1 (Spring, 1959), 26.

91 Ifigenia M. de Navarrete, *La distribución del ingreso y el desarrollo ecónomico de Mexico,* University of Mexico, 1960, p. 70.

92 Sanford Mosk, *The Industrial Revolution in Mexico.*

93 Frank Tannenbaum, *Mexico: The Struggle for Peace and Bread.*

Index

Achievement motivation, 17, 25–26, 34–48

Agrarian reform, 11, 24, 26–27, 52–71, 112, 119; and education, 30–31; and value system, 39, 41–43; and social mobility, 48–49; interpretations of, 53; and hacienda system, 56–59; and labor allocation, 57–58; and capital allocation and formation, 57–60; and agricultural credit, 62, 64–65, 147–49, 169–75; Carranza policy toward, 117; Cárdenas policy toward, 121; and development banking, 122–23, 152, 167

Agricultural mechanization, 66

Agricultural production: 1910–1940, 61–62; 1945–1959, 66–67

Alamán, Lucas, and development banking, 118

Alemán, Miguel, 46

Almacenes nacionales de depósito: description of, 189; mentioned, 71, 90, 138, 166, 173

Art, and Mexican Revolution, 30, 34

Ateneo de la juventuo, 24, 29

Attitudes, fostered by education, 31–32. See also Achievement motivation; Value system

Automobile industry, Mexicanization of, 90

Ávila Camacho, Manuel, relations to Cárdenas policies, 4, 11 ff., 56, 82 ff.

Banco del pequeño comercio del distrito federal (Small Merchants' Bank): support of lower-class aspirations, 42; establishment of, 72, 125–26; capital structure of, 137; and trust funds, 153–54; description of, 189–90; mentioned, 138, 142, 156

Banco de México (Bank of Mexico), 71, 116, 139, 155; and leadership, 121; capital structure of, 137; board of directors, 138; high prestige of, 157–58; description of, 186; mentioned, 137, 138, 139, 141, 146, 152, 157, 159–64 passim

Banco hipotecario urbano y de obras públicas (Public Works Bank): establishment of, 73; board of directors, 138; and federal system, 175–76; description of, 188; mentioned, 138, 141, 159, 160, 166

Banco nacional cinemategráfico (Movie Industry Bank), 71

Banco nacional de comercio exterior (Foreign Commerce Bank): and agrarian reform, 65; establishment of, 71; and economic elites, 124–25; capital structure of, 137; and trust funds, 153; and Ruiz Cortines' policy, 154–55; high prestige of, 158; description of, 188; mentioned, 137, 138, 149, 153, 155, 156, 159, 166

Banco nacional de crédito agrícola y granadero (Agrarian Credit Bank): establishment of, 71, 122–24; accusations against, 123; capital structure of, 137; board of directors of, 138; and agrarian reform, 147–49; and trust funds, 153; and Ruiz Cortines' policy, 154; description of, 188; mentioned, 137, 138, 141, 148, 152, 166, 171

Banco nacional de crédito ejidal (Ejido Bank), 71, 122; operating losses of, 43; board of directors, 138; and agrarian reform, 147–49; and Ruiz Cortines' policy, 154; description of, 189; mentioned, 138, 142, 149, 152, 157, 166, 171

Banco nacional de fomento cooperativo (Cooperative Development Bank): establishment of, 71; as descendent of Banco Obrero, 123; board of directors, 138–39; and trust funds, 153; description of, 189; mentioned, 138, 153, 156

Banco nacional del ejército y de la armada (Armed Forces Bank): establishment of, 72; and military influence, 126–27, 168; description of, 190; mentioned, 166

Banco nacional de transportes (Transport Bank), 72, 125–26, 156, 190

Banco nacional obrero de fomento industrial (Workers' Bank), 73, 123, 152

Banking, private, in Mexico, 115–18

Banking reform of 1932, 71

Bermúdez, A. J., 47, 90

Bracero remittances: and foreign exchange and domestic demand, 5, 15; and labor mobility, 19

Brady brothers, 47–48

Breceda, Alfredo, 47

Bureaucracy: interlocking of party and government, 12, 131; and leadership, 27–28; and social mobility, 45–46; public, 117; and agrarian reform, 122

Calles, Plutarco, 45, 113

Capital formation. *See* Investment

Capitalism and Mexican Revolution, 11–12, 22, 110, 117–29, 183

Cárdenas, Lázaro: general character of policy, 11 ff., 124; popular support, 41; and nationalism, 44; and agrarian reform, 54–55; and banking system, 73, 147–48; and industrialization, 82–83, 92; and Keynesian theory, 120–21; policy shift from Calles, 120–21; mentioned, 45–46, 123

Carranza, Venustiano, 13, 113, 115–16

Caudillos, 11, 26–27

Científicos, 15, 36, 40, 114

Class structure, changes in, 48–51. *See also* Social mobility

Comité coordinador de crédito, 140

Comité de importaciones del sector público, 140

Communism, and Mexican development, 183

Compañía exportadora e importadora Mexicana, S.A. (CEIMSA), 65, 166, 173; later known as Compañía nacional de subsistencias populares (CONASUPO), 65 note

Confederación de cámaras industriales de los Estados Unidos Mexicanos (CONCAMIN), 94, 132, 164

Confederación de cámaras nacionales de comercio (CONCANACO), 94, 132

Confederación de sindicatos de trabajadores al servicio del estado, 137

Confederación de trabajadores Mexicanos (CTM), 132

Confederación nacional campesina (CNC), 63, 132, 157

Porfiriato (*continued*)
dualism in, 32; distribution of wealth in, 52
Presidency, Mexican: 133–34; importance of, 129–30; control over development banks, 151–55; and economic planning, 182
Profit sharing law of 1962, 75
Programa Nacional Fronterizo, 90–91

Railways: in *Porfiriato*, 14; in Revolution, 76–78
Revolution and economic growth, relation between, 9–10
Río Fuerte Commission, 65
Ruiz Cortines, Adolfo, "March to the Sea" program, 56

Savings and loan institutions, 73
Sears, Roebuck and Co., 8
Secretary of Agriculture, and development banks, 138, 153–56 *passim,* 166, 168
Secretary of Economy, and interest groups, 94; and development banks, 139, 168
Secretary of Foreign Relations, 129
Secretary of Government, and development banks, 129
Secretary of Hacienda (Treasury), and development banks, 113, 116, 129, 136, 138–40 *passim,* 155, 158, 168
Secretary of Industry and Commerce, and development banks, 138, 155
Secretary of Labor, and development banks, 139
Secretary of Maritime Affairs, and development banks, 139
Secretary of National Patrimony (Property), and development banks, 136, 140, 162
Secretary of the Presidency, and development banks, 140, 162

Secretary of Public Works, and development banks, 139
Secretary of Water (Hydraulic) Resources, and development banks, 65, 139, 155
Socialism, and Mexican Revolution, 11, 75, 110
Social mobility: and education, 31–32; and *mestizaje,* 33; and value system, 44–51; and government programs, 45–46; and class structure, 48–51
Social Security Institute, 125, 135, 166
Statistical data, incompleteness, 3–5
Steel industry: growth, 8; in *Porfiriato,* 15; and railways, 78; and petroleum industry, 79
Stock exchange, 94

Take-off to sustained growth, 5, 13–14, 178–79
Tenochtitlán, 101
Tepalcatepec Commission, 65
Tourism, foreign exchange earnings of, 15, 19
Transportation, and agricultural conditions, 61–62, 64, 65
Trust funds, and development banks, 152–54

Ugarteche, Pedro, 126
United States, relations with Mexican economy, 6–8, 15–16, 67

Value system, 15; changes introduced by Revolution, 25–48; of ladinos, 36–37; of Indians, 37–38; of landowners, 37, 39; relation to social structure, 37–39, 44–51; rural, 41–43; and nationalism, 43–44

World depression, 3
World War II: an industrialization, 15, 19–20; and social mobility, 46; mentioned, 3, 105